Buffy the Vampire Slayer
and Philosophy

Popular Culture and Philosophy

General Editor: William Irwin

Buffy the Vampire Slayer and Philosophy

Fear and Trembling in Sunnydale

Edited by
JAMES B. SOUTH

OPEN COURT
Chicago and La Salle, Illinois

Volume 4 in the series, Popular Culture and Philosophy

To order books from Open Court, call toll free 1-800-815-2280, or visit our website at www.opencourtbooks.com.

Open Court Publishing Company is a division of Carus Publishing Company.

Copyright ©2003 by Carus Publishing Company

First printing 2003

Printed and bound in the United States of America

Cover design: Joan Sommers Design

Library of Congress Cataloging-in-Publication Data

Buffy the vampire slayer and philosophy : fear and trembling in Sunnydale / edited by James B. South.
     p. cm. — (Popular culture and philosophy ; v. 4)
    Includes bibliographical references and index.
    ISBN 0-8126-9530-5 (hardcover) — ISBN 0-8126-9531-3 (pbk.)
    1. Buffy, the vampire slayer (Television program)—
Moral and ethical aspects. I. South, James B., 1960- II.
Series.
PN1992.77.B84 B835 2003
791.45'72—dc21

                          2003001134

To Kelly
Si non confectus, non reficiat

Contents

Codex 3
You're really enjoying this whole moral superiority thing, aren't you?
Buffy and Ethics

Codex 4
That's the kind of of wooly-headed thinking that leads to being eaten
Religion and Politics in the Buffyverse

Codex 5
You're all slaves to the television
Watching Buffy.   269

What a lot of fun—you guys have been real swell

First, this project could not have come about without the enthusiastic participation of the contributors. I thank them for their creative work, professionalism, and timeliness. My colleagues in the Philosophy Department at Marquette University have provided me with a near-ideal environment in which to pursue my philosophical interests. I thank them for their collegiality over many years, their willingness to let me take pedagogical chances, and their bemused toleration of my interest in popular culture. Particular thanks are due to Kevin Gibson, Andrew Tallon, and Paul Neiman for their assistance with computer issues. Jacob Held read almost every paper with a careful eye and caught many mistakes that I did not. The remaining mistakes are, of course, my responsibility. Father Thaddeus Burch, S.J. provided me with a summer grant that helped in producing the final typescript.

I appreciate all the expertise, help, advice, and trust provided by Bill Irwin the series editor for Popular Culture and Philosophy and by David Ramsay Steele at Open Court. Carolyn Madia Gray deserves praise for all her work related to the promotion of this volume. Independently, Jim Wagner suggested a *Buffy* volume to Open Court, and his timing was influential in convincing them that this was a viable project. A group of friends (Betty, Bill, Carol, Cindy, Deb, Jan, Kate, Linda, Liza, Nancy, Nicky, and Sandy) have allowed me to blow off steam and discuss *BtVS*, while providing much good advice and stimulating conversation over the last two years. I gratefully take the opportunity here to thank them. David Lavery and Rhonda Wilcox have generously supported this project and welcomed me into the burgeoning field of Buffy Studies. I am happy to offer this book as an addition to the field. Finally, this book would never have seen print without the encouragement and support provided by Kelly Wilson; but then I can say that about all of the good things that have happened to me over the last fifteen years.

And was there a lesson in all this?

Thanks to the organized efforts of fans of *Buffy the Vampire Slayer* (*BtVS*), I know that the origins of this book can be traced to April 21st, 1997, when I watched my first episode of the series. I wish I could say that I had seen the show from its beginnings, but like so many viewers, then as well as now, I had a near-visceral reaction to the show's name. Why watch a show based on a harshly-reviewed movie from several years ago? Surely it was only a desperate attempt by a new network to curry favor with the coveted teen audience. And how are you supposed to take a character named Buffy seriously? However, in the five weeks between its premiere broadcast and the time I watched my first episode, I had heard enough from people whose judgment I respected to give the show a try.

In retrospect, it's hard for me to see the show with innocent eyes. I recently re-watched the episode I saw first, "Witch." I can see that there was some clever writing (BUFFY: Mom, I've accepted that you've had sex. I am not ready to know that you had Farrah hair. JOYCE: This is Gidget hair. Don't they teach you anything in history?), fast pacing, and a rather nice twist in the plot late in the episode. However, on first viewing I would not have had an inkling of what the show was (having missed the two-part series opener) or what it was going to become. I would have assumed that the central guest character in the episode was just that—a guest character; not a character who would occasionally recur and then play a pivotal role in Season Six over 100 episodes later.

I found myself tuning in to another episode of the series, and another, and another. By June 2nd I was hooked, yet nothing I had seen up to that point prepared me for the Season One finale, "Prophecy Girl," aired that evening. Joss Whedon, the series creator, has stated: "I designed *Buffy* to be an icon, to be an emotional experience, to be loved in a way that other shows

can't be loved."[1] It's certainly possible to take that statement as
hyperbole, as a way for a series creator to retrospectively justify
the fact that a show has been successful. Nonetheless, I recognize in that statement a grain of truth—after watching "Prophecy
Girl," a television show became something different for me: no
longer a form of entertainment or relaxation, but something
worth my thinking about. It quickly became apparent that I was
not alone in my response. It's because the show has developed
such a strong following, especially websites, mailing lists, and
such, that it was possible for me to specify the date I first
watched it.

The main point of this book is to demonstrate that philosophy can bring much to the watching of *BtVS* and that watching
BtVS can provide ample opportunity for philosophical reflection. The professionalization of philosophy as an academic discipline in the past century has been both a blessing and a curse.
Certainly, it has allowed philosophers an opportunity to write
for one another, and the level of sophistication of that writing
has led to much precision in demarcating philosophical issues.
At the same time, the non-philosopher or philosophical novice
interested in, for example, the questions of political philosophy
can be forgiven in feeling a bit resentful, or at the very least
intimidated, when faced with the technicalities present in John
Rawls's *A Theory of Justice*. Books like *Buffy the Vampire Slayer
and Philosophy*, and the others in the Popular Culture and
Philosophy series, can go some way towards mitigating that
resentment. After all, the first stirrings of philosophical interest
are always rooted in the events of our lives, and as Plato taught
us long ago, like it or not, we cannot easily escape the popular
culture around us. It is not a stretch to say that our thinking
about philosophy is always going to intersect with the popular
culture, though philosophers forget this lesson too easily.

The twenty-two chapters of this volume all bring sophisticated philosophical concepts in metaphysics, epistemology,
ethics, and political philosophy to bear on *BtVS*. Some chapters
start with a difficult philosophical issue, say friendship or punishment, and show how *BtVS* can help us to better understand
the issue by providing us with examples and themes from the

---

[1] Joss Whedon, *The Onion*, (5 September 2001), online at:
www.theonionavclub.com/avclub3731/avfeature_3731.html

show. In other chapters, the authors use philosophical concepts to understand the stories and motifs present in *BtVS*. In this latter task, the goal is to help the reader understand how philosophical concepts and theories intersect with particular cases. So, for example, we might wonder about the problem of human irrationality or the problem of nihilism and look to the series to see how *BtVS* has grappled with those themes, thereby deepening our understanding of the abstract philosophical concepts at issue. Finally, some of the chapters also reflect more explicitly on what it means to turn to a television show for philosophical stimulation. The hope of the editor and the authors is the straightforward one that this book will spur the reader's interest in philosophical themes. If, indirectly, it also raises issues for the reader about the relation of philosophy and popular culture more generally, the editor will be especially happy.

The contributors to this volume approach *BtVS* from a wide variety of perspectives and backgrounds. As a result, I doubt that any reader, including the contributors, would (or could, on pain of inconsistency) agree with the main argument of every chapter. As editor, I did not feel the need to agree with each chapter, and indeed there are chapters with which I disagree. However, I believe there is real value in bringing controversial topics and approaches into the conversation about *BtVS*. I trust the reader will be able to make her own evaluative decisions about each of the chapters, and that in running across arguments with which she disagrees, she will deepen her appreciation of the show and its extraordinary philosophical richness.

Aristotle famously distinguished between leisure and relaxation. If philosophy is a paradigmatic leisure activity, then it must be conceded that television watching is, usually, a paradigmatic means of relaxation. *BtVS* demonstrates, week in and week out, that we don't have to relax to watch television. We can interact philosophically with the series, remembering that, in the words of Aristotle, "it is peculiarly disgraceful not to be able to use [the goods of life] in time of leisure."[2] Nobody disputes that philosophy is a good of life, but one indirect argument of this project is that *BtVS* may be one of those goods as well.

---

[2] Aristotle, *Politics*, 1334a36–37.

Codex 1

*It's kind of a
Slayer thing.*

Buffy, Faith,
and Feminism

1

Faith and Plato:
"You're Nothing! Disgusting,
Murderous Bitch!"

GREG FORSTER

No fan of *Buffy the Vampire Slayer (BtVS)* needs to be told that
it is unlike any other vampire fiction ever produced. Traditional
vampire fiction has been heavily shaped by the worldview of
Christianity, whose strict metaphysical separation between good
and evil gives rise to images of vampires as demonic creatures
with seductive and corrupting power. An alternative type of
vampire fiction, which emerged over the past few decades and
is now the dominant form in the genre, forcefully rejects the
Christian worldview in favor of a nihilistic outlook with roots in
the thought of Friedrich Nietzsche. In these stories the vampire
appears as a hero (sometimes tragic, sometimes not) who overcomes conventional morality. However, the stories told in *BtVS*
and *Angel* (hereafter referred to collectively as "the Buffyverse")
do not take place in either of these literary worlds.

Because the Buffyverse does not fit neatly into any familiar
narrative framework, its dominant moral influences are not
obvious to the audience; we do not have a broadly familiar
worldview such as Christianity or nihilism to guide our understanding of the stories' moral structure. But the Buffyverse does
in fact have a moral structure: the school of ethics known as
"eudaimonism," which holds that the basis of moral goodness
is the fulfillment of human nature to its highest potential. In
particular, the eudaimonistic moral structure of the Buffyverse
becomes clear when we compare the Buffyverse with the ethi-

cal thought of Plato, one of the earliest and most important
eudaimonist philosophers. The Buffyverse consistently reflects
the Platonic view that a just person is always happier than an
unjust person.

This chapter analyzes the character of Faith, whose journey
from good to evil and back again most clearly represents the
Buffyverse's Platonic eudaimonism. From her first appearance,
the narrative emphasizes that Faith is motivated by pleasure. Her
eventual turn to evil seems natural to her, given that she takes
such pleasure from it. But, in a series of events that are a
remarkably close parallel to a hypothetical example Plato uses
to demonstrate his ethics, Faith realizes, to her horror, that Buffy
has a better, happier life than she does, and becomes disgusted
with herself for taking pleasure in shameful things.

Neither Christ nor Nietzsche

The Buffyverse does not fit comfortably into either the traditional Christian or the more recent Nietzschean literary styles of
vampire fiction. Viewers were tipped off that *BtVS* would not
rely on Christianity to supply a narrative universe as early as the
series premiere: in the big exposition scene, when Giles lays out
the history of the world according to the Buffyverse, he dismis-
sively refers to the biblical story of *Genesis* as "popular mythology" ("The Harvest"). In the Buffyverse, only villains (such as
the fanatical Knights of Byzantium or the twisted vampire hunter
Holtz) revere God. On *Angel*, our heroes clash frequently with
the higher forces of good, called "The Powers That Be." When
Buffy returns to earth from heaven in Season Six of *BtVS*, she is
not transported with elation at having discovered proof that
good does indeed rule the universe and that virtue will be
rewarded in the afterlife. Nor does she embark on a life of piety
and virtue in hopes of ensuring that when she dies again, she
will go back to heaven.

Even the strict metaphysical lines between good and evil,
which had been the most visible Christian influence on the
Buffyverse in its early years, have become more and more
blurred. One of the most fundamental features of the traditional,
Christian-influenced style of vampire fiction is a bright, shining
line between the supernatural forces of good and the supernat-

ural forces of evil. Try to imagine a Bible story about a good demon. When Whistler, a demon who serves good, was introduced in the finale of Season Two of *BtVS*, it was a novelty. A few years later, good demons were everywhere in the Buffyverse. On *Angel* it sometimes seemed as though you couldn't throw a stone in Los Angeles without hitting one. Angel himself was working with no fewer than three (Cordelia, Lorne, and Gru). On *BtVS*, Spike, despite the absence of a soul, was treated as a quasi-good-guy for two and a half seasons. Obviously, in the Buffyverse the war between good and evil does not correspond to a strict metaphysical distinction between good creatures and evil creatures.

Neither does the Buffyverse fit easily with the Nietzschean style of vampire fiction, in which good and evil are created through behavior rather than unchanging moral standards. Although the metaphysics of good and evil have become more and more jumbled in the Buffyverse, there has never been a moment's doubt that good and evil are permanent, objective landmarks rather than things that we make for ourselves. In the Buffyverse, people do not get to decide what shall be good and what shall be evil; protecting the weak is good, and preying on the weak is evil, period. Willow's embrace of evil at the end of Season Six of *BtVS* is not celebrated as a glorious act of Nietzschean self-creation in which she rejects the old, obsolete moral standards in order to create her own. It is treated as a corruption rather than a rebirth—her entanglement with magic is an addiction, a sort of super-alcoholism culminating in the mother of all benders.

In the Buffyverse, goodness is a burden we must bear. Nietzsche celebrated characters who threw off the shackles of other people's moralities in favor of inventing their own. Above all, he despised the "slave morality" that exalts service to others rather than the assertion of oneself, even—some might say especially—if asserting oneself meant preying upon others.[1] A great deal of recent vampire fiction fits this mold. Contrast this with the Buffyverse, a narrative world in which it is a terrible, soul-

---

[1] See especially Friedrich Nietzsche, *On the Genealogy of Morality*, edited by Keith Ansell Pearson, translated by Carol Diethe (Cambridge: Cambridge University Press, 1994).

crushing burden to be young, gorgeous, and strong enough to pulverize bricks with your bare hands. Buffy, as Faith sarcastically puts it, chooses to "feel the burden of slayerness" ("Who Are You?"). It is not hard to guess what Nietzsche would have thought of the finale of Season Six of *BtVS*, in which Willow recoils from the nihilistic abyss when confronted with Xander's refusal to stop loving her no matter how much suffering she inflicts.

All this is not to say that the Buffyverse has explicitly or specifically rejected either Christianity or Nietzsche. But the Buffyverse clearly does not seek to place itself in either the Christian or Nietzschean narrative frameworks of vampire fiction. The moral foundations of the Buffyverse are not laid out in easy view; we must do some digging to uncover them.

"The Work that I Have to Do"— Eudaimonism

The Buffyverse does have a recognizable moral structure. That structure is eudaimonism, a mode of ethical thought in which the fulfillment of human nature is the standard by which we recognize what is good. The word "eudaimonism" comes from the ancient Greek term *eudaimonia*, which is usually translated as "happiness." To put it briefly, eudaimonism arises from two premises: that people will always do whatever they think will make them happy, and that it is therefore the job of moral theory to show that the morally good life is also the happiest life. Eudaimonistic moral theories argue that human nature is ordered such that people are happier if they live morally good lives. Thus the moral life is the fulfillment of a moral plan or structure that is inherent in human nature.

This pattern has been seen countless times in the Buffyverse. Throughout Season One of *BtVS*, our heroine resists her calling as a vampire slayer. Giles's arguments that slaying is her duty because she is the chosen one fall upon deaf ears. And yet Buffy discovers time and again that she cannot live with herself if she turns her back on the suffering of others when she has the power to help them. In the Season One finale, when she is told that she must sacrifice her life to stop a cataclysmic vampire plot, she balks. But she cannot bear to see her peers continually preyed upon, and so she agrees to make the sacrifice. She does good not because she is called upon to do so by some higher power or duty, but because good, for all the very real pain and sacrifice it requires, is still less painful than the alternative.

She follows a very similar arc in the finale of Season Five. She announces in one scene that she is willing to refuse a supreme sacrifice even if it would be wrong to do so, rejecting moral arguments based on duty. But she ultimately makes just such a sacrifice, because it is, she explains, "the work that I have to do" ("The Gift"). Not "my duty," but "the work that I *have* to do." She has to do it not because the alternative is wrong—she has already rejected that argument—but because the alternative is unbearable. This good-people-are-happier-than-evil-people story has also been played out on *Angel* in the characters of Angel and Cordelia, who have each tried to turn away from the good life, only to find that they are miserable doing anything else.[2]

"The Real Tyrant Is . . . in Truth a Real Slave"—Plato and Eudaimonism

The school of thought we call "eudaimonism" actually includes an extraordinary variety of ethical thought. The label could reasonably be used to describe thinkers as diverse as the ultra-pious St. Augustine and the ultra-impious David Hume. However, the particular philosopher whose thought most directly illuminates the eudaimonism of the Buffyverse is Plato, specifically in the eudaimonist ethics he lays out in his most important work, the *Republic*.

The Buffyverse evokes the eudaimonism of the *Republic* for two reasons. First, in the *Republic* Plato's attention is focused directly on a moral question that the Buffyverse also frequently raises: who is happier, the just person (that is, the morally good person) or the unjust person? Early in the *Republic* Plato describes a magic ring, the Ring of Gyges, which will render its wearer invisible. Such a ring could be used to commit any crime

---

[2] "Darla," "Epiphany," "There's No Place Like Plrtz Glrb," "Birthday."

with no chance of being caught (359b–360d).[3] Plato uses this ring to focus our minds on the contrast between following the rules out of fear of punishment and following the rules because following them is really better. Given the opportunity to do evil with perfect impunity, would we be better off doing so? Second, several of the hypothetical examples Plato uses to illustrate his arguments are very closely mimicked or evoked by stories from the Buffyverse. For example, Buffy's invisible crime spree in the episode "Gone" bears a striking resemblance to Plato's argument concerning the Ring of Gyges.

Plato argues in the *Republic* that we should strive to be just rather than unjust because the just person is happier than the unjust person. We will have to simplify his argument to treat it in the limited space available here, but the Buffyverse does not exactly delve into great philosophic depth either, so hopefully the subtleties we will miss in this account won't make much difference for our purposes. Plato depicts the human soul as divided into three parts: reason, the source of contemplation, logic, and judgment; spirit, the source of anger, courage, and pride; and the appetites, the source of almost all our wants and desires. To reduce the account to a simple version, we can say that a just person listens to the voice of reason and controls his appetites, while an unjust person follows his appetites without control.

Plato's most important argument is that the just person is most happy because all the parts of his soul are under control and in harmony with one another (443c–445b). This harmony provides happiness for both internal and external reasons; it is a state of psychological peace and serenity, and it also facilitates the discipline and self-control necessary to achieve greater happiness in the world. The unjust person, by contrast, follows his appetites without control. He is miserable because he is constantly torn by the internal conflict among his uncontrolled appetites. He can never be at peace with himself, nor does he have the self-restraint necessary to live a truly happy life. If he is cunning, he can gain power, money, and influence by unjust methods, but his very injustice will make him far unhappier than

---

[3] Plato, *Republic*, translated by Allan Bloom (New York: Basic Books, 1968). References to the *Republic* will be noted with Stephanos numbers in parentheses.

those rewards can compensate for. Though he is master of all he surveys, he is a slave to his passions; the more powerful he becomes, the more miserable he will make himself. "The real tyrant is, even if he doesn't seem to be so . . . in truth a real slave" (579d). Deep in his heart, he knows it and detests himself for it.

There are, inevitably, important differences between Plato's eudaimonism and the moral framework of the Buffyverse. In particular, the moral role of reason gets very little attention in the Buffyverse. It seems safe to say that the Buffyverse favors a moral psychology similar to that of Rousseau, for whom moral behavior is achieved by a partnership between reason and compassion—a partnership in which compassion, not reason, is the more morally significant element. What is important for our purposes here is the similarity of emphasis in Plato and the Buffyverse on the fundamental question that defines ethics: who is happier, the just person or the unjust person? No other philosopher gives this question a more pivotal role in ethics than Plato does, and—as we have seen above, and will see further below—it is a question the Buffyverse also treats as the central ethical dilemma of human life.

"Living My Own Way, Having a Blast"— Faith's Corruption

The character whose story most clearly reveals the underlying eudaimonism of the Buffyverse is Faith, the rogue vampire slayer. Faith's unambiguous (and very self-conscious) pursuit of pleasure above all other things makes her the perfect illustration of eudaimonist ethics. She, unlike most characters in the Buffyverse, knows exactly what she wants and has no qualms about pursuing it. For this reason, her story is not subject to the complicating factors of confusion, self-deception, or indecision; her choices, whether good or evil, and the reasons she makes them are always clear and simple. And since Faith has moved from good to evil and back again, she is in a position to compare the two from experience, so her case most clearly illustrates the choice we face between good and evil.

When Faith is first introduced, her love of pleasure is heavily emphasized. She regales the group with a lurid story about slaying vampires in the nude, which she wraps up with, "God, I could eat a horse. Isn't it crazy how slayin' just always makes you hungry and horny?" She meets Giles and coos, "If I'd've known they came *that* young and cute, I would've requested a transfer." She assesses Buffy: "What's up with B? I mean, she seems wound kinda tight. Needs to find the fun a little?" Asked whether she likes slaying, she replies, "God, I love it! . . . When I'm fighting, it's like the whole world goes away and I only know one thing—that I'm gonna win and they're gonna lose. I like that feeling" ("Faith, Hope, and Trick"). The message is not subtle: Faith is interested in food, sex, "fun," and beating up her enemies—all very direct and basic sources of pleasure.

Faith is not a vampire slayer because it is her duty, nor because it is the work she has to do. Faith is positively joyful to be a vampire slayer. As she tells Buffy, "slaying is what we were built for. If you're not enjoying it, you're doing something wrong." However, her love of vampire slaying is entirely amoral; she doesn't appear to care very much that slaying serves a moral purpose. "Staking a vamp" gets her "juiced," and leaves her "hungry for more." Buffy denies that she feels the same way, and after a particularly hard-fought victory Faith turns to her and says, "Tell me you don't get off on this!" ("Bad Girls"). So at this point Faith is "good" only in an external sense. She is a force for good because her actions result in the promotion of good ends, such as the protection of the weak against predators. But she is not internally good. During her time in Sunnydale she never once utters a line reflecting any serious interest in the goals for which she is ostensibly fighting.

Because she's a pleasure-seeker and loves vampire slaying for the thrills it provides, naturally when she discovers something even more thrilling—namely, evil—she's hooked. When she accidentally kills a human, she defiantly refuses to acknowledge the incident's moral significance, telling Buffy point-blank, "I don't care" ("Bad Girls"). Buffy can't believe this; she accuses Faith of concealing the pain that she is sure Faith is feeling over the incident: "I know what you're feeling because I'm feeling it, too. . . . Like something sick creeped inside you and you can't get it out." We get some indication that Faith does feel this; her cool facade occasionally shows cracks. But Faith suppresses her guilt because feeling guilt is painful. Above all Faith loves pleasure and hates pain, so she decides to enjoy being a killer rather than regretting it. "We're warriors," she says defiantly. "We're built to kill." She tells Buffy that if she feels sad or guilty over the death of an innocent bystander, "that's your loss." Pleasure is Faith's only standard; to feel pain for any reason is, by definition, repugnant. When she makes her final leap to evil, she calls it "living my own way, having a blast . . . It feels good" ("Consequences"). All she needs to know is that evil is more enjoyable than good.

Or at least, so it seemed to her at the time. Never having been a truly good person, she had never experienced the pleasure of living a genuinely good life. Her comparison of the good life and the evil life at this point was therefore flawed; she compared the pleasure of the evil life not to the actual pleasure of the good life, which she had never experienced, but only to the pleasure of a life that was externally good but internally amoral. Naturally it seemed to her that evil was the more pleasurable life. She would have a long, dark road to travel before she learned her mistake.

"Disgusting, Murderous Bitch!"— Faith's Redemption

For a while after her conversion to evil, Faith lives it up. The villainous Mayor Wilkins puts her up in a posh apartment and showers her with gifts, and all she has to do for him in return is kill people, the one thing she loves to do most. But this is Sunnydale, after all, and so the villains' party ultimately comes to a crashing halt. Buffy defeats Faith in an epic fight, putting her into a coma, and goes on to ruin the mayor's master plan. For most of a season, Faith lies in a hospital bed, comatose and forgotten. Then she wakes up, and suddenly Faith's inner life gets really interesting.

Using a magical device left behind by the mayor, Faith switches bodies with Buffy. Faith gets to walk around in Buffy's body and live Buffy's life, while Buffy, trapped in Faith's body, is captured by agents of the Watchers' Council. This not only allows Faith to escape all punishment for her life of crime, it actually allows her to live the life of a hero—she, a professional murderess, will receive all the admiration and respect Buffy has earned through years of dangerous and painful self-sacrifice.

Meanwhile Buffy, who deserves to be treated as a hero, faces the prospect of spending the rest of her life in prison for a series of heinous crimes that she did not commit.

This episode enacts a hypothetical case used by Plato to set up the main argument of the *Republic*. Plato asks us to imagine two people: a perfectly just person who is mistakenly believed by everyone around him to be a perfectly unjust person (that is, a master criminal), and a perfectly unjust person who is mistakenly believed to be a perfectly just person. He luridly describes the fate of the just person mistaken for a criminal: he "will be whipped; he'll be racked; he'll be bound; he'll have both his eyes burned out; and, at the end, when he has undergone every sort of evil, he'll be crucified" (361e–362a). Next to this he places the fate of the unjust person mistaken for a just person: "First, he rules in the city because he seems to be just. Then he takes in marriage from whatever station he wants . . . he contracts and has partnerships with whomever he wants, and, besides benefiting himself in all this, he gains because he has no qualms about doing injustice. So then, when he enters contests, both private and public, he wins and gets the better of his enemies" (362b). Who wouldn't rather be king, sleep with anyone, prosper in business, and defeat his enemies, rather than be agonizingly tortured to death?

Well, as it turns out, Plato wouldn't. And, very much to her surprise and horror, Faith discovers that she wouldn't, either. Faith and Plato reach the same conclusion: the just person, punished for crimes he didn't commit, is happier than the unjust person who has everything he desires.

Right after the switch takes place, Faith (in Buffy's body) has a conversation with Joyce, Buffy's mother, about why Faith turned to evil. "Maybe she likes being that way," Faith says defensively. "I'll never believe that," says Joyce. "I think she's horribly unhappy." This remark sets the theme for the rest of Faith's story. Faith, noticeably, changes the subject rather than directly respond to Joyce's comment. She does still cling to her belief that she is happier being evil. Later, she puts it succinctly: rather than be "a stuck-up tight ass with no sense of fun," like Buffy, "I could be rich, I could be famous, I could have anything, anyone" ("Who Are You?"). This sounds quite a bit like Plato's description of the unjust person. And yet Faith seems taken aback by Joyce's observation that she is not, in fact, happy with her evil life. Faith's confrontation with her own unhappiness is just beginning, and she won't be able to deny it for much longer.

When Joyce hugs Faith, she becomes uncomfortable. When Faith saves an innocent girl from a vampire—strictly to avoid blowing her cover—and the girl thanks her, gazing at her with admiration and gratitude, she becomes even more intensely uncomfortable. The breaking moment comes when she offers Riley the opportunity to abuse Buffy's body for his sexual pleasure; he refuses, and instead makes love to her. If Faith's account of her love life in an earlier episode is to be believed, she has never been with a man who cared about her, or even— the hapless Xander excepted—with any man who met the most basic standards of decency. We are left to imagine what it must have been like for such a woman to spend her first night with a man who not only cared about her, but completely loved her.

When we rejoin them in bed, Riley whispers, "I love you," and Faith breaks down. "What do you want from her?" she cries out, apparently unable to believe that Riley's sexual generosity is sincere. As the truth dawns on her, she tries to deny it: "This is meaningless" ("Who Are You?"). But she can't deny what has just been so forcefully demonstrated to her. Buffy—stuck-up, repressed, joyless, moral, goody-two-shoes Buffy Summers—has a better sex life than she does. Coming as it does after demonstrations of the love and adoration Buffy inspires in her family and friends, and in those she protects, this finally forces Faith to confront a truth with deeply unpleasant consequences for her: Buffy has a better life. Buffy is happier.

This realization forces Faith to acknowledge that her decision to turn to evil was wrong even on its own terms. That is, even if duty and abstract morality are set aside, it simply isn't true that the evil life is more pleasant than the good life. Her elaborately concocted self-justification—that good people are all pleasure-hating hypocrites while she is simply an honest pleasure-seeker—falls apart, and she begins to see herself for what she really is.

In a fight with Buffy, she pins down her own body and begins to mercilessly pummel her own face, screaming, "You're nothing! Disgusting, murderous bitch! You're nothing! You're disgusting!" ("Who Are You?"). Her disgust with herself is so complete that after Buffy successfully switches their bodies back to normal, Faith flees to Los Angeles and tries to induce Angel to kill her. "I thought you were happy with the way you are," Angel says to her at one point, but they both know it isn't true. Finally knowing that evil will never make her happy, and believing that redemption is impossible for her after what she's done, Faith simply wants to end her pain. Ultimately, when Angel refuses to kill her, Faith drops all pretense and begs him: "I'm evil! I'm bad! I'm evil! Do you hear me? I'm bad! Angel, I'm bad! I'm bad. Do you hear me? I'm bad! I'm bad! I'm bad. Please. Angel, please, just do it. Angel please, just do it. Just do it. Just kill me. Just kill me" ("Five by Five").

Faith's disgust with herself is reminiscent of another story from Plato's *Republic*. A man walking along the city wall came upon the dead bodies of criminals, left there to rot by the public executioner as a warning to others. The man wanted to stare at the mutilated, decaying bodies, but was ashamed of this desire, so he turned away. However, the temptation to look overcame him, and so he looked. As he did, he angrily rebuked his own eyeballs: "Look, you damned wretches, take your fill of the fair sight!" (439e). Plato's point in telling this story is that it is a key feature of morally good personalities that they are ashamed and angry with themselves when they do wrong. To master one's own desires requires discipline and self-control, which is achieved not by seeking a Spock-like state of pure logic, but by harnessing the emotions of anger and pride on the side of reason and against the disorderly passions. Faith's disgust with herself, though she misguidedly followed it to what amounts to a suicide attempt, was the first crucial step to her redemption; it was, however halting and misdirected, her moral awakening.

The Buffyverse's Moral Compass

There are many important moral questions arising from its eudaimonist ethics that the Buffyverse leaves unanswered. One of the most intriguing is the role played by the soul in making the just person happier than the unjust person. Is it because humans have a soul that doing evil makes them miserable, while vampires and other soulless nasties tend to enjoy it so much? The evidence on this point is starkly conflicting; Angel's story would seem to confirm the suspicion that the soul is what connects moral goodness with happiness for a person, but Spike's story would tend to undermine that conclusion. Because the metaphysics of the Buffyverse are growing more jumbled and confused with each passing season, we will probably never have an answer.

But then, that is only to be expected, since eudaimonism is a school of thought that has always appealed to those who seek a morality firmly rooted in real experience, with as little dependence as possible on abstraction and metaphysics. The Buffyverse's eudaimonism dovetails perfectly with its longstanding ambivalence towards metaphysics, and particularly towards higher powers of good such as "The Powers that Be." In the Buffyverse, characters seeking moral guidance look not to the heavens but within; a person's happiness, or lack thereof, is his moral compass.[4]

---

[4] The author wishes to thank John Gould and Mark Stein for their comments on drafts of this chapter.

2

Also Sprach Faith: The Problem of the Happy Rogue Vampire Slayer

KARL SCHUDT

In *On The Genealogy of Morals* Nietzsche argues that morality is a creation of the weak; that the word "good" was originally defined in relation to the powerful, and was only later co-opted by the weak. The powerful only knew good and bad; that is, noble like themselves and weak unlike themselves. The weak apply the word "good" to themselves and invent the word "evil" to apply to the strong. They set up a moral system that defines the exercise of strength and power as evil as a means of self-protection and as a result of their resentment of the powerful. Such arguments have been made before, notably by opponents of Socrates, who used reason to show the inconsistency of this position. Nietzsche is immune to this tactic, since he denies reason itself. There is no such thing as pure reason, "There is only a perspective seeing, *only* a perspective 'knowing' . . . "[1] The nature of things is that the powerful should rule, and reason itself is just a tool invented by the weak to fight nature. Socrates used reason and logic to defeat the claim that might makes right, but Nietzsche denies the validity of reason and logic, since reason itself is a value judgment of the weak. It seems that there is no way to refute Nietzsche's argument.

---

[1] Friedrich Nietzsche, *On the Genealogy of Morals*, translated by Walter Kaufmann and R.J. Hollingdale, in *On the Genealogy of Morals and Ecce Homo*, edited by Walter Kaufmann (New York: Vintage, 1989), p. 119.

Perhaps there is a way. Even if reason is not allowed, one can appeal to the opponent's own nature. Those who do not discipline their desires are out of tune with themselves, and an argument may be successful that demonstrates the discord resulting from such a course. The happy tyrant or successfully selfish human being is not going to be convinced by any logical argument that he or she should renounce power; what is needed is persuasion, an enticement. This persuasion can be accomplished by an appeal to drama and popular culture. The appreciation of drama is an empathic project. The audience must be able to feel what the characters are feeling; in addition, the characters cannot act in any way the author likes, but must act in accord with human nature for the empathy to be possible. This empathy is the key to convincing a Nietzschean. There are examples in drama of characters who live the sort of life that Nietzsche advocates (but which Nietzsche himself did not live); one can watch these characters and follow what happens to them. If they flourish believably and live complete and desirable human lives, then Nietzsche is vindicated. However, if they end badly, and their endings ring true, the audience may be persuaded that the Nietzschean ideal is a dead end not to be pursued.

Faith, the rogue vampire slayer, can serve as an example. When in "Bad Girls" Faith accidentally kills a human being, she discovers the joy of the free exercise of her power. She embarks on an apparently successful career of evil, using her strength to take whatever she wants whenever she wants. But in the end, she discovers that the life she has chosen is empty. There is no possibility of true friendship, and she ends up as quite a mess. If the story of Faith, the rogue vampire slayer, is believable and true to human nature, her example can serve as a warning. If one follows the path laid out in *On the Genealogy of Morals*, one will come to a bad end. The persuasion here occurs not through dialectic and syllogism, but through empathy and emotion. First, I will examine Nietzsche's rejection of traditional morality and his alternative vision. Then, I will show how Faith can be identified with this ideal. Finally, I will show how Faith's self-chosen world collapses on her, and argue that this collapse, if it rings true to the watchers of the show, can be a warning against taking a similar path.

The Use of Drama in Persuasion

The commonality between the characters in the drama and human nature is what gives the key: we can look for examples of characters who act as if the claims of Nietzsche are true. If the drama is well executed, the characters will act as real humans would act, if they were in similar situations. So the inquirer can use the fictional character's life as an experiment, a test-case: what would this life be like? If the results are believable and if we are able to empathize with the character, then the characterization may be an accurate depiction of what would happen. If the results are negative, then we have reasons not to pursue the proposed course of life. As Aristotle puts it, in a tragedy "pity is occasioned by undeserved misfortune, and fear by that of one like ourselves."[2] If Faith presents the choices we would make if we had the power to get away with them, and if she comes to a bad end, we should experience a useful fear that will prevent us from following the same course. The benefit is that this can be done without suffering in one's own person the bad effects of that life.

Nietzsche's View of Morality

The clearest presentation of Nietzsche's argument on the true nature of morality can be found in *On the Genealogy of Morals*. He argues that the concepts of good and evil arise out of the resentment of the weak for the strong, and that these concepts constitute a reversal of the original and primal categories of good and bad. Nietzsche gives a linguistic argument designed to show that the word "good" was originally used of the powerful nobility. This is quite an insight, and is linguistically defensible: even in English, an admirable person will be described as being noble, having class, or respectable, all words which describe one as belonging to the propertied or powerful hierarchy.

Nietzsche describes the original good in various passages, and it is worthwhile to give some here. "The knightly-aristocratic value judgments presupposed a powerful physicality, a flourish-

---

[2] Aristotle, *Poetics* (1453a3), translated by I. Bywater in *The Complete Works of Aristotle*, edited by Jonathan Barnes (Princeton: Princeton University Press, 1991).

ing, abundant, even overflowing health, together with that which serves to preserve it: war, adventure, hunting, dancing, war games, and in general all that involves vigorous, free, joyful activity."[3] (This is a perfect description of Faith, as I will argue later.) The good are the rulers and masters. Noble morality "develops from a triumphant affirmation of itself."[4] The basic positive disposition of the primordial good is "filled with life and passion through and through."[5] The good man is forgetful, unable to hold grudges. Anger is expressed immediately in action.

So far, this is an attractive portrait. But Nietzsche goes further: those who are powerful and noble are also cruel without compunction. When these nobles leave the company of their equals (which for Faith would only include Buffy), "they go *back* to the innocent conscience of the beast of prey, as triumphant monsters who perhaps emerge from a disgusting procession of murder, arson, rape, and torture, exhilarated and undisturbed of soul, as if it were no more than a students' prank, convinced they have provided the poets with a lot more material for song and praise."[6] One can see examples of this sort of behavior in the *Iliad* or the *Odyssey*. In order to rid his house of the suitors of his wife, Odysseus locks them in a room and slaughters them. He is acting in a good way, according to noble morality. Greek morality is not the same as modern morality: As Alasdair MacIntyre notes, "Agamemnon in dishonoring Achilles did not cease to be *agathos*."[7] Agamemnon or Odysseus can still be good Greek heroes, even though they act in ways we would consider evil. There has been a shift in meaning.[8]

The shift has come about, says Nietzsche, as a result of a slave revolt. The nobles had power, but the weak were numerous. They began to define themselves and their weakness as good, and to define those different than themselves as evil. The

---

[3] Nietzsche, *On the Genealogy of Morals*, p. 33.

[4] *Ibid.*, p. 36.

[5] *Ibid.*, p. 37.

[6] *Ibid.*, p. 40.

[7] Alasdair MacIntyre, *Whose Justice? Which Rationality?* (Notre Dame: University of Notre Dame Press, 1988), p. 15.

[8] The modern view of morality that is expressed is the residue of the old Judaeo-Christian morality. But the modern practice of morality is Nietzschean.

noble were rechristened as evil, something to be pulled down and destroyed. This slave revolt in morality arises out of resentment, anger at the strength that one lacks, whereas the primeval noble morality arises out of the strength that nobles possess. Resentment makes new values by saying 'No' to what the weak are not, whereas noble morality says 'Yes' to what it itself is.

Strength is not to be exercised, say the weak, but Nietzsche rejects the possibility of self-restraint on ontological grounds: humans are nothing but the actions that they do. There is no soul, no substratum that can act to restrain what one is. If the strong ceases to act in a strong way, he or she is no longer strong. Expecting the strong not to exercise strength is like expecting an eagle not to eat mice. The concept of the soul that needs to be saved and that can conquer the instincts of the flesh (see St. Paul) is an invention of the slaves to justify their subjugation of the strong. There is no core to a human being that could restrain activity; there are only the effects of the will. Nietzsche says, "But there is no such substratum; there is no 'being' behind doing, effecting, becoming; 'the doer' is merely a fiction added to the deed—the deed is everything."[9] The only way one could restrain strength is by some sort of self-torture.

So far Nietzsche is describing the historical condition of morality as he sees it: there was a primordial morality of might makes right that has been overcome by a self-torturing morality of resentment, which is primarily embodied in Christianity. This is a historical claim, not a normative claim. It is one thing to describe the primordial noble morality; it is another thing to prescribe it as a good thing. But evidence is plentiful to show what the preferred course is. Nietzsche sees his destruction of morality not as a bad thing, but instead as choosing life: "It was precisely here that I saw the *great* danger to mankind, its sublimest enticement and seduction—but to what? to nothingness?—it was precisely here that I saw the beginning of the end, the dead stop, a retrospective weariness, the will turning *against* life."[10] The slave morality is a repression of the will to power, the will to do what one wants and to dare great things. It is rejected because it is a rejection of life. Nietzsche rejects this

---

[9] Nietzsche, *On the Genealogy of Morals*, p. 45.
[10] *Ibid.*, p. 19.

self-torturing man, and looks to the dawn of a new sort of man, the well-known *Übermensch*. The development of conscience, which is currently directed against life, into a force that is directed against enemies of life, will require a new sort of person: "This man of the future, who will redeem us not only from the hitherto reigning ideal but also from that which was bound to grow out of it, the great nausea, the will to nothingness, nihilism; this bell-stroke of noon and of the great decision that liberates the will again and restores its goal to the earth and his hope to man; this Antichrist and anti-nihilist; this victor over God and nothingness—*he must come one day*."[11]

Nietzsche desires that there come those who can go beyond good and evil and create their own values through strength of will. Nietzsche is not promoting despotism or mass murder: his ideal figure is not one who does evil for its own sake, but rather one who does not shrink from what is necessary for the satisfaction of his or her own desires. Nietzsche would probably be shocked to learn that his philosophy has been used to justify fascism and murder. But the fact remains that his destruction of conventional morality leaves no weapons to argue against murder: why not? It may be that Conard is right in saying that "Nietzsche's ideal is more the artist, the self-overcoming, self-creating individual, who forges new values, who makes an artwork out of his life."[12] But if the self-creation of this individual happens to involve murder and mayhem, there is no reason why one shouldn't commit murder and mayhem.

Nietzsche's argument is not refutable on rational grounds, since he denies rationality as a creation of slave morality. I propose a counter-argument not based on rationality, but based on empathy.

Faith As Nietzschean Ideal

I will focus on five primary characteristics of this ideal: strength, the search for satisfaction of one's desires, a ruthlessness or cruelty in the pursuit of these desires, a distrust of rational

---

[11] *Ibid.*, p. 96.
[12] Mark T. Conard, "Thus Spake Bart: On Nietzsche and the Virtue of Being Bad," in *The Simpsons and Philosophy: The D'Oh! of Homer*, edited by William Irwin, Mark T. Conard, and Aeon J. Skoble (Chicago: Open Court, 2001), p. 73.

argument, and a rejection of traditional morality. All of these will be seen quite clearly in the way Faith is portrayed.

As a vampire slayer, Faith possesses strength and health in abundance. She is something of a super-hero, with strength far beyond human beings and most non-human monsters that she encounters. In addition, slayers possess robust health: they can take punishment that would kill ordinary people and can heal quickly to fight again. At least on the physical level, Faith is a superb example of the sort of strength that Nietzsche extolled.

Faith is introduced as a vamp (not a vampire) in the episode "Faith, Hope, and Trick," dancing seductively on the dance floor. She is an image of sexual desire, without a care in the world. She leads a young man out behind the Bronze, apparently for a tryst; when he turns out to be a vampire, she kills him in an ecstasy of violence. The slaying of vampires takes on all the characteristics of a sexual rendezvous: the flirtation on the dance floor and the choosing of the mate are both there, with the sexual act replaced by the slaying.

When Faith arrives, she takes over the room. Names are reduced to nicknames without permission given: Buffy becomes "B." Faith tells stories of her various conquests, and the room is fascinated. In fact, her presence at the table and her stories are as much a contest for mastery as her slaying. She announces "Slaying always makes you hungry and horny." Slaying is just another desire to be satisfied, like hunger or sexual desire. She even flirts with Giles.

Buffy at this point has come to hate her job. She longs for a normal life, for freedom from the grave responsibilities that saving the world multiple times entails. She knows that her life is likely to be short and violent to the end. She only slays because of duty, not for any love for the job. Faith, on the other hand, loves her job: she loves the chase and the moment of the kill. Slaying is a desire, a lust to be fulfilled. This difference is shown in the first battle that the two of them fight together. Buffy takes on two vampires, while Faith fights another. Buffy's life is endangered because Faith pays more attention to the joy of killing than to the duty of getting the job done. So we have her presented clearly as a sort of Nietzschean: she is focused on the satisfaction of her lust for and joy in killing. In "Bad Girls" she insists to Buffy that one ought to enjoy the job: "Slaying's what we were built for. If you're not enjoying it, you're doing something wrong."

Faith is ruthless and cruel in her pursuit of her slaying, and is similarly disposed in her sexual habits. Men are simply animals to be made use of: she tells Buffy "Find a couple of studs, use them, and discard them. That's always fun" ("Homecoming"). A man is not to be valued as a person in his own right worthy of respect, but simply as a means to satisfying a physical desire. Once this desire has been satisfied, the man who is a means to this end is to be abandoned. In "The Zeppo," Faith beds Xander in order to work off some of the stress of hunting vampires. Xander is very excited: it is his first sexual experience, and as a result he thinks the two have made some kind of connection. But he is mistaking her intentions: she is merely scratching an itch with whatever is convenient, and to expect Faith to establish a relationship with him is like expecting the person with an itchy back to establish a relationship with the backscratcher.

Faith often remarks that truth and rational reflection are not necessary, which places her squarely in the Nietzschean camp. Nietzsche rejects the ability of reason to decide arguments, since reason is after all the product of any pre-existing value system. It is rather one's values that matter. Faith acts before she thinks, and doesn't value reflection. She asks Buffy if she has ever had sex with Xander, and when the reply is one of hesitation and doubt, tells Buffy "You think too much" ("Bad Girls"). Thinking gets in the way of action and satisfaction of desire. Thinking and reflection is a characteristic of slave morality, of those who cling to false ideals such as "duty" and "goodness," "right" and "wrong." One shouldn't think, but should act according to one's passions.

This lack of reflective thought continues. Buffy suggests to Faith that she needs to "Wait, stop, think," to which Faith responds "No. No. No." Just fight! Thinking is the enemy. Faith even manages to tempt Buffy with her carefree attitude, as they enjoy a wild night out on the town stealing whatever they need from the stores of Sunnydale. The exercise of strength without restraint of reason is exhilarating.

But at this point tragedy occurs. In the course of battle, Faith, who is carried away by the joy of slaying, doesn't stop to make sure that her victims are in fact vampires. She stakes and kills a human being by mistake. Horrified, Buffy tries to make things right, by trying to convince Faith to talk to the police. According to traditional morality, the killing of a human being is a serious matter, even when it occurs by accident or through negligence. But Faith has decided that she need not worry about such things. When Buffy confronts her saying "You killed a man," Faith responds with a smile: "No, you don't get it. I don't care."

This accidental killing becomes a moment of discovery for Faith. Having gotten away with one killing, she finds that any reason for her not to kill has vanished. She is stronger and better than the people of Sunnydale, and if anyone gets killed in the process of her satisfying her lust for battle, it is a small matter. In response to a call to duty by Buffy, Faith says: "We are better! That's right, better. People need us to survive. In the balance, no one is gonna cry over some random bystander that got caught in the crossfire" ("Consequences"). The morality of the slaves does not apply to the masters, those who are better and stronger. Faith and Buffy should be able to do what they feel they need to do in order to be good slayers, without being overly concerned about the fate of the ordinary humans that may get hurt in the process.

Faith abandons her job as a slayer, and hires on to work for the mayor, a human who has spent the last hundred years preparing for his ascension, whereby he can assume demonic strength and power. In order to make this ascension happen, the mayor needs to feed on a sufficiently large number of ordinary humans, which he plans to do at the high school graduation. It is worth noting that, although one cannot fail to see Faith as "the beast of prey, the splendid *blond beast* prowling about avidly in search of spoil and victory,"[13] it is the mayor who most closely approximates Nietzsche's concept of the *Übermensch*. This is the overman, the human who is to come, or at least ought to come, in order to justify the whole history of mankind. As Nietzsche puts it, "mankind in the mass sacrificed to the prosperity of a single *stronger* species of man—that *would* be an advance."[14] This is not done out of malice, but out of a search for beauty in life. Nietzsche gives a long description of the overman in *The Will to Power*:[15]

---

[13] Nietzsche, *On the Genealogy of Morals*, pp. 40–41.
[14] *Ibid.*, p. 78.
[15] A posthumously published work, and so a book of which to be suspicious, but still worthwhile in gathering good quotations.

A race with its own sphere of life, with an excess of strength for beauty, bravery, culture, manners to the highest peak of the spirit; an affirming race that may grant itself every great luxury—strong enough to have no need of the tyranny of the virtue-imperative, rich enough to have no need of thrift and pedantry, beyond good and evil; a hothouse for strange and choice plants.[16]

We can see in this an apt description of the mayor: he shows no malice, no evil desire to kill everyone. In fact, he is an exemplar of a decent man, with a taste for beauty, culture, family values, and good manners (often correcting Faith's own poor manners before sending her on a mission to kill an enemy). The only reason he wants to kill the students at the high school is to further his own desire to become a new and transcendent being. He wants to go beyond mankind, to be an overman, or at least an over-snake. Faith is simply along for the ride, out of admiration for his strength.

So it seems clear that Faith is an example of the type of person Nietzsche admired: strong, ruthless, not bothered by rational debates, and beyond traditional morality. She has even found herself a genuine *Übermensch* to work for in the mayor. The test will now be to see what happens to her. Two questions need to be answered: 1) is the depiction of her fate believable? 2) Is her fate one worth seeking? The answer to the first question will depend largely on the individual's reaction to the drama and sense of the character. I cannot argue someone into thinking that *BtVS* is well-written: one will either see that or not. So watch the show, and decide for yourself if the characters act as real humans do. I believe that it is in fact a very well-written show, and the evidence for this is the continued success it has had over the years, as well as the fact that one can find a sufficient number of philosophers to publish a whole book about it.

What Is Faith's Fate?

The climactic ending of Season Three involves the mayor's attempted ascension, foiled by Buffy and her friends. Faith is not there to see it, having been defeated in battle with Buffy. Faith spends the greater part of the next year comatose in the

---

[16] Nietzsche, *The Will to Power*, p. 478.

hospital. But things get interesting when she awakens. It turns out that the mayor has left her a gift, a magical device that allows one to switch bodies. She contrives to switch bodies with Buffy and attempts to take over Buffy's life, moving into her house, wearing her clothes, and attempting to form a relationship with Joyce Summers, Buffy's mother.

There is a striking scene in "This Year's Girl" that gives the key to Faith's thinking. She has possessed Buffy's body and is standing in front of the mirror, attempting to get used to her new face. As she is making faces, she begins to say things that she thinks Buffy would say. Faith gives a litany, delivered ironically: "You can't do that. It's wrong. You can't do that, because it's naughty, because it's wrong. I'll kick your ass. I'll kill you!" These statements of moral "oughts" seem empty and contrived when they are stripped to the bare words: why not do something? It is wrong! The word "wrong" becomes a magical symbol, a talisman before which evildoers must shudder. If one repeats it often enough and loudly enough, it must be respected. And if the malefactor doesn't desist, the magical word must be defended with force.

Faith has in these few sentences given her entire view of traditional morality. It consists of value statements that have no backing other than the might of the weak majority. The strong are told not to exercise their strength, but no reason can be given. All of the intricacies of moral reasoning, that one shouldn't harm others because of the categorical imperative or the innate natural law, ultimately resolves itself into a statement of the mysterious quality of "wrongness." For example, Faith (wearing Buffy's body) goes to the Bronze, the local nightspot, and encounters Spike, a vampire who has recently been "defanged" by means of a computer chip in his head. Faith teases him, telling Spike that she could have sex with him in ways that he couldn't possibly imagine, flirting explicitly and shamelessly. She then asks whether Spike knows why she will not do it. In a mock little-girl voice, complete with pout, she says, "Because it's wrong." Once again, the word "wrong" is an empty, emotivistic claim, which only has any meaning because of the force behind it, as Faith had said before: "I'll kick your ass."

It seems at this point as if Faith is prepared to live out her life happily occupying Buffy's body, with no compunction, following her desires as she wills. But in order to keep up her disguise, Faith needs to act as a slayer: Willow points out a vampire stalking a kill in the Bronze, and sends Faith out to save her. She has to comply in order not to blow her cover, and so saves the girl. The girl expresses heartfelt and sincere gratitude, to which a flustered Faith responds, "Yeah, it's cool." This is the beginning of the piercing of her Nietzschean shell. She has done an act that however motivated by prudence, connects her to a broader reality. The girl's gratitude and the feelings it engenders in Faith start to show her that her good may involve more than just herself.

Later in the episode one of Riley's friends claims that Faith/Buffy is just a killer, to which Faith angrily responds that she is the slayer. Afterwards, she says to herself that she doesn't care. But it appears she is experiencing the call of conscience. A starker example: a band of vampires have barricaded themselves in a church to kill parishioners. Faith shows up in Buffy's body. She has seen people in need and comes to their rescue. Why? It is a basic moral truth, missed by Nietzsche, that the other somehow makes a claim on us. Somehow, the good of the other *is* the good for me. Of course, the existence of this basic demand of the other cannot be proved by a rational argument since the commitment to reason is a value judgment that arises out of the very slave morality he is attacking. But it can be pointed to: one can see Faith experiencing it, and one can, if the drama is well executed, *co*-experience it with her.

Faith (still wearing Buffy's body) tells Riley, "Don't tell me what to do. I'm Buffy. I have to do this." She then proceeds to save the parishioners of the church who are being held hostage by vampires. Confronting the bad guy, she says,

FAITH: You're not gonna kill these people.
VAMPIRE: Why not?
FAITH: Because it's wrong.

Recall the earlier scene where she was looking into the window, getting used to Buffy's face. Then she was pretending to utter moral maxims, providing what she thought was its sanction: "I'll kick your ass!" Then the only reason that something was right or wrong was the threat of force. Now, she is making the same statement, "Because it's wrong," but with an entirely different meaning. Right and wrong is not a matter of the will of the strong, but is an independent reality, a brute fact that must be dealt with, whether one wants to or not. Faith is going to defend the people with force, but this action does not become right because of the threat of force. Rather, the force is employed because the action is right. Slayers must defend, not because of some weakness on their part, but because it is simply the right thing to do. It doesn't matter whether Faith is strong or not, or whether she likes the people in the church or not. She has strength and the means to defend the defenseless, and therefore has the duty to do so. Furthermore, she must save the people because the sort of person she will be if she doesn't is unacceptable.

Why does Faith change her mind? She is confronted with the true shape of her life. While she is wearing Buffy's body, Joyce asks her why Faith is the way she is. Faith responds that perhaps she likes being that way. In other words, Faith is strong enough to do what she likes, and is happy because she is doing it. But Joyce will have none of it and responds, "I'll never believe that. I think she's horribly unhappy." For Faith, happiness means to do what one wants. How could she be unhappy if she is doing what she wants? Joyce's claim argues that happiness does not consist in merely doing what one wants, but in *flourishing*.

These rival conceptions of the good for humans, to follow one's own desires as well as one can, or to work to develop the whole person are what is at stake. Can we resolve this dispute rationally? Nietzsche quite correctly points out that we cannot. But what I have attempted to do is show that an empathetic evaluation of the two alternatives will lead most people to reject Nietzsche. Look closely at the sort of person Faith is. She has become a hired killer, and has no friends, no society. It seems that Faith herself recognizes the undesirability of her position. When she fights the real Buffy in her own body, Faith yells "You're nothing, disgusting, murderous bitch!" ("Who Are You?") The words do not apply to Buffy, but to Faith herself. She is attempting to distance herself from the life that she has made for herself. She sees the shape of her own life course, and it disgusts her. She makes an aesthetic evaluation of herself and doesn't like what she sees. Rival moralities may not be able to be resolved rationally, but the results of choices in accord with them differ greatly. Faith's life has become *ugly*.

Faith recognizes this fact, and in the conclusion to her story works to rectify the problem. In an episode of *Angel*, "Five by Five," she shows up in Los Angeles, at first determined to show that she has no problems: she takes a contract to kill Angel, and proceeds to torture Wesley, her former watcher. When Angel finally counters her plans, she shouts at him "I'm evil, I'm bad, I'm evil! Do you hear me?" She wants Angel to kill her, to rid her of the terrible life she has formed, a life that resulted directly from her unabashed pursuit of her own ends without regard for her responsibilities to others.

In the end, Faith after much difficulty acknowledges that she needs to make things right. At Angel's urging, she makes a confession to the police, and begins to serve a jail sentence for her crimes. The change is dramatic: she has completed the leap from Nietzsche to Socrates, accepting the Socratic dictum that "a man who acts unjustly, a man who is unjust, is thoroughly miserable, the more so if he doesn't get his due punishment for the wrongdoing he commits."[17] There is, after all, a moral order beyond one's desires, and the good of the person involves more than just the desires of the person, but the state of that person's relationship to self and others.

Persuasion As Drama

It may be that the triumphant view of the world today is that morality is a matter of personal choice. Furthermore, the claim that moral statements are not factual, but rather are value judgments makes debate on the issue impossible: what one values is a matter of one's tastes, and as the old adage goes, there is no accounting for taste. If moral judgments are merely expressions of individual preferences, how can one dispute it? It's like arguing over the best flavor of ice cream. One cannot even argue that morality is a matter of rationality rather than values, because the opponent will respond that rationality itself is a value judgment.

I have argued that persuasion can be attempted not by means of reason, but by means of drama. A well-told story can

---

[17] Plato, *Gorgias* (472e), translated by Donald J. Zeyl, in *Complete Works*, edited by John M. Cooper (Indianapolis: Hackett, 1997).

often reach deeper into the human heart than a rational argument. For this reason I have proposed the example of Faith from *BtVS*. An examination of her decisions and course of life will resonate with the viewer, and serve not as an argument, but as a persuasion or enticement to reject a morality based merely on personal choice. The questions for the watcher: Do you feel what Faith feels? Do you sorrow over her evil actions? Would you want to be her? Do you cheer her final rehabilitation? If the answer to these questions is yes, then perhaps Nietzsche is not the best guide for your life.

3

"The I in Team": Buffy and Feminist Ethics

JESSICA PRATA MILLER

Buffy Summers is, like any superhero, incredibly strong, highly intelligent, and dedicated to fighting evil. Unlike most superheroes, though, she's a young woman, and fans know that this is no coincidence. Series creator Joss Whedon deliberately created a show that would turn the horror cliché of the blonde bimbo victim on its head, a show that "can make teenage boys feel comfortable with a girl who takes charge of a situation."[1] In a recent interview, Whedon reaffirms a commitment to "the very first mission statement of the show, which was the joy of female power: having it, using it, sharing it."[2] This chapter explores the question of whether there is something gendered in the way Buffy's strength and goodness are portrayed. This is a question for that school of ethics known as feminist ethics.

Feminist Ethics

Feminist ethics is an investigation of the basic ethical questions (questions like "What is the best life for human beings? How should I act? What is good? Evil?") that is grounded in—and foregrounds—feminism, defined loosely as a commitment to

---

[1] Quoted in R. Fudge, "The Buffy Effect: Or a Tale of Cleavage and Marketing," *Bitch* 10 (1999), at www.bitchmagazine.com/bitch.htm.
[2] Quoted from "Buffy's Not Too Cool for School" at nypost.com (21 June 2002).

ending sexism and oppression. Some feminist ethicists focus on
those practical problems that the women's movement first
brought to public awareness, such as domestic violence, sexual
assault, sexual harassment, and economic discrimination. And,
indeed, several *Buffy the Vampire Slayer* (*BtVS*) episodes deal
with these topics.[3] But other feminist ethicists focus on what is
called "moral orientation," that is, how gender affects the way
people see themselves and others as moral beings, the way they
construct moral issues and dilemmas, and the resources they use
to solve them. This kind of focus is closely associated with the
work of Harvard psychologist Carol Gilligan.

In her best-selling 1982 book, *In A Different Voice,*[4] Gilligan
presented empirical research that seemed to demonstrate a striking correlation between gender and moral orientation. In inter-
viewing subjects about moral dilemmas, Gilligan discovered two
different approaches to moral life, the "justice perspective" and
the "care perspective," that are connected to the two genders,
masculinity and femininity. People who approach moral issues
from the justice perspective are impartial, use reason to determine their rights and duties, and deduce moral behavior from
abstract, universal principles. They are concerned with rights
and obligations, with taking responsibility for actions, and view
themselves as essentially separate and independent from other
people.

In contrast, people who approach moral issues from the care
perspective are interested in preserving concrete relationships,
and in coming to understand how to care for themselves and
others. They believe that emotion and feeling are relevant to
moral life and they tend to make contextual judgments based on
particular features of people and situations. They are concerned
with avoiding harm and hurt, and with working out their
responsibilities to persons. They view themselves as embedded
in relationships, essentially interdependent with other people.

An argument between Buffy and her boyfriend Riley, a U.S.
soldier who works undercover for the Initiative, a secret gov-

---

[3] See, for example, "Go Fish" and "Reptile Boy" from Season Two; "Anne," "I
Only Have Eyes for You," and "Beauty and the Beasts" from Season Three; and
"Dead Things" and "Seeing Red" from Season Six.
[4] Carol Gilligan, *In a Different Voice: Psychological Theory and Women's
Development* (Cambridge: Harvard University Press, 1982).

ernment-sponsored demon-hunting outfit, nicely illustrates the difference between the care and justice perspectives. When Riley criticizes Buffy's best friend Willow for dating a werewolf (Oz), Buffy calls him a bigot, adding, "Love isn't logical, Riley. It's not like you can be Mister Joe Sensible about it all the time"("New Moon Rising").[5] Later, they have the following exchange:

> BUFFY: You sounded like Mr. Initiative. Demons bad, people good.
> RILEY: Something wrong with that theorem?
> (Buffy is exasperated. She takes a few steps away.)
> BUFFY: There's different degrees of—
> RILEY: Evil?
> BUFFY: It's just . . . different with different demons. There are creatures—vampires, for example—that aren't evil at all. ("New Moon Rising")

Buffy views Oz as a unique individual, a view which is informed by her friendship with Willow, by her own past (falling in love with Angel, a vampire with a soul), and by the confidence she places in the ability of love and concern to serve as moral guides. Riley, on the other hand, initially views Oz in the abstract, as a demon, the whole category of which has been labeled evil by the Initiative.

The justice perspective, with its abstract focus on reason and impersonal rules and authority, echoes cultural ideals of masculinity, while the care perspective, with its contextual focus on personal relationships, including feelings and emotions, fits with ideals of femininity.[6] And, indeed, while Gilligan is clear that the care perspective is not a "woman's morality" (because two-thirds of her female subjects used the justice perspective most or some of the time), her research showed that one-third of women, and

---

[5] All dialogue is from the website www.studiesinwords.de.

[6] This chapter follows feminist tradition in using the terms "male" and "female" to refer to biological categories (that is, sexes) and "masculine" and "feminine" to refer to social categories, that is, to how sex differences are elaborated in society and culture (that is, genders). In this chapter, genders are idealized types. An individual female may be more or less feminine, more or less masculine.

no men, were primarily care reasoners while two-thirds of men, but only one-third of women, were primarily justice reasoners.[7] Perhaps the most important result was that, unlike previous researchers, who had found women's moral reasoning deficient to the extent that it differed from the justice tradition, Gilligan insisted that the care perspective is a worthy moral orientation in its own right. Today, the empirical status of Gilligan's findings is the subject of debate, but the basic idea that women and men, based on their differing socialization and life experiences, may bring different, but equally valuable, perspectives to the moral table, still resonates with many people. In the rest of this chapter, I'll explore three interconnected themes in feminist ethics which are featured very strongly in the character of Buffy. These are: (1) a view of the self as embedded in relationships; (2) an emphasis on the moral importance of personal relationships; and (3) a new definition of what it means to be an autonomous, or self-governed, individual.

"The I In Team": Buffy's Relational Self

From Superman to Spiderman, the superhero typically hides his true self from even his closest loved ones. And according to the Slayer Handbook, this is no less the case for the Slayer. Rupert Giles, Buffy's Watcher, tells her that "if your identity as the Slayer is revealed it could put you and all those around you in grave danger" ("Never Kill A Boy on the First Date"). And in a dream encounter, the First Slayer (a.k.a. "The Primitive") tells Buffy: "No . . . friends . . . just the kill . . . we . . . are . . . *alone*" ("Restless").

Despite all this, Buffy's sense of self is deeply relational. Her identity as the Slayer was revealed very early on to best pals Willow and Xander, and then to a widening circle of friends. Buffy considers the "Scooby Gang," as her friends are known, crucial to her ability to fight evil. And this is another way of saying she sees them as essential to her very identity, since slaying for Buffy is not just a job, but rather who she is.

---

[7] Carol Gilligan, "Moral Orientation and Moral Development," in *Women and Moral Theory,* edited by Eva Feder Kittay and Diana T. Meyers (Totowa: Rowman and Littlefield, 1987).

The importance of mutual interdependence is brought home forcefully when Buffy and the gang face Adam, a Frankenstein-like creature made with demon, human, and electronic parts. After graduating from high school, the "Scooby Gang" had begun to drift apart. Adam manages to exploit the situation, pitting them against one another. Scooby relations become so strained during an argument about how to fight Adam that Buffy says, "I guess I'm starting to understand why there's no ancient prophecy about a Chosen One . . . and her friends" ("The Yoko Factor"). But Buffy and her pals soon realize that they have played into the hands of their enemy. They eventually defeat Adam with an enjoining spell that combines their various skills by merging their essences.

Family members are also key to Buffy's sense of self. When her mother dies from an aneurysm Buffy becomes so disoriented that she says, "I don't even know if I'm . . . here. . . . I don't know what's going on" ("The Body"). Soon after, Buffy faces her most formidable foe yet, the god Glory, who plans to use the blood of Buffy's sister, Dawn, to open a portal between human and demon dimensions, causing mass destruction. After a violent battle, Glory defeats Buffy and captures Dawn. Buffy, whose sense of self has been partly defined by her role as Dawn's "big sister" and protector, becomes catatonic. Later, when Giles suggests that they may be forced to kill Dawn to stop the ritual, Buffy refuses, saying: "She's more than [a sister]. She's me. . . . Dawn . . . is a part of me" ("The Gift").

While Buffy is her own person (and who *else* would say "If the Apocalypse comes—beep me"?), her sense of self is intricately bound up with her relationships, and it changes as they change. This is a point that many feminist ethicists make: relationships are not (necessarily) threats to individual uniqueness. Rather, they are crucial for maturity and individuation. This may seem obvious, but there is a long tradition in philosophy of treating the self as a kind of unchanging innate inner core that is constantly in danger of being corrupted by the influences and ideas of others.

It is important to emphasize, however, that for both Buffy and for feminist ethicists, a subservient identity that is constructed solely around meeting another's needs is very morally problematic. This is the theme of "I Was Made to Love You," in which Buffy suffers from a brief and humorous bout of desperation for a boyfriend ("Maybe I could change . . . I could spend less time slaying, I could laugh at his jokes, I mean, men like that, right, the, the joke-laughing-at?"). Buffy's longing is the counterpoint to the main plotline, in which the socially inept Warren Mears creates a robot ('April') programmed only to love him. Unfortunately, April nearly kills several people in pursuit of this objective. When Warren rejects the robot ("She got boring"), she wonders: "I'm only supposed to love him. If I can't do that, what am I for? What do I exist for?" The lesson is not lost on Buffy, who says: "look at me obsessing about being with someone. It's like . . . I don't need a guy right now. I need me. I need to get comfortable being alone with Buffy."

I'll have more to say on the subject of autonomy, but for now it is enough to note that feminist ethicists stress the importance of *mutual* dependency, not one-sided dependence. One must care for *oneself*, as well as for others. For women, this requires rejecting the feminine stereotype of the selfless giver.[8]

"Once More, with Feeling": The Moral Importance of Personal Relationships

As a result of her relational sense of self, Buffy tends to view moral problems through the prism of her own life history as it is bound up in relation with others. Buffy frequently works through moral questions in context rather than trying to abstract away from the details. And if this context includes people she knows well, then their unique attributes, situation and features also get taken into account. Carol Gilligan and others have argued that this approach can lead to very imaginative solutions to moral dilemmas, thereby promoting moral innovation.

We can see how this works by looking again at the case of Oz the werewolf. As a werewolf, Oz is irrational, violent and very dangerous. From the justice perspective, Oz is too great a threat to the life and security of other human beings to be

---

[8] Fans of *BtVS* might wonder how I reconcile this claim with Buffy's ultimate sacrifice—her death in the Season Five finale, "The Gift." The story arc of Buffy's death and revivification is worth extended analysis, but I can note here that her heroic dive from a hundred-foot tower into a whirling ball of energy in order to save the world is hardly the stuff of domesticated femininity.

allowed to live, or at least to be allowed a normal life. In contrast, while Buffy never downplays the threat Oz poses, her understanding of Oz's unique condition, his many positive qualities, and her best friend Willow's love for him lead her to devise a solution which meets everyone's needs and keeps each of the salient relationships intact: Oz is voluntarily caged each month during the full moon.

This feature of Buffy's moral orientation, like her sense of self, also dovetails with feminist ethics. Moral philosophy has not placed caring personal relationships at the forefront, tending instead to emphasize the moral rules for interactions between relative strangers of equal status. But both at home and in paid employment, the daily care of dependents such as children, the elderly, the sick, and the disabled is still largely women's work, and emotional attunement is identified with femininity. So feminists have sought to place caring relationships, especially among unequals, at center stage in moral theory. And this would include, of course, a philosophical exploration of the emotions and capacities (such as caring, empathy, and trust) required for being in such relationships.

In this regard, an exchange between Buffy and fellow Slayer Kendra is revealing:

> KENDRA: Your life is very different than mine.
> BUFFY: You mean the part where I occasionally have one? Yeah, I guess it is.
> KENDRA: The things you do and have, I was taught, distract from my calling. Friends, school . . . even family.
> BUFFY: Even family?
> KENDRA: My parents, they sent me to my Watcher when I was very young.

And later in the same conversation:

> KENDRA: Emotions are weakness, Buffy. You shouldn't entertain them.
> BUFFY: Kendra, my emotions give me power. They're total assets! ("What's My Line?, Part Two")

Kendra is taking the position of the justice perspective here, in which strict impartiality is required at all times for fairness and justice. Buffy's reply echoes the claim of feminist ethicists, that emotions—running the gamut from empathy to anger—can help a person be more sensitive to other's needs, to the presence of moral wrong, and to the kind of creative moral solutions that prevent, or at least minimize, harm and hurt.

All of this doesn't mean, of course, that Buffy's moral universe excludes strangers. Quite the contrary—most of her heroic activity is spent saving complete strangers from horrors they can barely imagine. In fact, feminist ethicists might claim that the emotional repertoire and attention to detail which are hallmarks of Buffy's moral orientation actually result—at least sometimes—in *better* treatment of strangers than the justice perspective.

For example, in the following discussion, Buffy explicitly rejects a form of justice reasoning called utilitarianism. According to utilitarianism, a person should take the action that brings about the best consequences for everyone affected. "Best consequences" usually get cashed out in terms of overall happiness, or overall satisfaction of desires. A utilitarian is supposed to deal with others (and oneself) on a strictly impartial basis.

In "Bad Girls," fellow Slayer Faith (called when Kendra is killed) accidentally kills a human being. Rather than face the tragedy, she dumps the body and conceals what has happened. In a heated argument with an appalled Buffy, Faith uses utilitarian calculation to defend her actions:

> BUFFY: And that's it? You just live with it? You see the dead guy in your head every day for the rest of your life?
> FAITH: Buffy, I'm not gonna "*see*" anything. I missed the mark last night and I'm sorry about the guy. I really am! But it happens! Anyway, how many people do you think we've saved by now, thousands? And didn't you stop the world from ending? Because in my book, that puts you and me in the plus column.
> BUFFY: We help people! It doesn't mean we can do whatever we want.
>
> FAITH: . . . People need us to survive. In the balance, nobody's gonna cry over some random bystander who got caught in the crossfire.
> BUFFY: I am.[9]

---

[9] From Season Three's "Consequences."

Here, Buffy rejects the kind of reasoning that would justify hiding a death by calculating the costs in revealing it. Unlike Faith—who is probably right in assuming that concealing the bodies would result in the best consequences overall—Buffy never loses sight of the human tragedy, the loss of a unique individual, however imperfect. Her main concern is not maximizing overall happiness or following universal rules, but how to respect each individual while acting in a way that fits with her own conception of who she is.

"Fool for Love": Criticisms of Care Ethics

In this section, I want to raise two kinds of criticism that philosophers sometimes level at the ethics of care. The first criticism is that the ethics of care leads to unfair favoritism. Buffy's relationship with her boyfriend Angel provides a good example. When Kendra discovers that Angel is a vampire, she accuses Buffy of foolishly allowing the relationship to cloud Buffy's judgment, saying, "He's a vampire. He should die" ("What's My Line?, Part Two").

But Kendra's "vampires bad" reasoning is, like that of the Initiative discussed above, too simplistic to be helpful in this complex situation. For Angel, as viewers know, is a vampire with a "soul," code in the show for moral conscience. He deeply regrets his evil past and now fights alongside Buffy for good.

Later, however, Angel again loses his soul. For months Angel torments Buffy and her friends, and gleefully kills many innocents, including Giles's lover. Buffy shows remarkable strength—both physical and emotional—when she brings herself to stake him. But when Angel reappears, Buffy, still in love, carries on with him in secret.

In Season Three's "Revelations", the Scooby Gang discovers Buffy's duplicity, and they are outraged. Not only has Buffy lied to them, but she has put them all in danger. Giles quietly communicates the seriousness of Buffy's selfish behavior:

> I won't remind you that the fate of the world often lies with the Slayer. What would be the point? Nor shall I remind you that you've jeopardized the lives of all that you hold dear by harboring a known murderer. But sadly, I must remind you that Angel tortured me . . . for hours . . . for pleasure. You should have told me he was alive. You didn't. You have no respect for me, or the job I perform.

Buffy's love for Angel has led her to act selfishly and immorally. Powerful emotions like love—which Joss Whedon calls "messy, delightful and dangerous"—will sometimes do that.[10] And this is exactly why the justice tradition requires that the moral actor use reason, not feelings, and that he treat everyone in the same manner. If only Buffy had asked herself impartially which course of action would have the best consequences overall, or whether she was treating people as she would want to be treated, she might have acted differently.

This is a significant concern, and I can't settle the debate between partialist and impartialist ethical systems here. But it is important to point out that even within an ethics of care, Buffy had the resources to identify her course of action as wrong. The care perspective promotes maintaining relationships, and, although Buffy was trying to do just that by tending to Angel, her actions caused a tearing of the fabric of trust among a much larger group of her loved ones. At one point, Buffy allows Oz to becomes the prime suspect, and thus object of distrust, in a brutal slaying rather than reveal that Angel—at least as likely a suspect—has returned. Finally, since it is happiness with Buffy that jeopardizes Angel's ensoulment, Buffy's love for Angel itself should have prompted more introspection on the wisdom of becoming close to him again.

A second criticism of the ethics of care has been leveled by feminists themselves. While few, if any, feminists quibble with the idea of raising the visibility and value of the emotional labor that women perform, or with extolling the neglected virtues that are associated with femininity, some question whether this perspective takes seriously enough the political context in which all of this occurs. They wonder what kind of moral damage women have suffered within the context of sexism and sexual oppression. Perhaps the so-called "women's virtues" are merely the traits women have developed to survive under patriarchy.[11]

---

[10] Joss Whedon, in a posting to the Bronze VIP posting board (4 May 2000, archived at www.cise.ufl.edu/cgi-bin/cgiwrap/hsiao/buffy/get-archive?date= 20000504).

[11] As Claudia Card has put it, "Is Gilligan picking up on something Nietzsche identified as 'slave morality'?" See Claudia Card, "Virtues and Moral Luck", *Working Series I*, No. 4 (November 1985), Institute for Legal Studies, University of Wisconsin, Madison, Law School, as paraphrased by Barbara Houston,

The great moral wrong is sexism, so what women really need to be moral, some feminists assert, are the kinds of qualities, skills, and strategies that will allow them to resist sexism and sexual domination. In other words, where's the "feminist" in feminist ethics? How can women whose moral orientation reflects current standards of femininity be moral innovators, especially in the area of gender relations? These questions raise the issue of autonomy, and it is to that which I now turn.

"The Graduation": Autonomy and the Relational Self

Traditionally, moral philosophers have defined the autonomous person as one who lives his or her own life by his or her own moral values. Until recently, mainstream philosophy has tended to interpret this as requiring social detachment and adherence to self-discovered and self-verified universal moral rules. The truly autonomous person would be literally "self-made"—independent of others to the greatest possible extent. In effect, moral autonomy has been defined in such a way that only certain kinds of men can achieve it. And this has, of course, fit with a social reality in which, until the twentieth century, only certain men had the freedom and power in various public realms (religion, education, employment, government, etc.) to exercise fully their moral capacities and live out their moral ideals.

Today, feminist and non-feminist philosophers agree that moral autonomy is a social achievement, at least in the sense that socialization is required for a person to learn a moral language, to develop moral virtues, skills and capacities, and to recognize which situations are morally problematic. Some worry, though, that when feminists combine this emphasis on socialization and relationships with the "feminine virtues," they end up with a recipe for subservience. Their concern is that heterosexual women tend to overidentify with the moral perspective

---

"Rescuing Womanly Virtues: Some Dangers of Moral Reclamation", in *Science, Morality and Feminist Theory,* edited by. Marsha Hanen and Kai Nielsen (Calgary: University of Calgary Press, 1987), p. 248. For a related discussion, see Sandra Lee Bartky, *Femininity and Domination: Studies in the Phenomenology of Oppression*, (New York: Routledge, 1990), especially p. 109.

and worldview of their male partners, preventing both true moral autonomy and any chance for criticism of the sexist status quo.

The best way to meet this criticism is by comparing moral autonomy in the three slayers, Buffy, Kendra, and Faith. All Vampire Slayers are female and yet the Watchers are, from what viewers have seen of them, mostly male. Slayers are supposed to follow the Slayer Handbook and take orders from their Watchers. One Watcher condescendingly informs Buffy that "The Council fights evil. The Slayer is the instrument by which we fight. The Council remains, the Slayers change" ("Checkpoint").

Kendra is a perfect example of an obedient Slayer. As we saw above, Kendra allows herself no friends, lovers, or distractions of any kind—Slayerhood consumes her life. Kendra lacks moral autonomy not because she memorized the handbook and follows the rules, but because she does so unquestioningly. She defends all of her strategies and actions by referring to procedure and orders, never asking, as Buffy frequently does, whether they make sense. For Kendra, morality is imposed entirely from the outside, by the Watchers' Council. Perhaps it is of symbolic significance that Kendra, always a follower, lacks the strength of will to resist the hypnotic gaze of a vampire who whispers "Be in my eyes. Be in me." before brutally slashing her throat ("Becoming, Part Two").[12]

The third Slayer, Faith, is in many ways Kendra's exact opposite. When we meet Faith, she is without a Watcher, and remains so despite the Council's best efforts to assign one to her. Faith is a loner who believes no one is to be trusted. Faith explicitly rejects Buffy's relational mode of Slaying, saying, "*I'm* on my side, and that's enough" ("Revelations"). Apparent similarities between Buffy and Faith quickly prove to be superficial: Buffy breaks the rules when necessary, but Faith breaks rules just for the thrill of it; Buffy draws on emotions to help her negotiate

---

[12] Kendra also literally bows down before men. When she meets Buffy's friend Xander, the script calls for Kendra to look "like a deer caught in the headlights, totally flustered, mortified by his attention". Ordinarily Kendra is a super-powerful woman, but in the face of a cute boy she can only nervously stammer: "I will be of service" ("What's My Line?, Part Two").

personal moral quandaries and to fight evil, but Faith literally gets high off of anger and vengeance.

Despite being female, Faith embodies an ideal of *masculine* autonomy that still has a powerful hold on society. Just think of action heroes played by Sylvester Stallone, Arnold Schwarzenegger, or, more recently, the appropriately named "The Rock." Faith's crack that "I just have this problem with authority figures" could easily be an action picture tagline. But, paradoxically, this hyper-individualistic, super self-reliant mode of autonomy makes Faith vulnerable to destructive emotions like jealousy, as when she tells Buffy: "I do my job kicking ass better than anyone. What do I hear about everywhere I go? Buffy. So I slay, I behave, I do the good little girl routine. And who's everybody thank? Buffy" ("Enemies"). Faith's very isolation and her inability to work through her insecurities with others make her susceptible to the call of evil, and she slides inexorably toward tragedy and self-destruction.

The Watchers' Council is an authoritarian, impersonal organization slavishly devoted to keeping its ancient rules and traditions—and thus its power, as Buffy eventually surmises—intact. Like Faith, Buffy comes to reject the Watchers' Council, but only after a series of morally inept and dangerous judgments on its part: rendering Buffy helpless as part of a "test"; sending an unstable Faith over the edge by kidnapping her in order to send her to England to hear "the judgment of the disciplinary committee"; and refusing to help a poisoned Angel, because "It's not Council policy to cure vampires" ("Graduation Day, Part One").

When Buffy finally rejects the Watchers' Council's moral authority, she is accused of mutiny, but replies, "I like to think of it as graduation" ("Graduation Day, Part One"). While the Council sees only a shift in power, Buffy sees the situation in terms of her growth as a Slayer and as a young woman. Rejecting the Council is part of a long process of gaining moral maturity. Buffy now understands how to balance the demands of self and others, how to give care, and how to avoid harm and exploitation, without forfeiting either her cherished relationships or her own integrity. Clearly, Buffy has attained autonomy—most notably moral autonomy—without sacrificing her sense of self-in-relation.

I have tried to show that autonomy is possible within an ethic of care, but I have not addressed the connection between moral autonomy and feminism *per se*. It is true that Buffy eventually comes to understand her independence of the Council in an overtly political way ("You're Watchers. Without a Slayer, you're pretty much just watchin' *Masterpiece Theatre*" ["Checkpoint"]). But whether Buffy is a feminist role model is a much larger question.[13] Still, I set out to address the narrower question of whether there is something uniquely feminine in the way Buffy's strength and goodness are portrayed. And when we reflect on her self-understanding, her emotional attunement, her capacity for empathy, and her relational brand of moral autonomy, the answer is clearly yes.

---

[13] Indeed, is Buffy any kind of role model at all? See Chapter 11 in this volume.

4
Buffy the Vampire Slayer as Feminist Noir

THOMAS HIBBS

In the opening episodes of Season Six of *Buffy the Vampire Slayer (BtVS)*, Buffy's town of Sunnydale, the cosmic center for the battle between good and evil, is bereft of its slayer, who died in the previous season's finale, "The Gift", sacrificing her own life to avert yet another impending apocalypse. Buffy's friends, affectionately known as the Scooby Gang, are disconsolate, their only hope being a tricky spell that might resurrect their dead friend. When the charm works, Buffy's lack of gratitude miffs her friends. Unable to tell them the truth, Buffy manages a feeble expression of thanks for being rescued from her awful existence beyond the grave. As she leaves them, she runs into Spike, a vampire and her longtime nemesis, now deprived of his vampire skills by a high-tech experiment. Buffy confesses to Spike that her experience of death was akin to paradise; having been "torn out of there by her friends," she now experiences life on earth as a living hell ("After Life"). Among the darkest moments ever on *BtVS*, the scene portrays Buffy's sense of entrapment in an alien and hostile world, her isolation from those who know her best and care for her most, and her uncertain quest to discover her place and purpose. It also foreshadows her decline into a self-lacerating sexual alliance with Spike.

The dark themes of *BtVS* call to mind film *noir*, whose definitive entries in the genre were produced by Hollywood in the mid-twentieth century and which has enjoyed something of a resurgence in recent years.[1] Operating as a counter to the super-ficial and optimistic visions of the American dream, the charac-teristic styles and themes of *noir* constitute a "set of conditions producing amazement," symptomatic of "meaning's multiplicity and elusiveness." *Noir* productions depict their characters as trapped in a kind of labyrinth or maze in which they attempt to decipher clues to the resolution of their quest and signs of exit. *Noir* offers "a disturbing vision . . . that qualifies all hope and suggests a potentially fatal vulnerability."[2]

Yet *noir* is never simply a repudiation or denial of properly human longing. In its accentuation of darkness and mystery, its rejection of standard characters and clear-cut happy endings, *noir* counters the naive American and Enlightenment faith in inevitable progress and transparent objectivity. At their most ambitious, modern conceptions of progress presuppose that we have a clear idea of where we are, where we are headed, and precisely how we are to reach the goal. A related Enlightenment theme is that of freedom from the bonds and superstitions of the past, a detachment from tradition, history, and religion. *Noir* productions are not typically religious nor are they particularly nostalgic, but they do depict the past as bearing down inex-orably upon the present. Memories and forgotten events from the past haunt and afflict human beings, circumscribing, if not utterly destroying, their possibilities in the present and their hope for the future.[3]

Although *noir* rarely exhibits the fulfillment of the human desires for truth and love, it does not mock longing itself. Instead, *noir* depicts these desires as noble and admirable. The

---

[1] Although there is some variation among film critics, the original set of films labeled *noir* typically includes: *The Maltese Falcon* (1941), *Double Indemnity* (1944), *Murder, My Sweet* (1944), and *The Lost Weekend* (1945). The era of clas-sic *noir* runs from these early films until roughly the late 1950s, with *A Touch of Evil* (1958) often being identified as the last entry. On the early period, the best treatment is Foster Hirsch's *The Dark Side of the Screen: Film Noir* (San Diego: Barnes, 1981). Hirsch's sequel *Detours and Lost Highways: A Map of Neo-Noir* (New York: Limelight, 1999) is also indispensable.

[2] J.P. Telotte, *Voices in the Dark: The Narrative Patterns of Film Noir* (Urbana: University of Illinois Press, 1989), pp. 17, 86.

[3] For a discussion of *noir*'s treatment of these themes, see my *Shows About Nothing: Nihilism in Popular Culture from The Exorcist to Seinfeld* (Dallas: Spence Publishing, 1999), pp. 10–53.

quest theme is prominent in *noir*. Always tenuous and often deadly, the quest of classical *noir* is twofold: "to solve the mystery of the villain and of the woman."[4] Thus, the quest is always about something more than the mere discovery of who did what to whom. It is also a search for love, communication, intelligibility, and truthfulness. However much classic *noir* raises questions about the purpose of human life, about the elusiveness of love and justice, it does not typically embrace nihilism. There are no superhuman anti-heroes in the world of classic *noir*; no one escapes the unyielding limits of the human condition. Nietzsche's vision of an overman standing beyond good and evil and transcending the petty conventions of morality by aesthetic self-creation finds no place in classic *noir*, a world where every aspiration is qualified, constrained, and limited by circumstances and by others, beyond the control of any particular individual. As one critic aptly puts it, in its attempt at achieving a "talking cure," *noir* seeks to "formulate our place in the cultural landscape" and thus it is a "genre of life."[5]

As we shall see shortly, the mythic structure and leitmotifs of *BtVS* reflect *noir* themes: the central role of the labyrinth and the quest, the influence of history and memory on the present, and the repudiation of Enlightenment autonomy and progress.

BtVS As Feminist *Noir:* A Hypothesis

Despite these similarities, there is no neat overlap between *BtVS* and classic *noir*. One difference concerns the setting of the productions. The definitive films of the classic *noir* era are set in cities. Both in their visual depiction of the city and in their narratives of city life, they put in question the vision of the city as modern utopia. According to the precepts of scientific rationalism, the city would be the place where desires could be tabulated and satisfied, where human life would become transparent to inspection and amenable to rational management. Moreover, *noir* often depicts those who play key societal roles in the city as morally compromised or at least as seriously tempted by vice

---

[4] Nicholas Christopher, *Somewhere in the Night: Film Noir and the American City* (New York: The Free Press, 1997), p. 20.
[5] *Voices in the Dark*, pp. 220, 222.

of one sort of another, usually lust or greed. In this respect, the
BtVS spin-off *Angel* is a more typical *noir*. Set in Los Angeles,
with most of the action at night, in a city run by a corrupt,
greedy corporation of lawyers, *Angel* also reflects the detective
story lines so prominent in *noir*. But the *noir* pattern of trans-
forming the American dream into a peculiarly American night-
mare is present in *BtVS* as well. Buffy's hometown of Sunnydale
sits atop the Hellmouth and officials such as the high school
principal and the mayor are dominated by a lust for power and
in league with dark forces. On *BtVS*, suburban paradise is but a
storm drain resting over the cauldron of hell.

Another difference between classic *noir* and *BtVS* has to do
with the overt feminism of the latter. Although classic *noir* provided some of the most complex parts for women in Hollywood
history, most female leads remained subordinate in the plot line
to the male leads. Some neo-*noir* films, such as *Body Heat*
(1981), often identified as initiating the period of neo-*noir*, and
Thelma and Louise (1991), break with these conventions and
reverse the standard *noir* relationship between males and
females. But these films violate fundamental assumptions of
classic *noir*, even as their excesses run counter to the dramatic
restraint of that era. In one case (*Thelma and Louise*), the story
is overly moralistic and in the other (*Body Heat*), flatly amoral.
In *Body Heat*, Matty (Kathleen Turner) is a kind of Nietzschean
superwomen residing beyond good and evil, akin to her male
counterparts in the neo-*noir* genre, such as Keyser Soze (Kevin
Spacey) in *The Usual Suspects*. Driven by a feminist mantra
about the evil that men do, *Thelma and Louise* presents a "cartoon version of real-world grievances." The film ends up painting itself into a "corner from which the only solution seems to
be killing off characters who have become steeped irreversibly
in *noir*."[6] More explicit than classic *noir* about the sexual desires
and activities of its protagonists, the films nonetheless provide
shallow, reductionist visions of sex. In *Body Heat*, Matty's sexual allure is all performance and her high octane sensuality is
"fatal to her male victim but not to herself."[7] Conversely, *Thelma
and Louise* reduces sex to a form of male sadism, the only ratio-

---

[6] *Detours and Lost Highways*, p. 244.
[7] *Detours and Lost Highways*, p. 183.

nal response to which is for women to fight physically for their rights not to be raped by male predators.

BtVS certainly deserves the label of feminist *noir*. Joss Whedon's original idea for the show encapsulates central themes of contemporary pop feminism. Musing on the obligatory horror movie scene where a monster chases a screeching, beautiful, teenage girl, Whedon thought, "I'd love to see a movie where (she) kills the monster."[8] Buffy replaces the standard male lead of classic *noir*. Here the female crime fighter is on her own quest to solve mysteries, concerning the crime, the fidelity of her male assistants, and her own identity. Buffy has inevitably been linked with male figures (Giles, her watcher, Xander, her friend, Angel and Riley, her lovers, and Spike, her nemesis and s-m sex tool), who often assist and sometimes thwart her quests.

But *BtVS* is feminism in a different key. It is a contemporary feminist drama cast in a classic *noir* mold. *BtVS* avoids both the preachy moralism of *Thelma and Louise* and the amoralism of *Body Heat*. *BtVS* is always tinged with a tragic, often sorrowful, sense of limitation, of the vulnerability of all human, even feminine, longing. It avoids reducing women to mere victim status, labeling men as evil or stupid, or granting the feminine—whatever that might be—icon status. *BtVS* also reckons with the consequences of vice, especially of violations of truthfulness, friendship, and love, in ways reminiscent of classic *noir*. The series, as Whedon insists, is all about "girl power," but it is not in the grip of illusory feminist theories of autonomous freedom or unbridled self-creation. In a more reflective and more sober way than *Ally McBeal*, Buffy is the greater counter to the mainstream feminist, and optimistic American, mantra: "You can have it all!"

The *Noir* Quest: Entrapment and Hope in the Labyrinth

Like many classic *noir* films, *BtVS* portrays human life as a quest, whose success depends largely on our ability to decipher uncertain clues and on the often dubious help of others. It thus counters Enlightenment themes of transparent certitude with

---

[8] Interview with Whedon in *Entertainment Weekly* (25 April 1997).

shadowy mystery and of independent autonomy with inescapable dependency. *BtVS* presents human life itself as part of a cosmic labyrinth, a universal battle between forces of good and evil, whose outcome for individuals and for humanity is perpetually in doubt.

For all its probing of themes excluded from other Hollywood genres, classic *noir* has a deeply conservative strain, affirming a clear set of limits to human aspiration and a warning of the dangers of transgressing boundaries. *BtVS* repeatedly affirms a clear structure to the cosmos, a sense of boundaries that cannot be crossed without dire consequences. At the end of Season Six, Willow's wiccan lover, Tara, is accidentally killed by a stray bullet intended for the slayer. Willow, whose use of magic has increasingly served her own aggrandizement, deploys all her powers to revenge Tara's murder. Buffy comments: "We can't change the universe . . . if we could, magic wouldn't be changing Willow the way it is. There are limits to what we can do. Willow ignored that and now the powers want to hurt her . . . to hurt all of us" ("Two To Go").

Implicitly affirming the classical teaching on vice as intrinsically corrupting of the perpetrator of evil, Buffy worries that, if Willow continues down the path of vengeance, she will "cross a line." For all of its allure and appearance of power, evil itself is, as Angel confesses at one point, "simple." Demons themselves have no soul. As Giles puts it, "A vampire isn't a person at all. It may have the movements, even the personality, of the person it takes over, but it is a demon at the core. There's no halfway" ("Angel"). As Angel, the vampire with the soul, says, "No conscience, no remorse . . . it's an easy way to live" ("Angel").

Some see the metaphor of the soul, particularly of the vampire with a soul as illustrative of ambiguities about good and evil, perhaps as teaching that all is ultimately gray. But this confuses the teaching of *BtVS* about good and evil, which has been consistent and clear throughout, with the question of whether characters can be neatly categorized as good or evil in a peremptory fashion. *BtVS* portrays a scale or spectrum of good and evil characters, along which the position of individual characters is never permanently fixed.

As is true of the complex characters in classic *noir*, so too on *BtVS* the complexity of humanity is as much curse as blessing.

Indeed, the story of Angel's recovery of his soul illustrates precisely this point; along with his soul, comes a conscience, a sense of remorse, and an insatiable longing to atone for his sins. As he confesses, "You have no idea what it's like to have done the things I've done and to care" ("Angel").

With some regularity both *BtVS* and *Angel* edge beyond the motif of entrapment and hint at the possibility of redemption. Seasons Five and Six ended on precisely this note: first, with Buffy offering her own life in place of her sister, Dawn, and then with Xander subjecting himself to Willow's wrath as a way of deterring her from destroying the world.

The True Essence of Magic

The Season Six finale contained a systematic reversal of conventional gender roles. The female leads (Willow and Buffy) are the chief protagonists who appear as warriors, seeking resolution through a violent attack on their opponents. Meanwhile, the male characters (Giles and Xander) play roles on the margins of the drama, until crucial moments when they confront Willow. But even then, they see that the use of direct force is futile. Thus, they opt for another response to evil and allow themselves to be subjected to unjust violence in an appeal to the residual humanity latent in Willow's soul. Although *BtVS* never rules out, and often insists on, the use of violence to fend off threats to the innocent, the show depicts a higher, more active, and more noble way of fighting evil: the sacrificial offering of oneself.

Giles calls this a higher magic or power, superior not only to dark magic, but also to the ordinary and virtuous use of violence to fend off evil and protect the innocent. So, for example, Buffy's slaying powers prove no match for Willow, whose comment that "there's no one with the power to stop me now," greets the return of Giles from England. Giles responds with his usual reserve, "I'd like to test that theory" ("Two To Go"). Giles proves no more successful than Buffy at combating Willow's ever-growing wrath and bellicose skill. When Willow drains all the power from Giles and leaves him for dead, the most able combatants have been rendered useless.

Willow, Giles warns, is "going to finish . . . the world." This, Willow herself admits, is the only way to "stop the pain"

("Grave"). Just as she begins to put these plans in motion, Xander, Willow's longtime friend and a guy not known for his courage, arrives. Willow mocks his presence and his powerlessness. But Xander is not here to fight Willow; instead, he is present to be with his old friend as she destroys the world. He recalls the events in their friendship, dating all the way back to "the first day of kindergarten." He reminds Willow, "you cried because you broke that yellow crayon . . . and you were too afraid to tell anyone. . . . You've come pretty far. . . . Ending the world, not a terrific notion, but the thing is . . . yeah, I love you. So if I'm going out, it's here. If you want to kill the world, then start with me. I've earned that." As she lacerates Xander's flesh, he is undeterred. The combination of his pitiful willingness to endure her wrath and his protestations of love cause Willow to relent in a torrent of tears.

Meanwhile, Giles recovers and explains how Xander saved the day. Since Giles knew that he would be defeated by Willow and that she would steal whatever power he possessed, he had himself infused with a different kind of magic, the "true essence of magic," which revived whatever "spark of humanity she had left in her" ("Grave"). The residue of humanity was precisely what allowed Xander's appeals to be heard. The true essence of magic has to do with sacrificial love, with a willingness to lay down one's life, not just for the innocent but also as a way of bearing the sufferings of others, even of converting those who have begun to cross the line.

Of course, Angel himself is the great example of a character seeking redemption. In one of the early episodes of his spin-off, an enemy traps Angel and tortures him as he probes Angel's soul. He repeatedly asks Angel what he most wants; unsatisfied with Angel's responses, he warns him to tell the truth because he will know if Angel lies. Angel responds, "I want forgiveness."

But redemption, like justice, seems always to be postponed in the *noir* worlds of *Angel* and *BtVS*. Angel has a long and tortuous path to travel before he recovers his humanity, while Buffy's return from the dead has only exacerbated her anguish. She now lives with the burdensome memory of paradise lost. Another episode from Season Six featured a despondent Buffy, desperately seeking to escape from a life she now detests ("Normal Again"). She retreats into a fantasy world, where her parents and psychiatrist treat her slayer world as a delusion of grandeur from which they hope she will return to her normal life. Buffy becomes torn between the two worlds. She ultimately opts for life as a slayer, but a final shot of a catatonic Buffy in a psych-ward leaves us wondering whether the entire *BtVS* series might simply be our window on Buffy's imaginary cosmos. Now, that's *noir*.

Season Six witnessed the near shattering of Buffy's identity. The show has always focused on the question and problem of Buffy's identity. Early episodes dealt with the obvious tensions between the demands of Buffy's calling as a slayer and her desire to lead a normal teen life. Even these episodes probed deeper questions about the identity and mission of the slayer. In the Season Six finale, Willow's most piercing rejoinder to Buffy touched on Buffy's own loss of purpose: "You hate it here as much as I do. . . . You know you were happier in the ground." Alluding to Buffy's sexual escapades with Spike, Willow taunts her need to "screw a vampire to feel" anything ("Two To Go").

Being plucked out of heaven to return to earth, failures in love and romance, the death of her mother, uncertainty about whether she is now mom or still big sister to Dawn, and the return of Giles to England—all these weigh heavily upon her, creating doubt and resentment. If early on in the series, Buffy seemed at times to be cursed by the inordinate burden of her duties as the chosen one, she seems increasingly cursed by an absence of a sense of what she is chosen or might choose to do. She is also afflicted by memories of what has or might have been. Buffy's *noir* labyrinth is increasingly an interior maze of her own soul.

The *Noir* Consequences of Sex: Eros, Death, and the Possibility of Love

The most demoralizing subplot in the sixth season was the sado-masochistic sexual relationship with the vampire, Spike, previously a most vicious nemesis. Being drawn inescapably to the sort of love that can only bring one harm and perhaps even destruction is a central motif in *noir*. The sexual liaison with Spike brings shame and a desire for secrecy. Although Spike shows glimmers of affection and is occasionally helpful to Buffy, their sexual chemistry is characterized mostly by violent genital stimulation. Toward the end of the season, as Buffy seeks to come to terms with what she's doing with Spike, she admits that she's been "in love with the pain" and that she's just been "using" Spike ("Wrecked"). To her repeated assertions that "it's over," Spike responds with knowing skepticism and then with a violence that culminates in attempted rape.

Of course, Buffy's love for men has always been tinged with elements of sadomasochism, a result of her own deeply competitive, physical prowess and the superheroes to whom she's attracted. Prior to the pre-eminently s-m relationship with Spike, Buffy's boyfriends, most notably her first and greatest love, Angel, had been noble sorts, committed to visions of justice and sacrifice. But Buffy's love for Angel underscores the contingency of love and human identity, their susceptibility to radical reversal. During Season Two, Buffy and Angel are an exclusive couple, and on Buffy's seventeenth birthday, in an episode entitled "Surprise," they consummate their love. The next day Angel is full of mocking wrath. Angel is thus a stand-in for the predatory male, whose true and truly vile self is revealed only after he gets what he wants.

But Angel's true self is more elusive and complex than this. His life illustrates the importance of history for *BtVS*, its embrace of the *noir* theme of the past's continued resonance in the present. Angel's life dates to mid-eighteenth-century Galway, where a simple bite from a vampire named Darla granted Angel membership among the undead. Known not so much for the number of his conquests as for the peculiarly cruel manner in which he inflicts evil, Angel becomes one of the most notorious vampires in history. After Angel kills the daughter of a gypsy family, the gypsies plot revenge. In a flashback to events unfolding in the Romanian woods in 1898, we witness the gypsies cursing Angel with the return of his soul, whose presence will bring back his memory and his conscience. He will thus be tormented by the memories of his innocent victims and "know true suffering." To keep the ensouled Angel from experiencing the pleasures of which humans are capable, the curse includes a caveat. If Angel ever experiences a moment of true pleasure or happiness, he will immediately be deprived of his soul and revert to his vampire ways ("Innocence").

But the curse is also a potential blessing. When Angel appears in Manhattan in 1996, a demon named Whistler meets him and tells him that "he can become a person." He then guides Angel to observe a novice slayer named Buffy Summers. Whistler's suggestion is that Angel can begin the process of redemption by assisting the slayer in her assigned duties. Angel complies and an unusual partnership, friendship, and love is born. But Angel's experience of true happiness activates the rider to the gypsy curse. He loses his soul and then sets out to torture and destroy the slayer.

Thus, *BtVS* replays themes about eros, sex, and love from classic *noir*, where sexual desire is typically seen as incompatible with conventional American life. Acting on that desire unleashes unanticipated consequences and rarely brings the happiness or even the pleasure sought. When he regains his soul yet again and returns to the margins of the human world, Angel, agreeing with Buffy that their love is impossible, departs for Los Angeles.

The last installment in the Buffy-Angel chronicles was entitled "I Will Remember You," a crossover episode in which Buffy travels to Los Angeles to chastise Angel for secretly returning to Sunnydale and spying on her. Angel's visit was prompted by word that Buffy was in grave danger and his secrecy by his unwillingness to stir up old passions and memories. As Buffy and Angel engage in verbal sparring, a demon appears to attack them. When the demon's blood splashes on Angel, he magically recovers his human state, with a heartbeat and an enormous hunger, for food and sex. He and Buffy get, as Cordy puts it, all "groiny." But like Samson without his hair, Angel is now useless as a warrior against evil. Meanwhile, Buffy, distracted by her enjoyment of the love that had for so long been forbidden and by her worries over Angel's vulnerable state, is losing her sense of duty as a slayer. So, Angel returns to the oracles, creatures that call to mind the Fates of ancient Greek mythology, and works out a deal to return Angel and Buffy to their prior states. The oracles agree to wipe out the previous day. The catch is that, while Buffy will have no memory of the blissful events, Angel will privately bear their memory. The end of the episode depicts Angel explaining this deal to a teary-eyed Buffy as they count down the seconds to the moment when the oracles will erase the past and forever alter their future. If in this episode, Angel appears as a sort of male protector of Buffy, it is also the case that the conclusion leaves Buffy once again alone, enduring the isolation proper to many a *noir* character.

With Season Six's explicit depiction of the sexual activities of Buffy and Spike and the lesbian romance of Willow and Tara, *BtVS* seems quite contemporary. Sexual desire has always been a staple of *noir*. In its insistence on the inevitable and usually destructive consequences of sex, *BtVS* once again reflects classic rather than neo-*noir*. *BtVS* is certainly feminist in its reflection of relaxed social constraints on the sexual activity of women. But it eschews the amoral sexual domination of women over men (*Body Heat*) and the flight from male sexuality (*Thelma and Louise*). Indeed, it is deeply skeptical about the very notion of sexual liberation. On *BtVS*, there is no free sex; consequences, usually unpleasant, always accompany sex.

BtVS is remarkably frank about the problematic complexity of sexual desire, about the way it conflicts with other human desire and goods, renders individuals susceptible to self-deception and vulnerable to the pain of being used for another's pleasure, and the way it tends toward excess and potentially lethal destruction. If, as critics have insisted, *noir* is an attempt to articulate our place in a confusing social and cultural landscape, then it would seem that in the contemporary *noir* world of *BtVS* nothing is more uncertain or more volatile than our sexual mores.

Of course, much contemporary art, literature, and film is precisely about this sort of issue. But *BtVS*'s feminist *noir* with a difference sees something else, our desperate need to see our erotic attractions to others in something more and other than merely genital terms. In this, *BtVS* revives a classical sense of eros, however tragically unfulfilled that desire may remain. It recovers eros as a longing for beauty, for wholeness, for discovering one's place both within the grand sweep of cosmic history and within the specific human community in which one finds oneself.

In its treatment of sexuality, as in its depiction of so many other themes, *BtVS* distinguishes itself as a dramatically successful and intellectually captivating feminist *noir*.

5
Feminism and the Ethics of Violence: Why Buffy Kicks Ass

MIMI MARINUCCI

> FAITH: Something made us different. We're warriors. We're built to kill.
>
> BUFFY: To kill *demons*. But it does not mean that we can pass judgment on people like we're better than everybody else.
>
> FAITH: We *are* better. That's right, better. People need us to survive. In the balance, nobody's gonna cry over some random bystander who got caught in the cross-fire.
>
> BUFFY: I am.
>
> FAITH: Well, that's your loss.[1]

The use of violence is central to Buffy's role as the Vampire Slayer. Although she displays greater respect for human life than Faith, Buffy is nevertheless willing, when necessary, to use violence against human beings. The thorough treatment of philosophy and *Buffy the Vampire Slayer (BtVS)* that this book aims to provide would be incomplete without an analysis of the ethics of violence.

My use of the term "violence" is consistent with its standard usage, and should not be confused with any idiosyncratic definitions developed within various philosophical discussions.

---

[1] This exchange occurs in the episode, "Consequences." Buffy confronts Faith, who has mistakenly killed a human being in "Bad Girls."

Quite simply, I conceive of violence as the use of physical force as an intentional means of inflicting pain or causing bodily harm. I regard the use of such force to inflict death as the ultimate expression of violence. For the sake of simplicity and continuity, I refer to the use of violence to destroy a vampire as killing, despite the technical inadequacy of this usage. I realize that vampires are not alive, at least not in the customary sense, but my imprecise application of terms relating to life and death in connection with vampires mirrors similar usage by Buffy and other characters from the show. In addition, I distinguish between vampires and demons because, although the show sometimes refers to vampires as a particular type of demon, there are significant differences between vampires and other demons. In particular, demons are depicted as members of species that are not human, but are capable of possessing or interbreeding with humans to create human-demon hybrids. In contrast, vampires are humans who have undergone a transformation through a ritualistic bloodsucking in which they are sired by an existing vampire. I refer to any and all other beasts not encountered in the real world as monsters. Finally, I refer, when appropriate, to "ordinary vampires" and "ordinary human beings" in recognition of the fact that, while vampires usually are evil and humans usually are not, there are occasional exceptions in both cases.

Violence and Vampires

Buffy offers a powerful commentary on violence in the episode "Anne." Ken, a demon disguised as a friendly human being, reaches out to healthy teenagers, usually runaways, and lures them into a Hell dimension. In this Hell dimension, they are convinced of their worthlessness and put to work as slaves until, drained of life and strength, they are returned to the streets, much weaker, much older, and much more confused. Buffy's search for Lily, yet another missing teenager, leads her through the portal into Hell, where she leads a revolt. Before passing back through the portal, she asks a thoroughly defeated Ken, "Wanna see my impression of Gandhi?" and bashes his head with a club. "Gandhi?" wonders Lily. Buffy explains, "Well, you know, he was really pissed off." It is possible, of course, that Buffy skipped one too many history classes and is, therefore, unaware of Gandhi's stance against violence. It seems more likely, however, that she is aware of Gandhi's pacifism and is expressing her own belief that violence is an appropriate, even necessary, response to certain forms of injustice. Moreover, by drawing this comparison between Gandhi's plight and her own, she invites us to conceive of the evil actions of the vampires, demons, and monsters that she faces as symbolically equivalent to the evil actions of human beings.

It might be tempting to dismiss Buffy's use of violence as irrelevant to questions about violence in the real world. After all, Buffy does not live in the real world, but in a world inhabited by vampires, demons, and monsters. It is not the case, however, that Buffy *always* uses violence against vampires, demons, and monsters, nor is it the case that she *never* uses violence against human beings. There are rare exceptions in which vampires, demons, and monsters warrant moral consideration, and rarer exceptions in which human beings do not. Unlike the more common cases in which Buffy slays the vampires and spares the humans, such exceptions convey a conception of justice with applications beyond the realm of fantasy.

Angel is the earliest and most obvious example of a vampire to whom Buffy extends the moral consideration usually reserved for human beings. After committing unconscionable evil during his first century as a vampire, Angel's soul was restored by a gypsy curse. With his soul intact, he is condemned to experience the pain of guilt over his past cruelty. In a futile attempt to compensate for his evil deeds, he begins protecting the innocent and "helping the helpless."[2] Angel is no ordinary vampire, and, for obvious reasons, Buffy does not slay him. Instead, Buffy and Angel find themselves in love and, eventually, in bed together. In a tragic turn of events, Buffy's love costs Angel his soul, as stipulated by the curse, when he experiences a moment of "true happiness" ("Surprise"). Without his soul, Angel reverts to his former vampire behavior, focusing the brunt of his cruelty on Buffy and her friends. Because there is a chance, albeit a slight one, of translating the curse and returning his soul, Buffy is

---

[2] In "Lonely Hearts," an early episode of the series *Angel*, Cordelia appoints herself as the business manager of Angel Investigations and supplies this slogan to describe Angel's mission.

reluctant to kill him. In fact, she finally kills him only when doing so becomes necessary for the continued existence of the world as we know it.[3] Fortunately, Angel eventually returns, soul intact, to resume his heroic mission.[4] As revealed by Angel's story, the straightforward principle that all and only vampires should be killed is overly simplistic. Although Buffy ultimately chooses the world over Angel,[5] she does not disregard him as she would disregard an ordinary vampire.

Like Angel, Spike is a vampire to whom Buffy extends moral consideration. Spike has been rendered incapable of harming human beings, thanks to a computer chip implanted in his brain as part of a scientific experiment in "The Initiative." Although this procedure did not restore his soul, it did change his behavior. When he begins satisfying his lust for violence by fighting the bad guys with Buffy and the gang, she loses her motivation to kill him. Buffy's treatment of Angel and Spike suggests that it is right for Buffy to kill vampires (when it is right) not because of what they are, but because of what they do. Vampires who are unwilling or unable to commit evil deeds are given the moral consideration that ordinary vampires are denied.

Buffy's treatment of vampires, demons, and monsters is relative to, and reflective of, their propensity to commit evil willingly. For example, before learning that the werewolf roaming Sunnydale is actually her friend Oz, Buffy refuses to kill the beast because, by day, it is just an ordinary human being ("Phases"). In contrast, when Buffy discovers that Ethan Rayne has fled shortly after putting her life in danger, she laments, "Darn. I really wanted to hit him 'til he bled" ("The Dark Age"). Such examples suggest that Buffy does not use violence against vampires, demons, and monsters insofar as they are vampires, demons, and monsters. Instead, she uses violence against will-

---

[3] Sadly, because Willow translates the curse in time to restore Angel's soul just moments before Buffy drives the stake through his heart, Angel is no longer evil when Buffy kills him in "Becoming, Part Two."

[4] Angel's return appears to have been triggered when Buffy returned his Claddagh ring to his mansion at the end of "Faith, Hope and Trick."

[5] It should not be assumed, however, that Buffy adopts a strict utilitarian principle that the good of the many outweighs the good of the individual. After all, she later refuses to sacrifice her sister, Dawn, in order to save the world yet again. Instead, she takes a chance by sacrificing herself in Dawn's place, with no guarantee that her plan will succeed.

ing agents of evil. While a consciously vicious person like Ethan Rayne fits this description, a werewolf whose actions are the result of an unwelcome monthly transformation does not.

More often than not, the willing agents of evil just happen to be vampires, demons, or monsters, rather than human beings. Nevertheless, if Buffy's tendency to slay the vampires and spare the humans is attributable to what they do and why they do it, then she should be no less willing to kill a human being, under the relevant circumstances, than to kill a vampire, demon, or monster. Indeed, the relevant circumstances arise in the episode, "Lie to Me." After learning that he has terminal cancer, Buffy's childhood boyfriend, Ford, conspires to trade Buffy's life for the opportunity to become a vampire. Buffy thwarts his plan by trapping him in a nest of hungry vampires, knowing that he will be eaten. Later, Buffy also demonstrates that she is willing to sacrifice Faith in order to save Angel. Faith is a Slayer who was called after the death of Kendra,[6] who was called after Buffy's own death.[7] In "Graduation Day, Part One," Faith, now fighting on the side of evil, poisons Angel, and the only way to save him is with the blood of a Slayer. Buffy stabs Faith, who escapes before her blood can be used to revive Angel.[8] Though unsuccessful, Buffy's attempt to kill Faith violates the moral stricture against taking human life. Buffy is rarely in a position to kill ordinary human beings, however, precisely because human beings who become willing agents of evil are far from ordinary. Human beings with no remaining trace of humanity do not warrant the moral consideration that ordinary human beings deserve. Indeed, they are the moral equivalent of ordinary vampires.

Just as human beings can enter the realm of nonhuman evil, nonhuman beings can also enter the realm of human evil. In fact, some of the evils that we normally associate with human beings and human institutions are represented, almost

---

[6] Kendra first appears in the episode, "What's My Line?, Part One." She is killed in "Becoming, Part One," and her replacement arrives in "Faith, Hope, and Trick."

[7] Fortunately, Buffy's death in "Prophecy Girl" was merely a technicality. She was revived within seconds, thanks to Xander's knowledge of CPR.

[8] Angel survives when Buffy commands him to drink her own blood, trusting him to stop before she is completely drained ("Graduation Day, Part Two").

exclusively, as forms of evil that transcend human agency. In particular, where there is political corruption, vampires or demons are usually involved. The abuse of power, including political power, is situated in opposition to humanity, and humanity is both necessary and sufficient for moral consideration. Consider the network of vampires and demons, especially Mayor Richard Wilkins III, in the government of Buffy's Sunnydale, as well as Wolfram and Hart, the law firm that controls much of what happens in Angel's Los Angeles. There is an analogy between power and the forces of darkness, and the resulting implication is that any abuse of power, be it the Mayor's abuse of political power or Willow's abuse of magical power, signals the loss of humanity. In fact, as Willow's use of magic turns to abuse, her friends fear that she will be lost to the forces of darkness. Their concern increases when Willow begins using magic to control the minds and memories of her friends, including Tara.[9] Tara breaks up with her, but they reunite after Willow finally stops using magic altogether. In "Villains," Willow returns to magic in order to punish Warren, the ringleader of Buffy's self-appointed trio of arch nemeses, who has accidentally killed Tara with a bullet intended for Buffy. Willow tortures and kills Warren, thus embarking upon a rampage that culminates in her attempt to destroy the world by resurrecting the buried temple of Proserpexa in the episode, "Grave." Resisting the use of violence, Buffy tells Willow, "I don't want to hurt you." Willow does not relent, however, and Buffy adds, "I said I didn't want to. I didn't say I wouldn't." In the end, Buffy is unable to defeat Willow with physical strength,[10] but her willingness to embrace the necessity of doing so is revealing. Unlike Gandhi, Buffy is willing to "fight the power."[11]

---

[9] In "All the Way," Willow erases Tara's memory of a recent argument. Tara discovers what Willow has done and considers leaving her in "Once More, with Feeling." The last straw comes when, in an effort to sooth Buffy's transition back from the grave, she accidentally erases the memory of the whole gang in "Tabula Rasa."

[10] This time, Xander is the one who saves the world. By expressing his love for Willow, he reaches that last spark of humanity that has not yet been destroyed by the evil forces inside her.

[11] I borrow this slogan from the song by Public Enemy, "Fight the Power," from *Fear of a Black Planet* (Def Jam, 1989, 1990).

Violence and Oppression

Through her attitude, if not through her actions, Buffy violates the popular and familiar stricture against violence. Most discussions of violence regard it, at best, as a necessary evil. In contrast, Buffy's use of violence is depicted, not as the lesser evil, but as the ultimate expression of her superheroic nature. Insofar as violence is a fundamental feature of Buffy's strategy, rather than a forgivable infraction of her moral code, she accepts William R. Jones's invitation to reconsider the moral status of violence as an instrument of social change.[12] Jones suggests that the ethic of nonviolence advanced by Martin Luther King, Jr. is not necessarily the best, and certainly not the only, model for fighting racial oppression. Nevertheless, King has become the ethical standard by which all Black leaders are judged, and moderate perspectives on violence have been misidentified as extremist. Jones compares the views of Martin Luther King, Jr., Malcolm X, and Mao Tse Tung. In contrast to King's belief that violence is an unacceptable response to oppression, Mao Tse Tung believes that violence is a necessary first response to oppression. Malcolm X, for whom violence is acceptable only as a last resort, occupies the philosophical middle ground between Martin and Mao, despite a widespread tendency to characterize him as a violent extremist.

Jones notes that the passive resistance recommended by Gandhi and King rests on the assumption that the sight of human suffering will "convert the oppressor by pricking his reason and conscience."[13] Following the moderate perspective of Malcolm X, Jones believes that, in the event that the conscience of the oppressor is not pricked, violence is both warranted and necessary. Thus, the oppressor warrants moral consideration only to the extent that the oppressor retains some vestige of humanity, as evidenced by the ability to respond with sympathy to the suffering of other human beings. Once again, moral consideration is directly proportionate to the humanity of the agent.

---

[12] William R. Jones, "Liberation Strategies in Black Theology: Mao, Martin, or Malcolm?" in *Philosophy Born of Struggle: Anthology of Afro-American Philosophy from 1917*, edited by Leonard Harris (Dubuque: Kendall/Hunt, 1983), pp. 229–241.

[13] Jones, p. 234.

As we have already seen, the abuse of political power is evidence of the loss of humanity in Buffy's world. Were Buffy to acknowledge both the fundamental evil of racism and the underlying abuse of political power through which it is maintained, she would surely endorse the use of violence against racial oppression.[14]

The moral stricture against violence serves the interests of the dominant culture, and those who employ or endorse violence in response to oppression threaten the status quo. Reactions typically include fear, hostility, and charges of immorality. This draws attention to the violence of the oppressed and renders the violence of the oppressor virtually invisible. Consider the public outrage over violence in rap music, which led to the 1990 introduction of the now familiar "Parental Advisory" that accompanies the cover art of many albums. While it is not my intention to defend the actions referenced in the lyrics of such songs as "Cop Killer,"[15] I will point out that the controversy following its 1992 release was focused entirely on the violence *mentioned* in the lyrics, while the violence that is actually *used* by so many police officers was largely ignored.

A similar double standard surrounds the issue of violence in response to women's oppression. Women's uses of violence against men draw far more attention than men's uses of violence against women, despite the infrequency of the former relative to the latter. Consider particularly the public outrage when Lorena Bobbit took a butcher knife to her husband's penis in 1993. While there is no denying the brutality of her actions, there is also no denying the comparable brutality of countless men who use violence against women at a rate of 5.9 million assaults per year.[16] The severity of Lorena Bobbit's violence was far from unique, but the reversal of gendered expectations rendered it highly visible. Also consider the critical response to the 1991

---

[14] Unfortunately, Buffy seems utterly unaware of the problem of racism. In her world, which is almost exclusively white, the question of race simply does not arise.

[15] "Cop Killer" was released by Ice-T (with Body Count) on the album *Body Count* (Time-Warner, 1992).

[16] Patricia Tjaden and Nancy Thoennes, "Full Report of the Prevalence, Incidence, and Consequences of Violence Against Women" (Washington, D.C.: U.S. Department of Justice, 2000).

film, *Thelma and Louise*.[17] Once again, the severity of the violence was unremarkable, but the gender of the agents of that violence was quite remarkable.[18] Even assertive attitudes among women, without any corresponding physical violence or threat thereof, are misidentified as intensely violent. For example, women who are verbally critical of sexism are often accused of "male bashing." What this accusation overlooks, of course, is the distinction between the literal and prevalent bashing of women by men, on the one hand, and the figurative and far less prevalent bashing of men by women, on the other hand.[19] Like racism, sexism exploits the moral stricture against violence to its own advantage.

Although Buffy's primary concern is not sexism, her perspective on violence is relevant to questions about the use of violence in response to women's oppression. As a woman empowered by the weapon of violence in a world that expects women to be passive, Buffy's role is not unlike the role of a similarly empowered Black leader in a world that expects Blacks to be passive. The feminist content of Buffy's struggle runs much deeper than the mere fact that she happens to be a woman who totally, and literally, kicks ass. Given the sexualized nature of so much of the violence that she faces, her mission is symbolic of the fight against sexual violence, for example, rape. As the Vampire Slayer, it is her duty to battle the strangers lurking in shadows and dark alleys, eager to prey on the enticing bodies of innocent and unwilling human beings. She prevents and punishes their attempts to "have," "take," "taste," "make" (and so on) their "desirable," "tempting," "luscious," "enticing" (and so on) victims. The interplay between bloodsucking and sex is especially clear when Buffy nearly "gives it up" (her passion as well as her blood) to the legendary and charming Dracula in "Buffy vs. Dracula." It is also clear when Riley visits the vampire's

---

[17] The title characters take a road trip, committing various crimes, including murder, along the way in *Thelma and Louise*, directed by Ridley Scott (MGM, 1991).

[18] For a thorough treatment of the connection between violence and the gender construction of masculinity, see Jackson Katz's film, *Tough Guise*, directed by Shut Jhally (Media Education, 1999).

[19] For a thorough treatment of these and related issues, see Suzanne Pharr, *Homophobia: A Weapon of Sexism* (Women's Project Publication, 1988).

answer to a prostitute in "Into the Woods." This vampire sucks his blood, without draining him completely, to satisfy her hunger and his fetish. It is noteworthy, as well, that being sired is reminiscent of the loss of virginity, and the resulting relationship carries an expectation of loyalty similar to that associated with sexual partnerships. This is evidenced by the relationship between Spike and Drusilla, as well as the relationship between Angel and Darla.[20] Such examples underscore the metaphor between bloodsucking and sex, thereby demonstrating that, when bloodsucking is unwelcome, as is usually the case, it is akin to rape.

Like rapists, vampires attempt to transfer responsibility for their actions onto the victims by describing their bodies as irresistible. In fact, however, it is possible for vampires, as it is for rapists, to resist temptation. Human blood is evidently much tastier than the blood of nonhuman animals, but vampires can survive without it. As evidenced by the exchange between Riley and his "prostitute," it is possible for vampires to feed on humans without killing them. Recall also that, when Angel drinks Buffy's blood in "Graduation Day, Part Two," he stops short of killing her. In "The Dark Age," vampires are caught stealing human blood from the hospital, which may interfere with the treatment of patients but is less violent than draining the blood of an unwilling human donor. When Angel has a soul and Spike has a chip, they exercise what is arguably the least objectionable means of satisfying their craving—they drink pig's blood. This suggests that, like a woman's sexuality, human blood is ultimately resistible. Consider Harmony's behavior when she visits Cordelia in Los Angeles. Cordelia senses that Harmony, her old friend from Sunnydale, is attracted to her, but she does not know that Harmony became a vampire in "Graduation Day, Part Two." Harmony refrains from biting Cordelia, who eventually realizes that Harmony was "coming out" to her, not as a lesbian, but as a vampire. This interaction highlights the eroticism implicit in the desire for human flesh, while simultaneously reminding us that vam-

---

[20] It is clear that Darla sired Angel and Angel sired Drusilla. In "Fool for Love," we see Drusilla sire Spike, but in "School Hard," Spike claims to have been sired by Angel. At any rate, the complex web of loyalties and vendettas among this group has a decidedly sexual character.

pires and, by extension, rapists are capable of resisting that desire.

A similar reminder underlies Spike's behavior toward Buffy when she returns from heaven after her second death.[21] She died by throwing herself into a magical force field, thereby sparing her sister, Dawn, and saving the world. Because Buffy was killed by magic, Willow was able to revive her with magic. Although a minor glitch in Buffy's resurrection permits Spike to harm her without activating the chip in his brain, he makes no effort to kill her. Instead, he treats her kindly, and she begins using him for violent sex, much to his apparent satisfaction. Realizing that her behavior demeans them both, Buffy ends her affair with Spike. Unwilling to accept that, this time, no really does mean no, he attempts to rape her. It is interesting that Spike's attempt to rape Buffy resembles an ordinary attempt to suck her blood.[22] It is also interesting that he chooses not to harm her until this particular scene. After demonstrating that he is capable of better behavior than ordinary vampires display, he responds to her rejection with rage. Like an ordinary human rapist, Spike is accountable for his own aggression.

Violence and Feminism

The primary form of evil that Buffy is called upon to fight is symbolic of rape, which is symbolic of women's oppression. For this reason, I suggest that Buffy's fight is, in turn, symbolic of the fight against women's oppression. Feminist discussions of the ethics of violence usually focus on men's violence against women. One exception is Bat-Ami Bar On's "Violent Bodies."[23] Bar On explores Hannah Arendt's *On Violence*, which warns that violence typically leads to more violence. Although this warning is reminiscent of King's "The old law of an eye for an eye leaves everybody blind,"[24] Arendt, unlike King, accepts the occasional necessity of violence. Her concern is that doing

---

[21] Buffy died in "The Gift," only to be resurrected again in "Bargaining, Part One."

[22] This resemblance was pointed out to me by Elizabeth Kissling.

[23] Bat-Ami Bar On, "Violent Bodies," in: *Feminists Doing Ethics*, edited by Peggy DesAutels and Joanne Waugh (Lanham: Rowman and Littlefield, 2001).

[24] Martin L. King, *Stride Toward Freedom* (New York: Harper and Row, 1964), p. 189.

violence habituates the agent, who then becomes more inclined to do violence the next time around. Because this is neither effective nor desirable, she believes that the use of violence is acceptable only in pursuit of short-term goals. According to Arendt, "If goals are not achieved rapidly, the result will be not merely defeat but the introduction of the practice of violence into the whole body politic."[25]

Similarly, Bar On suggests that a readiness to fight is the result of practice and habituation. For this reason, a readiness to fight entails a corresponding likelihood of fighting.[26] Obviously, Buffy is well practiced, well habituated, and ready to fight. Consistent with Bar On's description, Buffy is able to act quickly because she looks for danger. When she sees it before it becomes visible to others, however, she is often accused of blurring the boundary between fact and fiction. Consider her reaction to her Mother's new boyfriend in the episode, "Ted." Buffy does not realize that Ted is an evil cyborg, but she does realize that there is something very wrong about him. Her suspicions are not confirmed until after she fights him with sufficient force to kill an ordinary human being. Similarly, in "Living Conditions," her college roommate, Kathy, gets on her nerves, and Buffy concludes that she is evil. Her friends are understandably concerned when she resolves to fight what appears to be an unremarkable college student. They are not relieved of their concern when Buffy points out that Kathy's toenail clippings continue growing after they have been cut. Indeed, the fact that Buffy would examine her roommate's nail clippings strikes them as evidence of her paranoia. As it turns out, Kathy is, indeed, a demon. In Buffy's case, we can only hope that her Slayer senses are accurate enough to keep her from hurting innocent people.

Without the benefit of superpowers, however, a readiness to fight increases the likelihood of using violence when one should not. Bar On recognizes the complications associated with the production of violent bodies, even when it is justified by feminist ends:

A feminist cannot merely celebrate the transgressive excess that she creates through the production of her own or other violent women

---

[25] Hannah Arendt, *On Violence* (New York: Harcourt Brace, 1969, 1970), p. 80.
[26] Bar On, p. 64.

[sic] bodies. She must concern herself with quite complex questions about the possibility that, as women's bodies become habituated to violent action, they may act in ways that "inhumanely" and "destructively" transgress the boundaries that are specified by an ethico-political justification for the action that they are undertaking. This is a possibility that cannot be dismissed as too marginal to worry about, not in light of the extensive evidence regarding the enormity of past and present abusive or cruel violence in which women too have partaken. Women have acted violently not merely because they are not in control but also because, like men of the same socioculture, *they too can find something attractive about violence* [my emphasis].[27]

As the series progresses, it becomes more and more clear that Buffy does, in fact, find something attractive about violence, and this troubles her deeply. Her occasional comment that a Slayer is not simply a killer seems motivated by a desire to remind herself as much as anyone else. The revelation in "Restless" that the first Slayer's power, from which Buffy's own power descends, was based in primeval rage leaves her wondering if she is really very different from the evil forces she combats. While it is Faith who acknowledges in "Faith, Hope and Trick" that slaying arouses her sexually, Buffy does not disagree. Finally, the violent nature of her relationship with Spike suggests that Buffy is similarly aroused by her own aggression, particularly when she feels disengaged from humanity.

Indeed, one might argue that Buffy's readiness to fight the symbolic equivalent of rape yields a corresponding readiness to commit the symbolic equivalent of rape. This is illustrated most clearly through her treatment of Spike as an outlet for her simultaneously violent and sexual impulses. The theme of sexualized violence is reiterated, metaphorically, through Buffy's treatment of vampires under more typical circumstances. She slays them by penetrating their bodies, so to speak, with a sharpened phallic object—often, the aptly named "Mr. Pointy."[28] Thus, Buffy's use of violence can be interpreted as a disconcerting reflection

---

[27] Bar On, p. 71.
[28] Buffy chuckles when she learns that Kendra has named her favorite wooden stake. After Kendra's death, however, she occasionally refers to her own stake, presumably the same one that Kendra used, as "Mr. Pointy." See, for example, "Helpless," "Choices," and "The Freshman."

of the violence by which it is justified. Buffy's use of violence can be interpreted as a threat to her own humanity.

Despite these complications, I would reject the conclusion that Buffy is no better than the vampires against whom her violence is deployed. Regardless of the potential for abuse, there are good, moral reasons for Buffy to slay vampires, just as there are good, moral reasons for ordinary women to become empowered to defend ourselves against the violence to which we statistically are susceptible. Like Buffy's friends, we can develop the skills necessary to join the fight against evil. Nevertheless, our training must be sensitive to and reflective of the potential to abuse violence. When training to use appropriately violent measures, we must also train to avoid using excessively violent measures. This balance is implicit in many of the martial arts, including Tai Chi, which Buffy eventually adopts as part of her training. It is by no means surprising that Angel, who has been balancing the good and evil within himself for more than a hundred years, is the one to introduce Tai Chi into Buffy's regimen.

Rejecting the false dichotomy between passivity and hostility, I propose that the empowerment that comes with the ability to do violence can be tempered by the awareness of that ability. There may be some truth to the old stereotype that physically intimidating men, whose strength is not in question, are confident enough to walk away from challenges issued by men whose strength is less obvious. When threatened, a woman with intimate knowledge of her ability to cause harm is more likely to respond with appropriate violence than a woman who lacks such self-knowledge. At the same time, however, she is also less likely to respond with inappropriate violence, say, by attacking her sleeping husband's genitals with a butcher knife. A morally viable alternative to unwarranted passivity and unwarranted aggression alike is the readiness to use appropriate violence in response to inappropriate violence. If we are willing and able to defend ourselves "by any means necessary," we can transcend the choice between using means that are unnecessary or giving up entirely.

No Damsel in Distress

The gender construction of femininity as passive is reiterated in cultural ideals surrounding women and sexuality. Buffy's twofold status as both Slayer and sex symbol challenges the connection between women's vulnerability and women's sexuality. Buffy is sexy because of her strength, not in spite of it. To the extent that media images and role models have an impact on what we deem acceptable or desirable, it is important to construct alternatives to media images and role models that perpetuate oppression. Familiar representations of women as actual or potential victims of violence reinforce the link between femininity and passivity, particularly when such representations are sexualized. *BtVS* is a welcome alternative to countless books, movies, and television shows in which the male protagonist saves the damsel in distress and romance ensues. Although she accepts help when she needs it, Buffy is no damsel in distress.[29]

---

[29] I am grateful to Barry Messinger, both for general discussions of *Buffy the Vampire Slayer* and for helpful comments on multiple drafts of this manuscript. I am also grateful for discussions with Elizabeth Kissling and editorial suggestions by James South.

Codex 2

Don't speak Latin in front of the books

Knowledge, Rationality, and Science in the Buffyverse

6

Balderdash and Chicanery: Science and Beyond

ANDREW ABERDEIN

Magic? Magic is all balderdash and chicanery. I'm afraid we don't know a bloody thing. ("Tabula Rasa")

Practically the first thing that viewers of the first episode of *Buffy the Vampire Slayer* (*BtVS*) see is Sunnydale High's science lab. Before they have seen Buffy, or anyone else, they are shown a selection from the apparatus of empirical enquiry, or at least high school science instruction: a skeleton, specimens in formaldehyde, microscopes and a skull. It is dark, and a bit spooky, but quiet—until a window is broken from outside. A guy and a girl, vampire and victim (or *vice versa,* as it turns out), are making an illegal entry into the lab—and into the rational, naturalistic order it represents.

Confrontations such as this are a defining characteristic of the supernatural story: they mark the points at which the modern and scientific protagonists, and the audience, are allowed a glimpse of the uncanny. A classic example occurs as the dénouement of *The Hound of the Baskervilles,* when Holmes and Watson finally come face to face with the hound:

A hound it was, an enormous coal-black hound, but not such a hound as mortal eyes have ever seen. Fire burst from its open mouth, its eyes glowed with a smouldering glare, its muzzle and hackles and dewlap were outlined in flickering flame. Never in the delirious dream of a disordered brain could anything more savage, more appalling, more hellish be conceived than that dark form and savage face which broke upon us out of the wall of fog.[1]

But moments later and the impression of the supernatural has been vanquished, and the creature reduced to the natural order:

> Holmes and I both fired together, and the creature gave a hideous howl . . . that cry of pain from the hound had blown all our fears to the winds. If he was vulnerable he was mortal, and if we could wound him we could kill him.[2]

Not only has Watson's narration shifted from sublimity and terror to reiterated inferential reasoning, he has also described the successful application of appropriate scientific method. As Arthur Conan Doyle was writing, the International Congress of Zoology was establishing rules for the taxonomy of animal species.[3] These rules, which in an updated form obtain today, standardized the prevailing nineteenth-century practice that the discoverer of a new species should obtain a "type specimen" for deposit in the reference collection of a major natural history museum.[4] Strange animals are excluded from scientific consideration until someone succeeds in killing one, which may then be filed away appropriately to give the species its proper place in the natural order.

Doyle places this key confrontation at the end of his novel, decisively undercutting earlier suggestions of a supernatural explanation. But television series actively resist such closure, as novels cannot: the series format ensures that no resolution can ever be immune from revision; no confrontation final. In *BtVS*

---

[1] Sir Arthur Conan Doyle, *The Hound of the Baskervilles* in *Sherlock Holmes: The Complete Novels and Stories*. Volume II (New York: Bantam, 1986), p. 131.
[2] *Ibid*. Cf. Arnold Schwarzenegger's line "If it bleeds, we can kill it!" in *Predator* (1987).
[3] The 1895 congress appointed a committee to devise an international system. The committee's recommendations were adopted in 1901 and published in 1905 as *Règles Internationales de la Nominologie Zoologìque*. See E. Mayr, E.G. Linsley, and R.L. Usinger, *Methods and Principles of Systematic Ecology* (New York: McGraw-Hill, 1953). *Hound* was first published in *The Strand Magazine* between August 1901 and April 1902.
[4] As Stapleton, the hound's owner, had himself done with a Yorkshire moth (*Hound*, Chapter 15).

supernatural elements of an apparently irreducible character are present from the beginning and throughout. When Riley Finn, the Buffyverse's own soldier-scientist, finds a savage and hellish canine to train his gun on, the supernatural fights back, resisting reduction to the natural in an unexpected fashion:

> RILEY: What's the hold up? I thought Graham gave you a full description.
> SCIENTIST: The hold up is that he described characteristics present in about 40 varieties of known demons. So we're cross checking DNA evidence, hair, and fibers. . . .
> RILEY: And how long's that going to take?
> SCIENTIST: I have no idea. Now *back off*—
> RILEY: I don't need a bunch of tests to know this thing's a killer—so why don't you back off? ("New Moon Rising")

But just as Riley is about to shoot the creature, it turns human. Indeed, it transforms into Oz, Willow's werewolf ex-boyfriend. Riley's "Demons bad. People good." theorem takes another blow as he discovers that not only are some of the monsters not evil, but that some of them have dated his friends. The Initiative scientist is happy to set about matching Oz to the appropriate type specimen, but Riley appreciates that he knows Oz in a way that such tests cannot replicate. Even a specimen collection beyond the wildest dreams of the Smithsonian must leave whole areas of knowledge untouched. And Oz himself cannot help: taciturn at best, he has been drugged into temporary speechlessness by the very scientists seeking to identify him.

These confrontations between science and the supernatural can have three possible outcomes: the naturalistic view can win outright, reducing the (purportedly) supernatural to the world we know; or it can be vindicated in principle, by offering a reduction to some future or alternative science; or it can be defeated, faced down by something (some *thing*) which obdurately resists any such reduction. These different outcomes offer a three-fold taxonomy of popular representations of the supernatural: three grades of supernatural involvement, as it were. While many aspects of this distinction can be perceived in recent popular culture, from *Star Trek* to *The X-Files*, *BtVS* is notable for the depth of its engagement. In the next three sections we shall explore how it addresses each of these three grades.

Grade One

It's not magic. It's chemistry. You can tell by how damn slow it is. ("Doublemeat Palace")

The first grade is the reduction of the supernatural to contemporary science, as befell the hound of the Baskervilles. Another extraordinary hound, the animated great dane Scooby-Doo, was a standard bearer for this perspective: his original cartoon series is famous for always explaining away the supernatural elements as the machinations of people in rubber masks, who would have gotten away with it if it weren't for those meddling kids. However, the recent feature-length videos and live-action film have broken with this tradition—much to the dismay of the determined skeptics at the Committee for the Scientific Investigation of Claims of the Paranormal.[5] Buffy's friends ironically invoke these earlier meddling kids in naming themselves the Scooby Gang ("What's My Line?, Part One" and repeatedly, thereafter): but their monsters have always been real.

Nevertheless, the first grade is still the dominant view amongst the Buffyverse's human inhabitants: the population of Sunnydale repeatedly demonstrate their resilient "tendency to rationalize what they can and forget what they can't" ("The Harvest"). Since the underworld can prove swiftly lethal for the unwary meddler, this attitude has definite survival benefits. As Aimee Fifarek points out, while the essential conflict for the protagonists of *The X-Files* is over the truth of belief in the supernatural, in *BtVS* the concern is with its utility.[6] Even for the Scoobies, familiarity with the supernatural can be a mixed blessing. After Buffy escapes death at the hands of the Master, Xander and Willow assume her delayed trauma must be possession ("When She Was Bad"). Giles correctly identifies her real problem, but on other occasions he overcompensates: Buffy's roommate was a demon ("Living Conditions") and Xander was possessed by a hyena spirit ("The Pack"). For a third-generation watcher, Giles's skepticism is an unexpected ("I can't believe that you of all people are trying to Scully me," as Buffy puts it,

---

[5] Tim Madigan, "Scooby Doo, How Could You?," *Skeptical Briefs*, Volume 8, No. 4, www.csicop.org/sb/9812/scooby.html (December 1998).

[6] Aimee Fifarek, "'Mind and Heart with Spirit Joined': The Buffyverse as an Information System," *Slayage* 3, http://www.slayage.tv/ (June 2001).

["The Pack"]) but instinctive reaction, as his temporary amnesia reveals ("Tabula Rasa").

It would seem that the first grade could never provide a true explanation for all that goes on in the Buffyverse. But one episode, "Normal Again," challenges this notion. Apparently poisoned by a demon's toxin, Buffy begins to hallucinate that she is a patient in a mental ward and that all her experiences of the previous six years have been delusional. Characteristically, the show resists the comforting resolution of a clear falsification of this skeptical hypothesis: Buffy recovers, but the episode ends in the world of her hallucination. Radical skepticism has a substantial pedigree as a science-fictional storyline, but philosophers have known it for longer, and know how incorrigible it can be. Most famously, Descartes's "I think, therefore I am" is deduced by him as the one conclusion he could trust, even if he was deceived about everything else by the actions of a malicious demon.[7]

Grade Two

> Of course! I've been investigating mystical causes of invisibility when I should have looked to the quantum mechanical! ("Out of Mind, Out of Sight")

The second grade, reduction of the supernatural to a "future science" methodologically continuous with contemporary science, is a staple of science fiction. Some episodes of *BtVS* adopt this perspective, in the tradition of *Ghostbusters* (1984), imaginatively extending the modest achievements of parapsychology to explore traditionally supernatural themes in a "scientific" context. This device is intrinsically speculative and its plausibility can vary dramatically. Regrettably, there are no quantum-mechanical means of achieving invisibility and, while robotics and genetic modification are rapidly developing fields, they have not yet made possible robots such as Ted ("Ted") and April

---

[7] René Descartes, *Meditations on First Philosophy*, in *The Philosophical Writings of Descartes*, translated by John Cottingham, Robert Stoothoff, and Dugald Murdoch (Cambridge: Cambridge University Press) Volume I, pp. 15–17 (*Oeuvres de Descartes*, edited by Charles Adam and Paul Tannery (Paris 1964–1976, Volume VII, pp. 22, 25).

("I Was Made to Love You") or Coach Marin's application of Soviet fish DNA research to his swim team ("Go Fish"). However, the "science" behind these developments is never more than gestured at.

BtVS's most extensive treatment of Grade Two occurs as the principal plot arc of Season Four. The Initiative, as its shadowy head eventually tells us, "represent[s] the government's interest in not only controlling the Otherworldly Menace, but in harnessing its power for our own military purposes" ("Primeval"). In a story directly echoing both *The X-Files* and Joss Whedon's own script for the 1997 film *Alien: Resurrection*, a sinister government agency seeks to hybridize humans with monsters to produce unstoppable combatants, but loses control of its creations. The Initiative is a broad parody of the "big science" of the military-industrial complex, and as we saw above, their approach to the supernatural is profoundly reductive. Riley's colleague Forrest, ever the loyal company man, states the corporate line: demons are "just animals, man. Plain and simple. Granted, a little rarer than the ones you grew up with" ("Doomed").

This approach yields some technical successes but ultimately proves catastrophic. Dr. Angleman's "xenomorphic behavior modification" ("The I in Team"), has enduring effects, at least for Spike, who is rendered incapable of attacking humans. But the central, and most secret project, the "kinematically redundant, bio-mechanical demonoid" Adam ("Goodbye Iowa"), is a homicidal monster. Spike and Adam's predicaments both bring to mind Phineas Gage, who entered the history of cognitive science in 1848 when he was transfixed through the skull with a railroad spike.[8] Although he made an extraordinary physical recovery, the damage to his brain dramatically changed his character. His capacity for emotional engagement with the world was fatally compromised, to the unexpected, but philosophically revealing, detriment of his ability to make rational decisions.[9] Conversely, Spike, who was said to have "earned his nickname by torturing his victims with railroad spikes" ("School Hard"),

---

[8] Antonio R. Damasio, *Descartes's Error: Emotion, Reason, and the Human Brain* (New York: Putnam, 1994). Technically, Gage was struck by a tamping iron, not a spike, although that is how it is often described.
[9] *Ibid.*

also experienced a dramatic change of behavior after an unexpected neurological intervention, but for the better. Lack of emotional engagement was never his problem, although given his evil (in Buffyverse terms, soulless) nature, this tended to manifest as sadism. The external structure imposed on his actions by his chip eventually drives him to acquire his own soul. Adam, on the other hand, was made in the image of his creators' epistemology: he is technically perfect but devoid of precisely that emotional capacity necessary for sane decision making. When he is defeated, it is by the composite "über-Buffy" in which hand and mind are integrated with heart and spirit ("Primeval").

Grade Three

I don't believe in science. All those bits and molecules no one's ever seen. I trust eyes and heart alone. ("Crush")

At the third grade the supernatural is portrayed as irreducible. Sometimes this is a simple antithesis to the scientific attitude of the first two grades, as in Drusilla's remark above. Her perspective is the polar opposite of the Initiative's: while they are so rational as to exclude all emotion, she is so emotional as to exclude all reason. More typical of *BtVS*'s employment of this grade is an admonition that the supernatural can coexist with the scientific, to the enrichment of both perspectives. As Jenny Calendar reminds Giles, "bad old science" did not make the magic go away: "the divine exists in cyberspace same as out here" ("I Robot . . . You Jane"). Indeed the show's most characteristic ambience is "a creepy mix of magic and science" ("Beer Bad," shooting script direction). The astonishing success of malign scientific projects is frequently attributed to the scientific work having been conducted on the Hellmouth. Conversely, a surprising amount of spell casting takes place in science labs (crucial scenes in "The Witch"; "Bewitched, Bothered, and Bewildered"; "Lovers Walk"; and "Primeval," for instance). Jenny and, especially, Willow are portrayed as equally adept at both science and magic. Willow's irresponsible curiosity remains a constant throughout all the other changes she undergoes: from "accidentally decrypt[ing] the city council's security system" ("The Harvest") to scavenging parts from evil robots:

> BUFFY: Willow. Tell me you didn't keep any parts.
>
> WILLOW: (guiltily) Not any big ones. . . .
>
> BUFFY: Oh, Will, you're supposed to use your powers for good!
>
> WILLOW: I just wanna learn stuff. ("Ted")

and from "tinkering with the Tinkerbell" ("Out of My Mind") to commanding world-destroying magical power.

The conflict between Grades Two and Three is explicitly dramatized as the Initiative versus the Scoobies. For example, "Doomed" cuts between Giles reading a description of a demon as "Slick like gall, and gird in moonlight, father of portents and brother to blight . . ." from one of his "old, big, dusty and portentous-looking" books (shooting script direction) and Riley's "visual analysis" of the same demon as "three meters tall, approximately one hundred to one-twenty kilograms." Both groups seek to research and defeat the same phenomena, but deploy very different methodologies: the archive versus the laboratory; mystical powers versus military weaponry.[10] However, although the Scoobies can appropriate Initiative-style techniques when necessary (as in "Innocence"), the Initiative's Grade Two perspective always prevents them from reciprocating.

Learning from the Supernatural

The distinction among the three grades has several important parallels in philosophy and the history of ideas. For example, the contrast between the three grades directly mirrors that between three positions in the philosophy of mind which have been termed currentism, futurism and non-physicalism.[11] Currentists hold that all the operations of the mind could in principle be understood in terms of contemporary physics; futurists appeal to some hypothetical future completion of physics to

---

[10] For more detail, see William Wandless, "Undead Letters: Searches and Researches in *Buffy the Vampire Slayer*," *Slayage* 1, www.slayage.tv (January 2001).

[11] Seth Crook and Carl Gillett, "Why Physics Alone Cannot Define the 'Physical': Materialism, Metaphysics, and the Formulation of Physicalism," *Canadian Journal of Philosophy* 31 (2001), pp. 333–359.

perform the same explanatory task; whereas non-physicalists deny that the mental could ever be satisfactorily reduced to the physical.

But perhaps the most instructive parallel is with the enduring dispute between the sciences and the humanities. Recent manifestations of this dispute include the two cultures debate and the "science wars," but it goes back much further—ultimately perhaps to Plato's "old quarrel between philosophy and poetry."[12] However, one of its most important phases was the quarrel of the ancients and the moderns, which dominated seventeenth-century thought. Today we take it for granted that science is essentially cumulative, telling us new things about the world, but we forget how modern a perspective that is. Until the scientific revolution in the seventeenth century, the prevailing assumption was that the lost knowledge of past generations far exceeded our own. Myths of a "Golden Age" were widespread in the ancient world, while medieval Europeans were surrounded by ample evidence of the superior achievements of their ancestors. The new scientific methodology began to challenge this view, but for a century or more both positions remained tenable: the "moderns" stressed the novelty and importance of results that the "ancients" dismissed as trivial, useless, or essentially foreshadowed by earlier authorities.

Grades One and Two are explicitly modern: the first regards science as sufficiently complete to explain the supernatural; the second appeals to the future completion of science. Grade Three encompasses the ancient perspective, since it allows for the possibility of recovering a knowledge that transcends scientific explanation. The ancients promised a more nuanced and richly textured appreciation of the natural world than that available through the spartan scientific methodology of the moderns. Unfortunately, their research program was in steep decline and they were unable to fulfill this promise. As Voltaire remarked of die-hard ancient Sir William Temple,

> He goes so far as to pity us for having nothing left of the magic of the Indians, the Chaldeans, the Egyptians; and by this magic he understands a profound knowledge of nature, whereby they

---

[12] Plato, *The Republic*, Book X, 607b.

produced miracles: but he does not cite one miracle, because in fact there never were any.[13]

But Voltaire's wit oversimplifies: recent historians of science have focused attention on the magical practices and beliefs of early modern scientists. Although there were some resolute skeptics, such as Galileo and Huygens, many of their contemporaries believed in alchemy, astrology, witchcraft or even more esoteric practices: Kepler, Bacon, Boyle and Newton are only the most illustrious examples.[14] While this was once dismissed as embarrassing atavistic regression, it can also be understood as demonstrating their modernity: magical practices provided an alternative to the authority of Aristotle, and anticipated many of the characteristic features of scientific method. Hence, magical modes of thought may be understood as a synthesis of ancient and modern, and their surprising persistence as a desperate attempt to retain subtleties of interpretation that the modern paradigm would inevitably forfeit.[15] "Revolution" implies loss as well as innovation, and the scientific revolution is no exception. The survival of a Grade Three perspective in popular culture is a reminder of this loss, and a challenge to provide appropriate restitution.

This argument turns on the assumption that the distinction between Grades Two and Three is a real one. We have seen how *BtVS* argues that it is, but what of Arthur C. Clarke's "Third Law," that "any sufficiently advanced technology is indistinguishable from magic?"[16] This plausible aphorism implies that the irreducible supernatural of the third grade would be indistinguishable from the advanced technology of the second grade. Of course, "indistinguishable" is an epistemic assessment: it does not imply that the grades could not be separated, but only that they could not be told apart. Yet the distinction might still

---

[13] Voltaire, *The Philosophical Dictionary*, "Ancients and Moderns," selected and translated by H.I. Woolf (New York: Knopf, 1924).

[14] H. Floris Cohen, *The Scientific Revolution: A Historiographical Inquiry* (Chicago: University of Chicago Press, 1994), p. 174.

[15] *Ibid.* p. 182. Loss of scientific content in this fashion has latterly been called "Kuhn loss": see Thomas S. Kuhn, *The Structure of Scientific Revolutions* (Chicago: University of Chicago Press, 1970), p. 148.

[16] Arthur C. Clarke, "Technology and the Future" in *Report on Planet Three and Other Speculations* (London: Pan, 1984), p.147.

be thought to assume an unduly narrow account of scientific method. Critics of this notion, such as Paul Feyerabend, have argued that the content typically ascribed to scientific method is a bad description of what scientists do, and a poor guide for their future conduct.[17] Feyerabend's "methodological anarchism" controversially rejects the conventional exclusion of the magical from scientific technique. However, this exhortation to transcend the conventional limits of scientific enquiry is as readily understood as an endorsement of Grade Three as it is as a rejection of its distinction from Grade Two.

Smelly Knowledge

JENNY: Computers don't smell, Rupert.

GILES: I know! Smell is the most powerful trigger to the memory there is. A certain flower or a whiff of smoke can bring up experiences . . . long forgotten. Books smell. Musty and rich. The knowledge gained from a computer, . . . it has no texture, no context. It's there and then it's gone. If it's to last, then the getting of knowledge should be, uh, tangible, it should be, . . . smelly.[18] ("I Robot . . . You Jane")

Giles has many fans among professional librarians, yet his fogeyish technophobia is one aspect of his character with which they cannot identify.[19] But in this passage he is communicating a deeper insight. In the last section, we saw how Grade Three could be understood as a yearning for a richer conception of knowledge than the reductive rationalism which has been the enormously successful legacy of the scientific revolution. And in discussing Grade Two, we touched upon the unexpected

---

[17] Paul Feyerabend, *Against Method* (Atlantic Highlands: Humanities Press, 1975).

[18] For an interesting parallel to Giles's opinions, see the title story in: Elspeth Davie, *The Man Who Wanted to Smell Books and Other Stories* (Edinburgh: Canongate, 2001).

[19] GraceAnne A. DeCandido, "Rupert Giles and Search Tools for Wisdom in *Buffy the Vampire Slayer,*" www.well.com/user/ladyhawk/Giles.html. An earlier version of this article was published as "Bibliographic Good vs. Evil in *Buffy the Vampire Slayer,*" *American Libraries*, Volume 30, No. 8 (September 1999), pp. 44–47.

importance of emotional engagement for rationality. So Giles's desire for "smelly" knowledge is widely shared and perceptive: can we articulate something suitable?

One prospect lies in a further analogy with the Grade Two-Grade Three distinction. Some feminist commentators on science compare masculine and feminine "ways of knowing": sharply contrasted epistemic vices and virtues attributed to men and women respectively. We have seen enough to tell that this would be a simplistic characterization of the differences between the Initiative and the Scoobies: the latter happily exploit the methods of the former. However, feminist epistemology and philosophy of science are diverse fields and provide the resources for a more credible account. Specifically, the sensitivity to social and historical factors engendered by a feminist analysis has led to a rapprochement with the sociology of science. Social epistemologists in this tradition argue that the divisions of the "science wars" (in which we saw the Grade Two-Grade Three distinction reflected) can be overcome.[20] By decoupling the standard epistemological linkage of the social to the irrational, room can be made for a pluralist conception of knowledge in which the richly humanistic can coexist with the crisply formal. Such an account does justice to the insight that the emotional is inextricable from the rational, and allows us to enjoy the fruits of science without impoverishing our engagement with the world.

The status and limits of scientific enquiry have become the focus of urgent public debate. This chapter has explored how a philosophically informed reading of science and the supernatural in pop culture can contribute to this debate. Although *BtVS*'s employment of the supernatural might be construed as an anti-science attitude, we have seen that the initial plausibility of this perspective masks a commitment to an epistemology that can enrich our appreciation of the cultural status of science.

---

[20] Helen E. Longino, *The Fate of Knowledge* (Princeton: Princeton University Press, 2002). For more on *BtVS* and the "science wars" see Chapter 7 in this volume.

7
Pluralism, Pragmatism, and Pals: The Slayer Subverts the Science Wars

MADELINE MUNTERSBJORN

The "Science Wars" is a campus craze, more popular with professors than students. Upholders of objectivity, truth, and better living through chemistry battle defenders of subjectivity, value, and better living through narrative. Common cries of the former, "there is an objective world beyond human experience" and "scientists use rationality to discover reality," clash against the latter's insistence that, "there is no objectivity outside human experience" and "scientists use rhetoric to create reality." *Buffy the Vampire Slayer (BtVS)* invites us to consider our commitments to people and principles. Humanities scholars seeking to canonize a patron saint might consider *BtVS*'s creator, Joss Whedon. His television serials celebrate the vitality of literature, history, and art. But does Whedon's commitment to the humanities imply that he must champion the anti-science cause in the Science Wars? Not necessarily. *BtVS* is a subversive challenge to arbitrary battle lines drawn in a needless debate.

In Season Four, Buffy Summers enrolls as a freshman at UC-Sunnydale. She tries to find the fun in higher education, despite the fact that her roommate turns out to be a soul-sucking demon ("Living Conditions"), the local brew turns drinkers into Cro Mags ("Beer Bad"), and her first college crush dumps her after a one-night-stand ("The Harsh Light of Day"). "The Slayer vs. the Initiative" story arc that unfolds over the course of several episodes may be seen as the humanities' triumph over the sciences once the Chosen One arrives on campus.

The Initiative is an underground complex of laboratories and holding cells for vampires and other demons drawn to the Hellmouth under Sunnydale. This massive covert operation is funded by the U.S. government and is run by scientists and soldiers who masquerade as professors and students. Buffy's second college crush is Riley Finn, mild-mannered teaching assistant by day, audacious Initiative commando by night. In "Doomed" Riley refuses to reveal his true self to Buffy, even though she stared down the barrel of his gun before saving his life the night before:

RILEY: I can't tell you.
BUFFY: Well then let me. You're part of some military monster squad that captures demons, vampires, probably have some official-sounding euphemisms for them . . . like "unfriendlies" or "non-sapiens" . . .
RILEY: . . . Hostile Sub Terrestrials . . .
BUFFY: . . . so you deliver these HSTs to a bunch of lab coats who perform experiments on them which among other things turns some of them into harmless little bunnies. How am I doing so far?
RILEY: A little too well. ("Doomed")

For someone who has yet to be inside, Buffy knows a lot about the Initiative. Her knowledge comes from disreputable sources, namely, escaped Hostile Sub Terrestrials. Spike, a.k.a, Hostile 17, is a vampire who goes from vicious punk to vulnerable puppy after the Initiative puts a chip in his head. The Initiative surgically implants behavior modification circuitry into a vampire's brain that causes debilitating pain whenever said vampire tries to hurt a human. There is no such thing as informed consent inside the Initiative. When caught, Spike fumes: "I always worried what would happen when that bitch got some funding" ("The Initiative"). Unbeknownst to Spike, "that bitch" is not the Slayer but the Initiative's research scientist, Professor Maggie Walsh: tough as nails psychology professor by day, maternal demon tamer by night. Like Dr. Frankenstein, Professor Walsh manipulates dead body parts to compensate for human vulnerability. Her most gruesome creation is "Adam," a nuclear powered cyborg, part demon, part dead white male.

Buffy slays vampires one at a time by driving a wooden stake through their unbeating hearts. The Slayer and her band of mystical outsiders study old books, collect talismans, and utter incantations. Their knowledge of foreign languages and metaphysics allows them to defeat Adam, the monster created by computer science and biochemistry. *Human vulnerability is precious.* While some may view this story as "Dionysius defeats Apollo," the subversion of Season Four is not captured adequately by the "chaos vs. order" distinction. *BtVS*'s characters rely more on magic than on mathematics, not because of some deep distrust of logical reasoning, but because they are so busy trying to save the world (while living lives worth saving) that they have little time to develop complete and consistent systems of axioms. Further, magic is not chaotic: probabilistic causal laws govern the Buffyverse. Three philosophical ideals permeate Season Four: pluralism, pragmatism, and pals. If more academics took these ideals to heart, the Science Wars would dissolve like a freshly staked vampire into a pile of dust.

Pluralism

> My criticism of modern science is that it inhibits freedom of thought. If the reason is that it has found the truth and now follows it then I would say that there are better things than first finding, and then following such a monster. (Paul Feyerabend, "How to Defend Society Against Science")[1]

Pluralism is the name philosophers give to the view that reality consists in many kinds of interrelated things. The view may be contrasted with dualism and monism. Someone who insists that reality can be divided into two realms, the material and the mental, or two forces, order and chaos, is a kind of dualist. She who claims, "All things are physical" and he who replies, "All things are spiritual" disagree, but they are both kinds of monists. Some think that trying to decide which -ism is superior is a waste of time.[2] Those who disagree have social and epistemological

---

[1] Reprinted in *Scientific Revolutions,* edited by Ian Hacking (New York: Oxford University Press, 1981), p. 158.

[2] Rudolf Carnap: "It seems doubtful whether we can find any theoretical content in such philosophical questions as discussed by monism, dualism, and

concerns. Pluralists like Paul Feyerabend abhor dogma: Anyone who claims to have all the answers is probably wrong. For Feyerabend, this theory of knowledge is in the back seat while his politics drives. *Anyone who claims to know the truth is a danger to us all.*

In "The I in Team," the scientist and the superhero chat:

PROF. WALSH: We thought you were a myth.

BUFFY: Well . . . you were myth-taken.

PROF. WALSH: And to think that all that time you were sitting in my class—well most of those times. Now I understand your energies were directed to the same place as ours in fact. I always knew you could do better than a B-minus. It's only our methods that differ. We use the latest in scientific technology and state of the art weaponry and you, if I understand correctly, poke them with a sharp stick. ("The I in Team")

Is there room for the Slayer within the Initiative? To find out, Professor Walsh performs an experiment. Her armed patrol team takes forty-two minutes to locate Buffy who neutralizes them in twenty-eight seconds. Next thing you know, Buffy has a pager and an access code. Professor Walsh and Buffy appear to be allies. When her friends question the wisdom of enlisting, Buffy is nonplussed: "It just means that when I patrol I'll have a heavily armed team backing me up." Willow Rosenberg, who is good at magic (the fast way) and mathematics (the slow way), questions the Initiative's agenda. After all, what do you do with a "fangless" vampire like Spike? Get him a job at Wal-Mart ("The I in Team")?

Willow's misgivings prove prescient. The methods of Buffy's gang and the Initiative differ too much for them to work together. The Initiative is a large bureaucracy with a strict chain of command. You're either in or out. Loyalty to the cause consists in following orders without question. The question of who is in charge, or even a member, of Buffy's small cadre is always

pluralism," in *International Encyclopedia of Unified Science* Volume I, edited by Otto Neurath, Rudolf Carnap and Charles W. Morris. (Chicago: University of Chicago Press, 1955), p. 49.

open. From one season to the next, even from one episode to the next, the roster changes. People in the opening credits can die without warning. Buffy herself bows out more than once, while Spike switches allegiance within individual episodes. You don't need superpowers to be Buffy's pal and there's no test you have to pass. Potential Slayerettes need courage and a serious work ethic. They must be willing to ask questions, take risks, share ideas, jettison beliefs and spend hours doing research.

Karl Popper (1902–1994) rejected dualism by arguing for a "third world" beyond the mental and the physical, a realm populated by the viable products of human efforts to come to terms with reality. This realm includes works of art as well as science. He is most often remembered for his criterion of falsifiability, the position that all good scientific theories must be vulnerable, or susceptible to disconfirmation.[3] Good scientists must be willing to revise their theories in light of new evidence. According to Popper's view, Professor Walsh is a bad scientist. Buffy's unpredictability and incessant questioning of authority threaten to expose Professor Walsh's secret agenda. Professor Walsh refuses to abandon Project 314, the attempt to build a super-soldier, even after she learns that one already exists: The Slayer is *real*. Professor Walsh tries to have her killed, but underestimates her supernatural abilities. Buffy does not, however, underestimate the Initiative. As long as they're around, "It's not safe for any of us." The scope of the personal pronoun in Buffy's line is universal. Professor Walsh and her HST lab rats are not any safer than Buffy, her friends, or Spike. The scientist's faith that she alone knows what's in the best interest of the greater good places *everyone* in danger. Professor Walsh refuses to ally with the Slayer because the Slayer refuses to follow orders. Tragically, Professor Walsh's super-soldier has the same "flaw." When Adam awakes ahead of schedule, the first person he kills is "Mommy." He stabs her through the heart with a sharp stick.

Those who survive the Buffyverse learn to respect its rules. Buffy destroys vampires with *wooden* stakes, not metal or plastic ones. Audiences enjoy the show's creative interpretation of this rule—tennis rackets, fence posts, spatula handles, No. 2 pencils—any wieldy piece of wood is a potential weapon. The

---

[3] See his *Conjectures and Refutations* (London: Routledge, 1963).

target is the vampire's heart: location matters. When molecules of type A (wood) are in direct physical contact with molecules of type B (heart), the vampire dissolves—usually. Buffyverse rules are probabilistic rather than deterministic; they represent what happens most of the time, rather than all of the time. Exceptions to the natural order are possible, though only dire circumstances can induce wisdom to flout Nature. Exploring why these particular rules govern her universe doesn't concern Buffy. She's too busy. In "The Harsh Light of Day," Parker, Buffy's first college crush, suggests that we freely choose our actions:

> BUFFY: It doesn't feel like it. To me, a lot of the time, it feels like stuff's just coming at me, you know, and I'm reacting as fast as I can, just trying to keep going. Just—just trying to be on my feet before the next things hits.
> PARKER: That sounds exhausting.
> BUFFY: It really is.

In her haste to save the day (while living a life worth saving), Buffy makes mistakes. In "A New Man" she believes that an object is genuine silver when it is not. As a result, Giles, who is temporarily transformed into a demon susceptible to silver, survives being stabbed by the faux-sterling letter opener. The existence of rules makes mistakes possible. Moreover, departures from the rules may result in good things. Consequently, the value of a rule or an exception depends on the context in which it occurs and the context always changes. Giles teaches Buffy to ask, "What does it want?" when tracking demonic danger. Professor Walsh trains her commandos to track protein signatures and scan for hotspots of other worldly energy. Buffy is happy to follow a pheromone trail alongside the commandos, but she doesn't fear monsters as the sum of their molecular parts. A demon may smell different to a dog, but that fact alone doesn't make it a threat. Similarly, just because Buffy's roommate drives her crazy doesn't mean she's a demon. The fact that her roommate's toenail clippings grow does ("Living Conditions"). In order to champion the cause of good over evil, one must try to discern fact from fantasy; in order to pursue truth one must try to be good. Debating which is more important, objectivity or subjectivity, ignores the possibility that real heroes champion both causes simultaneously.

Pragmatism

So in contemplating a painting, there is a moment when we lose consciousness that it is not the thing, the distinction between the real and the copy disappears, and it is for the moment a pure dream—not any particular existence, and yet not general. At that moment we are contemplating an *icon*. (C.S. Peirce, "On the Algebra of Logic")[4]

A pragmatist considers the practical consequences of her beliefs. Scholarly Giles would never reduce a complex philosophical position to a slogan, but Buffy might define pragmatism as "whatever works." Pragmatism should not be confused with relativism. Relativists do not think any maxim is superior to others. Pragmatists strive to develop better understandings of reality. Relativists object that "better," "understanding" and "reality" are arbitrary cultural constructs that may not have anything to do with anything. Pragmatism's progenitors were C.S. Peirce (1839–1914) and William James (1842–1910). Peirce worked as an astronomer and physicist but called himself a logician, while James taught anatomy, psychology, and philosophy at Harvard. Pragmatism's parents were interested in the art of reasoning and the science of human behavior.

Pragmatism is hard to pin down precisely because pragmatists take seriously the idea that everything changes. Pragmatism itself is caught up in this flux, inspiring Peirce to rename his version of the view "pragmaticism." Pragmatists sometimes separate fact from fiction and the particular from the universal. At other times they blur together, as when we are contemplating an "icon." An icon resembles the thing it represents. Icons help us understand reality better when we take them at face value, temporarily losing sight of the distinction between representation and reality. Icons are found throughout the arts (paintings) and sciences (equations). *BtVS* is a television icon that teaches us to value the difference between fact and fiction. Yet, in order for the show to work as an icon, viewers must take it at face value. In "Hush" only the scream of a real live girl—not a recording— can destroy the fairytale "Gentlemen." Why? Buffy does not have

---

[4] Reprinted in *Collected Papers III,* edited by Charles Hartshorne and Paul Weiss (Cambridge: Harvard University Press, 1931), p. 211.

time to wonder why. The voices of everyone in town have been stolen and it's up to her to kick their creepy asses, get her voice back, and scream their heads off. Viewers may ask why her screams cause the Gentlemen's heads to explode. Watching the show as a "pure dream" suggests that embodied fact is more powerful than empty fiction.

BtVS's viewers endure unprecedented flux from their beloved series. Fans will surely recognize this Tuesday afternoon exchange:

> BELIEVER: I'm so worried one of my favorite characters will die tonight.
> NON-BELIEVER: Why worry? They all come back next week.
> BELIEVER: Not on *Buffy* they don't!
> NON-BELIEVER: Can't they just magic them back?
> BELIEVER: No! I mean, yeah, of course they can. Joss can do anything. But just because they *can* doesn't mean that they *should*.
> NON-BELIEVER: Why not?
> BELIEVER: Because it's wrong!

Admittedly the conversation is fantastic because, in reality, the non-believer gets bored and changes the subject before the dialogue ends. But as rogue Slayer Faith struggles to learn, she and Buffy are chosen to enforce mortality. Vampires must be stopped, not just because they prey on humans, but also because they violate Nature. Amidst the flux that carries us willy-nilly in its wake, death emerges as the exception to the rule that, "rules always have exceptions." The universality of death cannot be taken for granted, however. *Natural laws must be cultivated with care and defended with diligence.* The "whatever works" slogan dismays people who hear "whatever" as too arbitrary and "works" as too hard. Buffy works hard to defend the laws governing her universe using whatever means she can: Death is her gift.

The pro-science faction in the Science Wars rightly notes that there is more to reality than we comprehend. The anti-science faction rightly notes that we habitually transcend the borders of our experience. Artists and scientists have much to learn from each other as they try to make the implicit explicit and "eff the ineffable."[5] Folks should stop quibbling over whether the rules are created or discovered and pay more attention to the collaborative processes whereby they are cultivated and defended. Naïve realism and relativism are lazy philosophies, flourishing in an age of timid consumerism. People want to buy their beliefs off the rack and be done. The struggle to fashion flexible views, tailored to fit but subject to constant alternation, needs more brave and hard-working people like Buffy.

The Initiative ranks kinds of humans and then tampers with the best of them. The commandos are disciplined, brave, and darling young men—but they could be better. Professor Walsh implants behavior modification circuitry in Riley and doses her Commandos with performance-enhancing drugs: There is no such thing as informed consent inside the Initiative for men or monsters. Humans may be superior to HSTs, but they are also weak and vulnerable. The best creature ever is but a twinkle in the mind's eye of Professor Walsh until she gets government funding. Adam enjoys the best of the artificial, natural, and supernatural worlds and revels in his superiority. To make more cyborg-human-demon hybrids, he arranges a deadly battle between humans and demons to generate the necessary spare parts. Who can stop his diabolical plan? Adam has refrained from killing the Slayer because he wants her at his big showdown to even out the kill ratio. Buffy must defend the distinction between the natural and the supernatural by becoming even more of a hybrid than she already is. Luckily, she's not alone.

Pals

Our acts, our turning-places, where we seem to ourselves to make ourselves and grow, are the parts of the world to which we are closest, the parts of which our knowledge is the most intimate and complete. Why should we not take them at their face-value? (William James, "Pragmatism and Religion")[6]

---

[5] Gregory Benford is a physics professor and science-fiction writer. This *bon mot* comes from his, "Effing the Ineffable," in *Aliens: The Anthropology of Science Fiction,* edited by George E. Slusser and Eric S. Rabkin (Carbondale: Southern Illinois Press, 1987), pp. 13–25.

[6] Reprinted in *Pragmatism in Focus,* edited by Doris Olin (New York: Routledge, 1992), p. 136.

The title for my conclusion comes from dialogue between Adam and Spike. Professor Walsh's monster is a master motivational speaker. He talks HSTs into getting caught so they will be within the Initiative's walls during the battle. *The zealot spawns the con man*. Adam wants Spike to get the Slayer in position. In "The Yoko Factor" Adam promises to remove his chip:

> ADAM: I will restore you to what you once were when I have the Slayer how and where I want her.
> SPIKE: Easier said. She's crafty—her and her little friends.
> ADAM: Friends?
> SPIKE: There's your whatcha' call it, variable. The slayer's got pals. You want to even the odds in a fight you don't want the Slayerettes mucking about.
> ADAM: Take them away from her.
> SPIKE: Now there's a plan.

Spike's plan almost works. Everyone knows how hard it is to keep the old gang together after high school. Spike talks trash to Buffy's friends and before long she's screaming at them, "How can you possibly help?"

James defines pessimism as the view that nothing can save the world; optimism is the view that the world will be saved no matter what. He contrasts both with meliorism, the view that the world may or may not be saved but we should try for salvation anyway. A good meliorist depends on other meliorists. Anyone out to save the world needs friends who think the world is worth saving. Buffy saves the world—a lot. But she doesn't do it alone. In "Primeval" the metaphorical reliance of Buffy on her friends becomes literal. Adam's power source is a radioactive uranium core.[7] Buffy has the strength to yank it out of him if only he could be made to stand still:

> GILES: Perhaps a paralyzing spell. Only I can't perform the incantation of this.
> WILLOW: Right. Don't you have to speak it in Sumerian or something?

---

[7] Willow suggests a "uranium extracting spell," a reach we can measure by considering the cost of this particular "spell" as part of the Manhattan project. We have yet to experience the full blowback from that Initiative's monster.

GILES: I do speak Sumerian. It's not that. Only an experienced witch can incant it and you have to be within striking distance of the subject.

XANDER: See what you get for taking French instead of Sumerian?

BUFFY: What was I thinking?

XANDER: So, no problem. All we need is combo Buffy, her with Slayer strength, Giles's multilingual know-how, and Willow's witchy power. ("Primeval")

Xander Harris did not go to college. Throughout Season Four he frets that his role in the Scooby gang is limited to comic relief. His combo-Buffy joke gives Giles an idea. Why not take Xander's suggestion at face value? As Giles says, as they make their way to the Initiative, right on Adam's schedule, "Just because this is never going to work is no reason to be negative." The scene wherein "combo-Buffy" destroys Adam *rocks*—but it is not the season finale. Combo-Buffy violates Nature. Giles suggests that they flout nature's authority only because the circumstances are so dire. In "Restless," they suffer the consequences of their transgression, as the first Slayer stalks them in their sleep.

Pals are not those who agree to see the world the same way. Pals are those who agree to share with one another the world as they see it. In today's society, where the "truth" is whatever market research says and the "good" is whatever sells, old-fashioned values like honesty and humility are easy to disdain. Why bother trying to attain the unattainable? According to *BtVS*, we try because our lives depend on it. Pals do not keep secrets from each other. Professor Walsh does not have pals. She keeps secrets from Riley, even though she supposedly loves him like a son, and dies alone. Buffy and her pals struggle to be honest with one another and live to fight another day.

The last in a series of lectures on Pragmatism given by James in 1907 asks us to imagine a scenario in which the Creator pitches the following world:

I am going to make a world not certain to be saved, a world the perfection of which shall be conditional merely, the condition being that each agent does its own 'level best.' I offer you the chance of taking part in such a world. Its safety, you see, is unwarranted. It is a real adventure, with real danger, yet it may win through. It is a social scheme of co-operative work genuinely to be done. Will you join the procession? Will you trust yourself and trust the other agents enough to face the risk?[8]

Joss Whedon is not a soldier in the Science Wars. He is the guy who pitches James's meliorist scenario to a talented group of actors and artisans who continue to do their best in pursuit of perfection so that we may all live in better worlds.[9]

---

[8] Ibid., p. 138.

[9] My pals helped me write this chapter. Amy Larson assigned the paper and loaned me carefully labeled videotapes and her *Watcher's Guide Volume 2* so I could do it right. Dinah Larson, Karin Clarkson, and Kimberly Blessing made helpful suggestions. Estil Canterbury is an indulgent Non-believer. John Muntersbjorn is my favorite Watcher—even if he did hide behind a pillow during most of "Something Blue."

8

Between Heavens and Hells: The Multidimensional Universe in Kant and *Buffy the Vampire Slayer*

JAMES LAWLER

Philosopher as Vampire Slayer

In Plato's "Allegory of the Cave,"[1] the basic nature of human existence is portrayed through an imaginative fantasy. Picture people living their entire lives in a dark cave. Outlines of objects are projected from behind them on the cave wall. Because they don't know any better, they think these shadow-images are the true reality. One of the people leaves the cave, climbs out of the darkness and up to the sunlight, and discovers that there is more to reality than the shadow-world of ordinary experience.

For Plato, the person who recognizes that there is a higher dimension than that of ordinary sensible reality is the philosopher. This understanding of the multidimensional structure of reality imposes a duty: to dispel the darkness in order to bring its captives to the light of truth. In Plato's allegory, the person who has seen the sun returns to the cave to liberate the others from their ignorance. There follows a life and death struggle between the witness to the light and the forces of darkness that have established their grip on human minds. The viewer of *Buffy the Vampire Slayer (BtVS)* will readily recognize that the idea of the Vampire Slayer, aware of both higher and lower dimensions, can be seen as a contemporary allegory for Plato's philosopher.

---

[1] Plato, *Republic*, Book VII.

Kant's Multidimensional Universe

In one of his earliest works, *Universal Natural History and Theory of the Heavens*,[2] the eighteenth-century philosopher Immanuel Kant develops the Platonic vision of a multidimensional universe in terms of modern science. The universe begins, Kant thinks, as an infinitely extended gaseous cloud composed of elements of widely varying densities. Through the operation of the basic Newtonian forces of attraction and repulsion, the densest elements gravitate together first to form galaxies of especially heavy material. Worlds made of finer stuff, with less gravitational pull, evolve later.

The evolution of consciousness follows a parallel pattern. Consciousness naturally evolves in steps or stages, going from ignorance and limited practical ability to greater knowledge and skill. It is appropriate, therefore, that the very beginning of the history of spirit be situated in that very dense matter that constitutes the earliest world systems. The mental abilities found in such worlds would be of the densest kind in psychological terms. Perhaps the inhabitants are like the demons in "The Harvest" or in "Bargaining" whose idea of fun is sheer destruction. On the scale of evolution, they are like full-grown two-year-olds in their negative stage.

We can suppose, Kant thinks, that human beings exist in the mid-range of the spectrum of possibilities. This is suggested by the fact that most of our energies are devoted to physical survival, while the higher possibilities of creative spirit are realized very seldom, sporadically and in flashes, rather than consistently and forcefully.

Kant's early cosmology has one important difference from that of *BtVS*. He sees the different worlds as separated by immense temporal and spatial differences, whereas in *BtVS* the distances are reduced, the dimensions border closely on one another, and the transitions between them can be very rapid. In his later philosophical thought, however, Kant came to think that we are conditioned by our distinctly human physical and psychological make-up to subjectively *interpret* the multidimensional reality beyond our experience *as if* it were divided by

---

[2] Immanuel Kant, *Universal Natural History and Theory of the Heavens*, translated by Stanley L. Jaki (Edinburgh: Scottish Academic Press, 1981).

great distances, both spatial and temporal. But reality in itself may be quite different from the way we naturally think about it from our limited, mid-range, human perspective. It is practical moral experience, not theoretical speculation, that gives us insight into the true nature of reality—because reality is what we are creating.

We Make Our Own Reality

In his *Critique of Pure Reason*, Kant proposes this thought experiment: "Hitherto it has been assumed that all our knowledge must conform to objects. . . . We must make trial . . . whether we may not have more success in the tasks of metaphysics, if we suppose that objects must conform to our knowledge."[3] Let us think of time and space as subjective forms of our experiencing, not as features of reality in itself. While our human constitution obliges us to represent different worlds as separated from ours by great distances, in reality different densities or dimensions of the cosmic order may in fact impinge on one another in more proximate ways. Portals into other space-and-time dimensions may therefore really lurk in the recesses of high school libraries.

Following Kant's revolutionary thought experiment, instead of supposing that the world as we see it is fixed and independent of our consciousness, we should recognize that we create the world of our experience out of our basic beliefs. In "Out of Mind, Out of Sight," Marcie becomes invisible after being regularly ignored by her teacher and other students. Because she mentally and emotionally sees herself as invisible, she becomes physically invisible, and begins to work gruesome revenge on those who previously ignored her. When recognition of this causality finally dawns, Xander says: "What, she turned invisible because no one noticed her?" Giles suddenly sees the light: "Of course! I've been investigating the mystical causes of invisibility when I should have looked at the quantum mechanical! Physics." Giles explains the science: "It's a rudimentary concept that reality is shaped, even created, by our perception."

---

[3] Immanuel Kant, *Critique of Pure Reason,* translated by Norman Kemp Smith (London: Macmillan, 1961), p. 22; b xvii.

In quantum mechanics the way the observer approaches sub-atomic entities determines the form in which they appear, whether as a compact particle or a fluid wave-form. Here is a contemporary scientific validation of Kant's proposal that instead of thinking of our thoughts as reflections of an independent world, we should think of the world of our experience as constituted in fundamental ways by our thoughts. In "Nightmares" the energy barrier between dream life and waking life collapses through a contagion of fear arising out of the unleashed psyche of an abused child. In this dreaming reality, Buffy finds herself powerless and facing a vampire known as the Master. "This isn't real. You can't be free!" The Master replies: "You still don't understand, do you? I am free because you fear it. Because you fear it, the world is crumbling. Your nightmares are made flesh."

In the universe of *BtVS,* the structure and even the very existence of our world are determined by our basic choices. Fear and love are the two poles around which whole worlds are constructed. The fundamental tension between them grounds our basic choices and creates the dynamics of the evolution of our human world. Between these two poles is the duty of the Philosopher/Slayer, which is first of all to dispel the shadows cast by fear.

Life Is Short

In the first episode of the series, "Welcome to the Hellmouth," Buffy is standing with her Watcher, Giles, on a balcony in the favorite Sunnydale hangout, The Bronze. Below them, young people are pulsing to primal rhythms. Giles is aghast: "Look at them, throwing themselves about, completely unaware of the danger that surrounds them." Buffy replies with the wit, pathos and directness that characterize her anguished appraisal of life: "Lucky them."

Buffy had previously been talking to Willow, her new friend on campus. Seemingly luckless in love and scorned by the upwardly mobile fashion clique at the Sunnydale Public High School, Willow has been confessing her sense of social inadequacy: "I think boys are more interested in a girl who can talk." Willow believes Buffy belongs to the superior social set, with looks and money and guys. Buffy wants to set her right on this score by giving Willow a soulful glimpse into her philosophy.

"Well, my philosophy, do you wanna hear my philosophy?" Willow lights up: "Yeah, I do!" Buffy puts her philosophy—her basic view of life—in a nutshell: "Life is short. . . . Not original, I'll grant you, but it's true. You know? Why waste time being all shy and worrying about some guy, and if he's gonna laugh at you. Seize the moment, 'cause tomorrow you might be dead."

Buffy envies her seemingly happy peers, who are unaware that death lurks in every dark corner. Ignorance must be bliss. She proposes an unoriginal philosophy of life, but for her there is ultimate originality. She is the Slayer, the only one in a generation, "one girl in all the world, a Chosen One, one born with the strength and skill to hunt the vampires." With these words, Giles exhorts Buffy to recognize her unique destiny and high responsibility. Buffy breaks in: "to stop the spread of their evil blah, blah, blah . . . I've heard it, okay?" Disturbed by her attitude, Giles reminds her of her "duty." Buffy is not moved: "I've both been there and done that, and I'm moving on."

Despite such protests in the name of ordinary life as she understands it, Buffy does assume the burden of her duty—especially when friends and loved ones and vulnerable people in general are threatened or victimized. When death strikes her school mates, Willow says, "I knew those guys. I go to that room every day. And when I walked in there, it . . . it wasn't our world any more. They made it theirs. And they had fun. What are we gonna do?" Buffy knows her duty. Her fear and self-pity drop away. She answers, resolutely: "What we have to."

Moral Duty: Respect the Human Essence

As the Vampire Slayer, Buffy provides a powerful paradigm of moral responsibility. According to Kant, the essential feature of the moral point of view is the experience of duty. The moral person does what she has to do, what her duty requires. What duty fundamentally requires, Kant argues, is that we respect the humanity, the fundamental essence, of each individual. Kant too can put his moral philosophy in a nutshell: "Now I say that man, and in general every rational being, exists as an end in himself, not merely as a means for arbitrary use by this or that will."[4]

---

[4] Immanuel Kant, *Groundwork of the Metaphysics of Morals,* translated by H.J. Paton (New York: Harper, 1964), p. 95.

This moral philosophy is based on the assumption that there is in each human being something that is of infinite worth and therefore requires the utmost respect—both from others as well as oneself. Significantly for our interpretation of *BtVS*, Kant extends the scope of moral respect beyond "man" or members of the human species to "every rational being"—to members of other species who are also capable of governing their lives from the standpoint of moral duty. Kant distinguishes moral rationality from instrumental rationality—intellect employed for purely egotistical purposes. In *BtVS*, there are demonic beings whose intelligence is purely instrumental, wholly subordinate to egotistical goals of power and pleasure, and incapable of responding to duty.

It is the threat of death, Kant writes,[5] that brings to the fore the essential characteristics of morality. Aware of the infinite worth concealed in the individual, the morally committed person will sacrifice her life rather than cause the death of an innocent human person. And if the circumstances of her life—her destiny—make it her duty to protect others, then she will sacrifice her life to fulfill that duty. Kant writes solemnly: "Duty! Thou sublime and mighty name . . . "[6] Only the existence of a higher dimension than that of ordinary physical existence makes sense of moral experience. For why would an individual sacrifice her life, or even any of her desires or interests, unless she were somehow connected to something that transcends these desires and interests, that transcends her entire "sensible" existence?

This something Kant calls variously humanity, personality, or soul. He defines this higher personality as "freedom and independence from the mechanism of nature." In moral experience we "postulate," rather than scientifically know, a free essence or soul that does not belong to the "world of sense" but to an "intelligible world," that is, to a world that we don't directly perceive with our five senses, but that we relate to in moral experience. It is the sacred inner dimension of our own being before which the proper attitude is one of reverence. "Man is certainly unholy enough," Kant writes of the ordinary personality that

---

[5] Immanuel Kant, *Critique of Practical Reason,* translated by Lewis White Beck (New York: Macmillan, 1993), p. 30.
[6] *Ibid.,* p. 90.

belongs to the world of sense, "but humanity in the person must be holy to him."[7]

While Kant emphasizes the importance to morality of the postulate of a higher, "intelligible" world, his language suggests that morality postulates a lower world as well. In the projected lower world, sensible experience with the instrumental intelligence that is subordinate to its demands exists independently of all moral awareness. If moral experience points above us to higher, heavenly dimensions, it also points below—to the hell realms of demons who threaten to take over our world, and have fun in doing so. In moral experience we tend to suppose our involvement with two opposing worlds, two dimensions of being, out of which our intermediary, mixed human world is constructed. And the way it is constructed depends on us.

In "Anne," Buffy has once more attempted to abandon her Slayer duty because of the tremendous emotional pain it has cost her. She therefore stops being "Buffy" and becomes Anne, a waitress swallowed up by anonymous urban life. The ultimate logic of this world is not the elusive happiness of "ordinary life," but enslavement. Buffy finds herself a denizen of a hell governed by fear and force. Only through duty, Kant says, do we acquire the true freedom that stems from our sacred personality. Otherwise, if we seek merely to satisfy our physical needs and desires, we become slaves in a mechanistic underworld founded on our own cowardly acquiescence.

In this dark world, the higher personality is obliterated. A guard says to the prisoners: "You work, and you live. That is all. You do not complain or laugh or do anything besides work. Whatever you thought, whatever you were does not matter. You are no one now. You mean nothing." When he asks a young man his name, the young man replies, "Aaron," and is bashed to the ground. The others quickly learn the lesson, and reply, when asked their names, "No one." Buffy refuses to consent to this obliteration of her essential personality. With recovered pride and the sense of humour that always accompanies restored self-awareness, Buffy replies: "I am Buffy, the Vampire Slayer. And you are . . .?"

---

[7] *Ibid.*, p. 91.

Contradictions of the Middle World

Human life between two worlds has a paradoxical nature. Without our sensible desires and attachments, we could not experience duty. The desire to enjoy the full experience of sensible life is an indispensable condition for evoking all the pathos in which the needs of the sensible ego must sometimes be sacrificed in the name of duty.[8] Kant argues that moral experience ultimately demands that we reconcile these conflicting tendencies and create a kind of heaven on earth in which sensible demands are fulfilled on the basis of moral principles. We must therefore be fully embodied beings to fulfill our moral duty.

But by this very condition of morality we are constantly tempted to immerse ourselves wholly in the sensible world—to become creatures of the dark for whom sensibility is the only reality. One way of escaping the conflicting demands of the earth plane, in *BtVS*, is for individuals to give up their souls and become vampires. Similar temptations of sensuous gratification and physical power take both Angel and Spike down this path. While Angel never rejoins the human species, he does achieve the status that Kant intends by "rational being" when his soul is restored to his vampire physical form. At the end of Season Six, Spike too recovers his soul. Moreover, all of the Scooby Gang with the exception of Giles have relationships that put them in intimate connection with the demonic forces. Without knowledge of the dark, can we truly appreciate the light? Isn't the sun lovelier at dawn than at noonday?

In "The Initiative," Spike receives a substitute for the soul in the form of a behaviour-modifying computer chip that prevents him from directly assaulting humans. In "Crush," Buffy discovers that her sister Dawn has a crush on "cool" Spike: "He's a killer, Dawn. You cannot have a crush on something that is . . . dead, and, and evil, and a vampire." She could love Angel, she says, because he has a soul. Dawn replies: "Spike has a chip. Same diff." But it is not the same. The purely instrumental technology that treats human beings as things to be used and

---

[8] In "The Moral World of the Simpson Family," I illustrate this dynamic in relation to the character of Lisa Simpson. See *The Simpsons and Philosophy*, edited by Willian Irwin, Mark T. Conard, and Aeon J. Skoble (Chicago: Open Court, 2001), pp. 147–159.

controlled, rather than as "ends in themselves" with infinite value, cannot create a true substitute for the soul.

The Power of Teamwork and Love

As a paradigm of the moral experience, Buffy is not a lone, solitary superhero. She attracts Willow and Xander who recognize through her the demands of duty, and are uplifted and exhilarated by it. In "The Harvest" Buffy tells Willow and Xander: "You guys don't have to get involved." "What d'ya mean?" says Xander. "We're a team! Aren't we a team?" "Yeah!" says Willow. "You're the Slayer, and we're, like, the Slayerettes!"

Buffy could not fulfill her duty as an isolated heroine, for the world-saving tasks that confront the moral individual are too monumental to be taken on by one person alone. Entering the multidimensional universe through the portal of Buffy's courage and commitment, others too discover that they have a higher destiny and hidden abilities to fulfill that destiny. At the end of "The Harvest," Willow asks, "Did we win?" Buffy replies, nonchalantly, "Well, we averted the Apocalypse. I give us points for that." Xander is trying to grasp the import of his life-changing discoveries: "One thing's for sure: nothing's ever gonna be the same."

This theme culminates in "Primeval." In the symbolism of the Tarot, Willow as Spirit, Xander as Heart, Giles as Mind, and Buffy as Hand achieve a merging of essence (as Xander explains to Philip in "Checkpoint") that defeats Adam, the unnatural creation of purely instrumental science. The merging of souls is made possible by the mutual respect and love that conquers separation and fear. Science in the service of governmental power produces a super-demonic distortion of the forces of nature. Importantly, it is the vampire Spike who recognizes this ultimate secret weapon of the Slayer, and contracts with Adam to sow division among the Slayer group. Egotism, fear, and separation are the natural element of the vampire.

Too Much Heaven

While the first five seasons are devoted to threats from the forces of darkness, the sixth season suggests that too much light can be blinding. In "Bargaining, Part One" Xander states the facts about Buffy's death as these appear to sensible experience: "We saw her body, Will. We buried it." Willow, whose magical power taps into unseen dimensions, replies: "Her body, yeah. But her soul . . . her essence. . . . I mean, that could be some-where else. She could be trapped, in some sort of hell dimen-sion like Angel was."

Angel's descent into a hell realm was appropriate in the light of his sense of guilt and desire for atonement for his life as a vampire. But Buffy longs for a heaven in which she is freed from the burdens and contradictions of duty. "Death is your gift," says her Spirit Guide, taking the appearance of the First Slayer ("Intervention"). In "The Gift," Buffy plunges through the portal of death, simultaneously realizing her duty, and freeing herself from it. Buffy's death, motivated both by her duty as Slayer and by love of Dawn, turns out to be a gift to herself. It is her portal to heaven. And heaven is simply a direct experi-ence of her true self, her essence, her soul, unencumbered by the complexities of physical existence in the middle world of our earth. In "After Life," Buffy describes this experience: "I was happy. Wherever I was, I was happy. At peace. I knew that everyone I cared about was all right. I knew it. Time didn't mean anything. Nothing had form. But I was still me, you know? And I was warm, and I was loved, and I was finished, complete. I don't understand about theology or dimensions, or any of it, really, but I think I was in heaven."

Buffy has had a direct experience of her higher self, her true personality. Her Guide (in "Intervention") had told her: "You are full of love. You love with all of your soul. It's brighter than the fire . . . blinding. That's why you pull away from it." It is the inkling of this higher dimension of one's own being that moti-vates moral duty. But Buffy's experience has been so overpow-ering that, when she is dragged back into physical existence through Willow's magic, she has the opposite difficulty to the one she had on first assuming her responsibility as Slayer. From being overly attached to ordinary life, Buffy has become too detached from it. Relative to the higher reality, earthly life, with its natural estrangement among bodies and vulnerability to darkness, now seems like a descent into hell. "Everything here is hard, and bright, and violent," she says in "After Life." "Everything I feel, everything I touch. This is Hell, just getting through the next moment, and the one after that, knowing what I've lost."

Death is no longer a threat but a promise of liberation—liberation from the burden of her duty and the contradictions of this world. For Buffy, the balance between the worlds has shifted from one in which the "sensible world" has the greatest pull, to one in which the "intelligible world," the world of the soul, has overwhelming force. If we have a duty to fulfill in this lifetime, it is important not to be too intimately aware of the bliss of higher worlds. In the emotionally revelatory musical episode, "Once More, with Feeling," Buffy confesses that she has no feeling for life in this world: "Every single night, the same arrangement, I go out and fight the fight. Still I always feel this strange estrangement, nothing here is real, nothing here is right."

Only her explosive sexual connection with Spike ignites the vital flow of physical energy that ultimately makes it possible for her to realize her duty, while temporarily pulling her away from it. In "Dead Things," Buffy reveals to Tara her fear that she has "come back wrong." In the same episode, we see Buffy once again standing on the balcony of The Bronze, looking down wistfully on the dancers below. Only this time she is not estranged from ordinary life but from her Slayer companions who are practicing dance steps for Xander's and Anya's wedding. And it is not Giles at her side, urging her to realize her duty, but Spike, who whispers, "That's not your world. You belong in the shadows—with me." The shadows draw us in when the light has become too strong.

It is her sense of duty—above all now to herself—that pulls Buffy once more back out of the shadows into the light of her true identity. In "As You Were," she breaks up with Spike, evoking the central commandment of morality that forbids treating oneself or others, as Kant says, as "a means for arbitrary use by this or that will." "I'm using you. . . . and it's killing me." She realizes that in using Spike and letting herself be used by him, she, the Vampire Slayer, is being drawn into the darkness of the vampire.

It is her Christian, church-going,[9] soldier lover, Riley, who reminds her of who she really is. In "A New Man," he tells Professor Walsh, meaningfully, "She is the truest soul I've ever

---

[9] In "Who Are You?" Buffy asks Riley how he responded so quickly to the demon takeover of a church. Riley replies, "I didn't. I was just late for church."

known." In "As You Were," he tells Buffy, suggesting the dialectic of light and dark: "Wheel never stops turning, Buffy. You're up, you're down. It doesn't change what you are. And you are a hell of a woman." Buffy must continually remember her true nature. She is Buffy, the Vampire Slayer. No doubt, Riley's use of the term "hell" is not philosophically accurate. Buffy learns to live between both heavens and hells. If she takes on aspects of many dimensions, that is only as it should be.

Conquering the Inner Demon

The sixth season also shifts the focus from external battles with the demonic to internal ones. The requisite action arc involves "The Trio" of Warren, Jonathan and Andrew as comic relief from inner struggles until their bungling leads to tragedy. While Buffy, trying to come back from the heavenly bliss of her true self, is captivated by her bouts of sexual ecstasy with Spike, Willow seeks the bliss of self-obliteration brought about by the use of dark magic. "I . . . it took me away from myself. . . . I was out of my mind," she says in "Wrecked," as she laments the fact that she nearly caused the death of Dawn. She explains her motivation: "If you could be plain old Willow or super Willow, who would you be?" she asks Buffy. Buffy replies: "You don't need magic to be special."

In "Forever," Tara explains to Dawn, and indirectly to Willow, the ethics of magic: "witches can't be allowed to alter the fabric of life for selfish reasons. Wiccans took an oath a long time ago to honor that." Willow's use of magic, however, is partly governed by the sense of inferiority and insecurity that she expressed to Buffy in the first episode. She does not believe that she is lovable for herself. As the Master explained to Buffy, it is fear that empowers the demonic. Afraid to lose Tara's love, Willow uses magic to hold it. When she uses magic to control the person she loves, rather than respect the fundamental freedom of the higher personality, Willow only repels Tara.

The test of Willow's true power is in defeating the inner demonic force of fear and egotism that usurps her intrinsic humanity. She must find the inner soul power that makes her truly special. At first she struggles with the pain of withdrawal from her magical indulgences. But all such efforts cease when Tara is accidentally killed by Warren. In her rage for vengeance,

Willow turns against the whole of life, against this entire middle world with all its contradictions and suffering.

In "Two to Go," Buffy tries to express her recovered love of earthly life to Willow. Buffy will later tell Dawn ("Grave") her new insight into why she has been allowed back into this world. It wasn't because of Willow's magic, which is powerless against the death of Tara. It wasn't the duties of the Slayer, since she would have been replaced by another one. It was for the sake of Dawn herself. "Things have really sucked lately, but that's all going to change, and I want to be there when it does. I want to see my friends happy again. I want to see you grow up—the woman you're going to become. Because she's going to be beautiful. And she's going to be powerful. I got it so wrong. I don't want to protect you from the world. I want to show it to you. There's so much that I want to show you." Buffy promises a new dawn for Dawn.

But Willow will not have it, blaming herself for all Buffy's troubles: "You're trying to sell me on the world? . . . This world? Buffy, it's me! I know you were happier when you were in the ground. The only time you were ever at peace in your whole life is when you were dead. Until Willow brought you back."

In "Grave," the world is saved from the demonic power unleashed through Willow's fear by Xander, her oldest and truest friend—Xander the Heart. As Willow is about to open the gates of Hell, Xander evokes her intrinsically lovable essence: "You're Willow." "Willow" replies, "Don't call me that." She has rejected her true self, which she identifies with being a "loser" ("Two to Go"). As with Angel and Spike before her, Willow's fear and frustration with ordinary human life propel her toward egotism and darkness, which ultimately lead to the destruction of the vulnerable human world.[10]

Xander's heart is big enough for all of this. "The first day of kindergarten you cried 'cause you broke the yellow crayon and you were too afraid to tell anyone. You've come pretty far, ending the world—not a terrific notion. But the thing is, yeah, I love you. I love crayon-breaky Willow and I love scary veiny Willow." As Willow magically cuts him to ribbons, Xander repeats, "I love you, Willow," until Willow, in tears, collapses in

---

[10] For a discussion of Willow's choices, see Chapter 10 of this volume.

his arms. As Giles explains later, Xander was able to reach "the spark of humanity she had left." This "humanity" or "soul," as Kant argues, is the higher dimension of self that ennobles the ordinary human personality and is the source of our sense of moral duty.

In the final sequence, scenes of Willow crying in Xander's arms, while the others recover from the wreckage of her demonic rampage, are accompanied by the voice of Sarah McLachlan singing the *Prayer of St. Francis,* which includes the words: "Where there is hatred let me sow love. Where there is injury, pardon. Where there is doubt, faith. Where there is despair, hope. Where there is darkness, light." Francis of Assisi, like his compatriot Dante, would have been comfortable with the multidimensional universe of *BtVS*, while learning from its post-modern sensibility to bless the very darkness itself, without which the light of a new dawn would not be possible.[11]

[11] Much thanks to my colleague Carolyn Korsmeyer for many valuable contributions to this chapter, and appreciation to Jim Wagner for suggestions in his essay, "Prophecy Girl."

9

Buffy Goes to College, Adam Murders to Dissect: Education and Knowledge in Postmodernity

TOBY DASPIT

> WILLOW: "Images of Pop Culture." This is good. They watch movies, shows, even commercials.
> BUFFY: For credit?
> WILLOW: Isn't college cool? ("The Freshman")

Buffy Summers's transition to college life is anything but "cool" (not that high school was particularly easy for her!). In Season Four's opening episode, "The Freshman," Buffy faces numerous things that make her feel out of place at University of California Sunnydale: (in no particular order) she gets thrown out of an "Images of Pop Culture" class; she feels overwhelmed by the size of the library and the overall academic climate; she has a less than reassuring encounter with her new roommate Kathy; she meets the self-proclaimed "Evil Bitch-Monster of Death" Professor Maggie Walsh; and she encounters a powerful vampire, Sunday, who hands her quite a beating. Buffy does eventually rise to her sacred duty and slays Sunday and her minions (except for one who is captured by what is discovered later to be Initiative commandoes), feeling temporarily more comfortable in her new academic environment.[1] Despite Buffy's proclamation at the end of the episode that college is "turning out to

---

[1] In a symbolic break with her high school past, Buffy slays Sunday after Sunday breaks the Class Protector award given to Buffy in "The Prom."

be a lot like high school . . . at least I know what to expect," the change in educational setting and the introduction of the Initiative (foreshadowed in "The Freshman" and developed as the season progresses) illuminate essential components and tensions of the current historical period that has been termed post-modernity[2], which by definition is anything but predictable.

Postmodernity and the Allure of the Vampire (Slayer)

Defining postmodernity is no easy task, and the ambiguous nature of postmodernism guarantees multiple interpretations. Patrick Slattery, for example, identifies eleven different ways that postmodernism can be defined, and indicates that this list is not exhaustive.[3] In contextualizing postmodernity, William Doll, Jr. provides an overview of human thought that identifies two previous major intellectual movements, or "megaparadigms." The premodern world was characterized by belief in "a cosmological harmony that included an ecological, epistemological, and metaphysical sense of balance or proportion" and "covers the span of time from recorded Western history to the scientific and industrial revolutions of the seventeenth and eighteenth centuries." This premodern worldview was "slowly replaced by a new mathematical and mechanistic cosmology—a scientific one"—that came to characterize modernity (René Descartes and Isaac Newton are the two thinkers who most epitomize modernity according to Doll).[4]

---

[2] According to Terry Eagleton, "The word *postmodernism* generally refers to a form of contemporary culture, whereas the term *postmodernity* alludes to a specific historical period." See his *The Illusions of Postmodernism* (Oxford: Blackwell, 1996), p. vii. The terms postmodernity, postmodernism, and postmodern will be used interchangeably in this chapter. Additionally, while much has been written regarding whether "postmodern" should be hyphenated or not, analysis of the issue is beyond the scope of this chapter. An author's original inclusion or non-inclusion of the hyphen will be maintained in direct quotes. Otherwise, the hyphen is omitted.

[3] Patrick Slattery, *Curriculum Development in the Postmodern Era* (New York: Garland, 1995), pp. 15–16.

[4] William E. Doll, Jr., *A Post-Modern Perspective on Curriculum* (New York: Teachers' College Press, 1993), pp. 19–22.

Pinpointing the "origins" of postmodernity is also difficult, as such megaparadigms develop over long periods of time. Nevertheless, Slattery notes that various dates have been proposed (1875, 1914, 1945, or 1960 for example). The essential feature of postmodernity, particularly in the Western world, he contends, is a "rethinking (of) some very sacred beliefs and structures that have been firmly entrenched in human consciousness for at least the past five hundred years."[5] Perhaps one of the most comprehensive, at least for the purposes of this chapter, descriptions of postmodernity comes from Eagleton:

> Postmodernity is a style of thought which is suspicious of classical notions of truth, reason, identity and objectivity, of the idea of universal progress or emancipation, of single frameworks, grand narratives or ultimate grounds of explanation. Against these Enlightenment norms, it sees the world as contingent, ungrounded, diverse, unstable, indeterminate, a set of disunified cultures or interpretations which breed a degree of skepticism about the objectivity of truth, history and norms, the givenness of natures and the coherence of identities.[6]

In other words, postmodernity challenges many taken-for-granted assumptions of the classical Western mindset.

Buffy the Vampire Slayer (*BtVS*) illuminates many of these challenges, particularly as they concern knowledge (epistemology), and offers some alternatives to the dangers inherent in modernist educational viewpoints. Some of the more prominent postmodern features of *BtVS* include its analysis of the potential dangers of reason and science, its explorations of the ambiguous, chaotic natures of reality and identity, and its positing of possibilities for knowledge construction that reject modernist attempts to channel and control learning.

BtVS exists in a turn-of-the-millennium cultural milieu that is rife with the tensions inherent in such megaparadigm shifts. And although the show certainly focuses on more than just vampires, it nevertheless utilizes (and extends) aspects of this "monster" genre enough to qualify as a "vampire text." Veronica Hollinger notes that "some vampire texts 'mirror' aspects of that peculiar

---

[5] Slattery, pp. 16–17.
[6] Eagleton, p. vii.

human condition which has come to be termed 'postmodern,'" which she argues, "is one of the more productive—and challenging—paradigms through which contemporary Western reality is currently being conceptualized."[7] Noting that "certain previously sacrosanct boundaries—political, philosophical, conceptual, ethical, aesthetic—have tended to become problemitized" in postmodernity, Hollinger explains that

> This deconstruction of boundaries helps to explain why the vampire is a monster-of-choice these days, since it is itself an inherently deconstructive figure: it is the monster that used to be human; it is the undead that used to be alive; it is the monster that *looks like us*. For this reason, the figure of the vampire always has the potential to jeopardize conventional distinctions between human and monster, between life and death, between ourselves and others. We look into the mirror it provides and we see a version of ourselves. Or, more accurately, keeping in mind the orthodoxy that vampires cast no mirror reflections, we look into the mirror and see nothing *but* ourselves.[8]

As Buffy struggles to make sense of life after high school, viewers are invited to witness the transitional dissonance of shifting views of knowledge and education and to see themselves on the developing terrain of postmodernity.

The Wolf of Science and the Tyranny of Reason

BUFFY: Ever since we did that spell where we called on the First Slayer, I've been going out a lot, every night.
GILES: Patrolling?
BUFFY: Hunting. ("Buffy vs. Dracula")

From Plato and a tradition which lasted throughout the classical age, knowledge is a hunt. To know is to put to death. . . . To know

---

[7] Veronica Hollinger, "Fantasies of Absence: The Postmodern Vampire," in *Blood Read: The Vampire as Metaphor in Contemporary Culture*, edited by Joan Gordon and Veronica Hollinger (Philadelphia: University of Pennsylvania Press, 1997), p. 199.

[8] *Ibid.*, p. 201.

is to kill, to rely on death. . . . The reason of the strongest is reason *by itself*. Western man [*sic*] is a wolf of science. (Michel Serres)[9]

Thelma Lavine, in exploring aspects of Georg Wilhelm Frederich Hegel's philosophy, explains the role that "mastery" of an "other" had in both premodernist and modernist thought:

> We are beings . . . who take mastery as our goal . . . such mastering actions (are) the examples of the principle of negation, at work in all human thought . . . the same principle of negation is at work in the human subject, producing the subject's relation to all objects through the will to mastery . . . the principle of negation and death is at work in the self's characteristic relation to objects, in its desire to negate them, to overcome them in some way, to destroy them, to incorporate them, to cancel them out of existence.[10]

This principle of mastery, of negation, of the desire to *know*, manifests itself in Season Four especially through introduction of the Initiative, the secret U.S. military sponsored program supposedly aimed at removing the demon threat through research and rehabilitation. In *knowing* the "true" nature of demons, the Initiative's goal appears to be to "solve" the demon problem, echoing modernism's faith in the ability of science and reason to remedy all ills.

In "Doomed," Buffy begins to come to terms with Riley's (and Professor Walsh's) involvement with the Initiative, and the Initiative's purpose in Sunnydale:

> BUFFY: You're part of some military monster squad that rounds up demons, vampires—probably have official-sounding euphemisms for them like "Unfriendlies" or "Nonsapiens" . . .
>
> RILEY: Hostile Sub-Terrestrials.
>
> BUFFY: There you go. So you deliver these . . . "HSTs" to a bunch of lab coats who perform experiments which,

---

[9] In Jacques Daignault, "Traces at Work from Different Places," in *Understanding Curriculum as Phenomenological and Deconstructed Text*, edited by William F. Pinar and William M. Reynolds (New York: Teachers' College Press, 1992), p. 198.

[10] Thelma Z. Lavine, *From Socrates to Sartre: The Philosophic Quest* (New York: Bantam, 1984), p. 220.

among other things, turn some into harmless bunnies. How am I doing so far?

RILEY: A little too well.

Maggie Walsh explains to Buffy the difference in the Initiative's approach from those of the Slayer:

> MAGGIE: Our goals are similar. We're each interested in curtailing the sub-terrestrial menace. It's only our methods that differ. We use the latest in scientific technology and state-of-the-art weaponry and you—if I understand this correctly—poke them with a sharp stick.
>
> BUFFY: It's more effective than it sounds.

Indeed, as will be explored in more detail later, Buffy's epistemological approach embodies many postmodern principles, whereas the Initiative clings to modernist desires to master and control, even if the goal of "curtailing" harmful demon activity seems similar to Buffy's.

When Romantic poet William Wordsworth wrote in "The Tables Turned," "Our meddling intellect/Misshapes the beauteous forms of things;/We murder to dissect," he undoubtedly could not have predicted the excesses that human attempts to understand, and control, "nature" would bring. This will to mastery most poignantly emerges in Adam, who defines himself in "Goodbye Iowa": "I am a kinematically redundant, bio-mechanical demonoid. Designed by Maggie Walsh." Indeed, in creating her Frankenstein's monster from demon, human, and mechanical parts, Walsh exemplifies the modernist reductionism to which Wordsworth alludes. That is, by "dissecting" demons, then putting together pieces as if solving some jigsaw puzzle, she believes that science can not only understand reality better, but in fact supersede that reality. Walsh and the "powers-that-be" behind the Initiative intend Adam to be a prototype of a slew of super-soldiers.

The Initiative's goals are hardly relevant in many respects, as Riley explains in a trenchant critique of modernist ethics: "She made you *because* she was a scientist." That is, the will to mastery intrinsic in modernist scientific inquiry is itself dangerous. Adam simply personifies that danger. The first glimpse of Adam is at the end of "The I in Team" when he kills his creator, Maggie

Walsh. The next major scene for Adam, in "Goodbye Iowa," and in a homage to the 1931 film *Frankenstein*, involves an encounter with a young boy. It is discovered later that Adam has not only killed the young boy, but mutilated him as well; or more accurately, dissected him, in an attempt to understand not only how the boy works, but also the world, and ultimately himself. Adam explains to Buffy, Riley, and Xander: "I've been thinking about the world. I wanted to see it, learn it. I saw the inside of that boy, and it was beautiful. . . . now I want to learn about me. Why I feel. What I am."

Postmodern Identity and Ambiguity

ADAM: What am I? ("Goodbye Iowa")

RILEY: (to Buffy) Who are you? ("Goodbye Iowa")

Western philosophy has often concerned itself with the search for the authentic "self," to answer the question, "who am I?" In Descartes's quest for a first principle upon which to build a unified philosophy, he ultimately believes he exists because he is a thinking, rational being (that is, *cogito ergo sum*, "I think, therefore, I am"). He then moves "outward" from this discovered self to "prove" the existence of God and, ultimately, the rest of the world.[11] In finding his existence primarily in his mind, Descartes introduces what has come to be known as the Cartesian split between mind and body (that is, the mind exists independent of the body and the rest of the material world). The mind, however, can be deceived by the senses, by the "subjective"—the only way to apprehend "objective" reality is through meticulous application of rational "rules." Furthermore, in Descartes's method for philosophical inquiry,

> there is the assumption of an external reality—set by a rational, geometrical, undeceiving God, unaffected by our personal ruminations and activities. This categorical separation between the external and the personal . . . is part of Descartes's legacy to modernism

---

[11] In "Earshot" Oz references Descartes by noting, after Buffy has acquired the ability to read minds, "I am my thoughts. . . . if they exist in her, Buffy contains everything that is me, and she becomes me. I cease to exist. Hmmm. . . . No one else exists either. Buffy is all of us. We think, therefore she is. . . ."

. . . nature . . . becomes an object to be manipulated by "reason."
. . . Descartes bequeathed to modernist thought a method for discovering a pre-existent world, not a method for dealing with an
emergent, evolutionary one.[12]

At first glance, the Buffyverse might appear to be the closed
universe Descartes envisioned, where the battle between Good
and Evil is played out in predetermined worlds, natural and
supernatural, governed by their own laws, and knowable
through prophecies (that is, all that needs to be known can be
discovered as that knowledge already exists, especially in various texts that require specific training to decipher, to *know*). The
institutional structures that *BtVS* initially lays out, a Slayer by
birthright under the tutelage of a Watcher (who is similarly
under the guidance of a governing body, the Watchers' Council)
equipped with seemingly endless access to ancient texts/knowl-
edge, support such a modernist interpretation. Note especially
in the first few seasons how frequently Giles consults his books
for "answers."

Yet *BtVS* constantly complicates such a simplistic reading. In
fact, the series's very first scene (and a scene Joss Whedon comments on in the Season One DVD) introduces the postmodern
significance of ambiguity. In that scene viewers are led to
believe that a stereotypical horror scene is set to unfold: a seemingly unwitting young blonde female is tempted into Sunnydale
High by a young male. Of course the "unwitting" woman is
Darla, a vampire who quickly foils expectations by being the
killer, not the prey.

The number of instances where Buffy and the Scooby Gang
thwart the expected unfolding of some demonic threat or
prophecy, a teleology in philosophic terms, are too numerous to
mention. To give but one example, in "Prophecy Girl," the literal meaning of a prophecy is fulfilled (Buffy *does* die), but the
overall "plan," or metanarrative, does not reach the desired ends
of the Master's rising. The future in the Buffyverse is indeed one,
as Doll noted previously as a neglected component of modernism, that is "emergent (and) evolutionary."

Furthermore, characters' identities in *BtVS* are constantly
blurred. Rarely is one simply as he or she appears to be, or often

---

[12] Doll, pp. 31–32.

even what one might think. Characters can rarely be defined by
the modernist binary of Good and Evil; instead they are complex and their actions often ambiguous. Identity is never fixed,
and the modernist quest for the authentic, or essential, self is
generally revealed to be the illusion that postmodernism contends. The self, in spite of attempts to understand one's "true"
nature (see Buffy's attempt to understand her "dark" side after
her encounter with Dracula in "Buffy vs. Dracula") is instead
contingent, multiple, and perpetually in flux. Three continuous
episodes in the fourth season, "This Year's Girl," "Who Are You?"
(where Faith is able to switch bodies with Buffy), and
"Superstar" (where Jonathan is able to assume the role of a
famous hero with everything revolving around him), are shining
examples of the way postmodernity challenges not only unitary
identity, but also a fixed frame for reality.[13]

BtVS displays a "diverse and mixed universe in which multiple and shifting regimes of knowledge are aligned with salutar-
ily multiple and shifting ethical domains."[14] These are
postmodern knowledges that those who surround Buffy eventually come to recognize. Buffy goes through her own process
of acknowledging the multi-faceted nature of reality in her relationship with Angel (she tells Giles in "Reptile Boy," "No, I think
you don't know what it's like to . . . stake vampires while you're
having fuzzy feelings toward one"), later during Season Six in
her sexual encounters with Spike, and with questions surrounding her resurrection.

Riley perhaps most clearly undergoes this transformation and
faces an identity crisis as he slowly begins to understand that
things are rarely black and white in the Buffyverse, that some
demons are indeed not evil, and that the rational world indoc-
trinated in him by the Initiative is significantly more complex. In
"Goodbye Iowa" he succinctly articulates what many identify as
the postmodern crisis: "I thought I knew . . . but I don't. I don't
know anything." Many critics of postmodernity fear that such
uncertainty borders on relativism, or perhaps more nefariously,

---

[13] Thanks to Lee Papa for pointing out that "Superstar" is an exemplary postmodern text.

[14] Brian Wall and Michael Zryd, "Vampire Dialectics: Knowledge, Institutions,
and Labor," in *Reading the Vampire Slayer: An Unofficial Companion to Buffy
and Angel*, edited by Roz Kaveney (London: Tauris Parke, 2001), p. 62.

nihilism. Yet, *BtVS* reveals that the lack of absolute Truth can in fact be constructive by highlighting a postmodern approach to knowledge and education that may be essential for survival in the new millennium.

Possibilities of Postmodern Education: Beyond Control

WESLEY: I have in fact faced two vampires—under controlled circumstances, of course.
GILES: Well, you're in no danger of finding any here.
WESLEY: Vampires?
GILES: Controlled circumstances. ("Bad Girls")

Educational philosophers, perhaps heeding Mark Twain's reminder that one should never allow schooling to get in the way of an education, are quick to note that schooling is an institutional activity that purports to educate but instead often serves other purposes as either part of the overt curriculum (those explicitly stated objectives and content) or the "hidden" curriculum (things that schools "teach," or reproduce, without expressly stating so, for example, racism, sexism, heteronormativity, competition, obedience to authority, etc.) William Doll identifies such a "ghost" lurking in the history of Western schooling: control.[15] That is, formal schooling, in the name of efficiency and progress, has attempted to provide "controlled circumstances" to supposedly maximize learning, or at least create docile bodies who accept institutional authority. Every schoolchild is accustomed to the myriad ways that the institution of schooling attempts to control learning—from lesson plans and seating charts, to grade levels and standardized tests.

Most of what has emerged in modernist schooling, practices still common today, are akin to what Paulo Freire terms the "banking model" of education:

The banking concept of education (is) an act of depositing in which students are the depositories and the teacher is the deposi-

---

[15] William E. Doll, Jr. "Curriculum and Concepts of Control," in *Curriculum: Toward New Identities*, edited by William F. Pinar (New York: Garland, 1998), pp. 295–323.

tor. . . . Instead of communicating, the teacher issues communiqués and makes deposits which the students patiently receive, memorize, and repeat. . . . Based on a mechanistic, static, naturalistic, spatialized view of consciousness, it transforms students into receiving objects. It attempts to control thinking and action, leads men [*sic*] to adjust to the world, and inhibits their creative power.[16]

The few classrooms that *BtVS* allows viewers into (at UC Sunnydale one brief classroom scene of "Images of Pop Culture" is shown in "The Freshman," and a few scenes of Professor Walsh's "Introduction to Psychology" course are interspersed throughout the first half of Season Four) reinforce Freire's concept of the banking model. In Professor Riegert's course on popular culture, unquestioned authority is clearly present:

PROFESSOR REIGERT: The point of this course is not to critique popular American culture. It is not to pick at it, or look down upon it. And it is not to watch videos for credit. The point is to examine—

BUFFY: (Whispers to student beside her) Do you know if this class is full yet?

PROFESSOR REIGERT: And there are two people talking at once, and I know that one of them is me. And the other is . . . a blonde girl. You, blonde girl. Stand up. I'm very excited to hear what you have to say that's worth interrupting my lecture for.

BUFFY: I was just asking if the class was still open, if I could still sign up.

PROFESSOR REIGERT: If your name isn't on this sheet then you are wasting everyone's time. Are you on the sheet?

BUFFY: They told me that if I just—

PROFESSOR REIGERT: Do you understand? You are sucking energy from everyone in this room. They came here to learn. Get out!

BUFFY: I didn't mean to suck.

PROFESSOR REIGERT: Leave!

---

[16] Paulo Freire, *Pedagogy of the Oppressed* (New York: Herder and Herder, 1970), pp. 64–66.

Buffy's first encounter with Maggie Walsh in her "Introduction to Psychology" course also reinforces what is called a "transmission" pedagogy, a hallmark of modernist education. Knowledge, in the context of the institutional classroom setting, is possessed by the teacher, whose job it is to impart this knowledge into passive students, generally through lectures:

> PROFESSOR WALSH: OK. This is Psych 105, "Introduction to Psychology," I'm Professor Walsh. Those of you who fall under my good graces will come to know me as Maggie. Those of you who don't will come to know me by the name my TAs use, and think I don't know about, "The Evil Bitch Monster of Death." Make no mistake, I run a hard class, I assign a lot of work, I talk fast and I expect you to keep up.

Again, authority is not to be questioned, and in most of Maggie Walsh's classes (at least those shown), students' roles are relegated to note-taking, with the occasional question and answer session or demonstration.

In fact, although *BtVS* has used educational institutions as its primary setting (Sunnydale High School before UC Sunnydale), the relative rarity of actually being inside a classroom is perhaps not accidental. That is, the type of knowledge necessary for survival on the Hellmouth is not discovered (to use modernist terminology), or created (an essential feature of postmodern knowledge is that it is socially constructed), within a banking model. Instead, other modes of knowledge, and of education, are explored.

At Sunnydale High, the most common setting for *BtVS* was the school library (located on the Hellmouth), which although institutional, is subverted by Giles (who somehow finds room for his multiple resource texts and weapons as well as space in which to "train" Buffy) and the Scooby gang who hold meetings and research sessions there (in Season Four Giles's home takes the place of the library which is destroyed with the rest of the school in "Graduation Day, Part Two," and in Seasons Five and Six the Magic Box serves as such a gathering place). But it is the *actions* of the characters within the library that gesture toward postmodern possibilities for education. As Wall and Zryd note, in *BtVS* "knowledge is the product of labor and, unlike much else in the shows, is not 'magical.' That is, knowledge results from *work*, from the research and the collective experience of the characters."[17]

The "collective experience of the characters" becomes increasingly important in *BtVS*, in spite of instances where Buffy becomes estranged from the group. This postmodern collective and relational view of knowledge/education is illustrated most prominently in "Primeval" when Willow, Xander, and Giles magically unite with Buffy to defeat Adam. This relational, as opposed to hierarchical, view of knowledge/education as process and creation, rather than method and discovery, is also reproduced in Buffy's relationship with Giles. Other slayers, most notably Kendra, do things by "the book," mimicking modernist acceptance of authority and the transmission of knowledge. However, Buffy and Giles develop a more fluid, postmodern dynamic:

> Consider the narrative of Buffy's relationship with Giles, her "Watcher." At once such a title seems tinged with values of supervision and hierarchy—as if the Slayer, the Chose One, were little more than a resentful worker on the assembly line . . . The authenticity of (Giles's) relationship with Buffy—based as it seems to be on a mutual trust and respect—also includes an idealization of the teacher/student relationship . . . Both *Buffy* and Buffy know knowledge to be always interested, so the Giles/Buffy teacher/student relationship is consistently at odds with institutionally validated forms of knowledge production.[18]

Buffy and Giles (as well as the Scooby Gang) offer an alternative to Freire's banking model, and echo William Doll's postmodern educational creed:

> In a reflective relationship between teacher and student, the teacher . . . asks the student . . . to join with the teacher in inquiry, into that which the student is experiencing. The teacher agrees to help the student understand the meaning of the advice given, to be readily confrontable by the student, and to work with the student in reflecting on the tacit understanding each has.[19]

---

[17] Wall and Zryd, p. 54.
[18] *Ibid.*, pp. 71–73.
[19] Doll, *Post-Modern Perspective on Curriculum*, p. 160.

While the question of whether postmodern *education* can occur in *schools* created under modernist ideologies remains unanswerable, *BtVS* certainly offers intriguing possibilities for modes of knowledge/education that more effectively represent the dynamics of a world still evolving, still emerging—a post-modern one.

10

"My God, It's Like a Greek Tragedy": Willow Rosenberg and Human Irrationality

JAMES B. SOUTH

> What we need to know is that there is in everyone a terrible, untamed and lawless class of desires—even in those of us who appear to be completely normal.
> — PLATO, *The Republic* IX, 572b

> The past influences everything and dictates nothing.
> — ADAM PHILLIPS, *Darwin's Worms*

Any student who has ever taken a philosophy course has heard the claim that one is born either a Platonist or an Aristotelian. In one respect this is a very helpful disjunction, pointing towards whether one finds philosophy to have more to do with everyday experience (Aristotle) or as providing access to an experience of transcendent reality (Plato). Raphael's famous painting *The School of Athens* captures this distinction nicely. He portrays Plato pointing upward with his index finger while he shows Aristotle with his hand splayed and fingers directed towards the earth. Plato is, in the popular imagination, the philosopher concerned with trying to explain our worldly experiences by reference to some unifying feature that stands apart from them while Aristotle emphasizes the priority of this world. As useful (or unuseful) as this popular contrast between Plato and Aristotle might be, it does a real disservice to Plato, since he also stands at the beginning of another philosophical tradition that I think is equally, or even more, important than the tradition that emphasizes the transcendent. This other tradition is one in which the human mind is thought to be a mystery to itself because it possesses hidden depths that can lead the mind to act in ways that cannot always be explained by an appeal to reason. It is this aspect of Plato's thought that Jonathan Lear has captured:

> How shall we live?" is, for Socrates, the fundamental question of human existence—and the attempt to answer that question is, for him, what makes human life worthwhile. And it is Plato and Shakespeare, Proust, Nietzsche, and, most recently, Freud who complicated the issue by insisting that there are deep currents of meaning, often crosscurrents, running through the human soul which can at best be glimpsed through a glass darkly.[1]

By appealing to "deep currents" in the human mind, philosophers such as Plato and Freud are trying to come to grips with the fact of human irrationality. Despite the rather obvious fact of human irrationality, philosophers have been resistant to recognize that what makes an irrational act irrational is precisely that it cannot be explained. After all, any explanation we might give would have to be intelligible and bringing an act under the grasp of intelligibility is equivalent to finding a reason for the action's occurrence, that is, showing that the action is rational.

One useful example of the tendency to bring irrationality under the banner of intelligibility is Aristotle's account of tragedy in which the emotion of pity plays a central role. Pity, Aristotle argues,[2] is something we can feel only when the object of our pity is basically like us where "like us" means, at a minimum, the pity we are experiencing must be due to the character acting in ways intelligible to us. The primary way that intelligibility manifests itself is in being able to see when the apparently "irrational" person made a mistake. Once we see the mistake, we can have pity on the person, but at the same time be reassured that the

---

[1] Jonathan Lear, "On Killing Freud (Again)," in *Open Minded: Working Out the Logic of the Soul* (Cambridge, MA: Harvard University Press, 1998), p. 28.
[2] In this discussion of Aristotle, I am dependent on Lear, "Testing the Limits: The Place of Tragedy in Aristotle's Ethics," in *Open Minded*, pp. 167–190.

tragic outcome is intelligible precisely because we have an explanation at hand for the "irrational" outcome.

Willow Rosenberg's character trajectory over six seasons provides us with a compelling study of the issue of irrationality, and forces us to confront the possibility that irrationality can be unintelligible, not just a mistake. Briefly, the question before us concerns how Willow, someone who is "very seldom naughty" ("Restless") managed to make a set of decisions that resulted in her attempt to destroy the world. Throughout the first five seasons of the show, Willow is repeatedly seen as the best of the Scooby Gang. When it is thought that she has been turned into a vampire, the group stands around devastated:

> GILES: She was truly the finest of all of us.
> XANDER: Way better than me.
> GILES: Much, much better. ("Doppelgängland")

When Buffy dies at the end of Season Five, the gang gets together and decides to make Willow "boss:"

> XANDER: Excuse me? Who made you the boss of the group?
> ANYA: You did.
> TARA: You said Willow should be boss.
> ANYA: And then you said "Let's vote," and it was unanimous
>   . . . .
> TARA: . . . and then you made her this little plaque, that said "Boss of Us," you put little sparkles on it. ("Bargaining, Part One")

I will argue that when we study Willow's character and the choices she makes throughout the series, we will see two different sorts of unconscious mental processes at work. In providing a framework for understanding Willow's choices, I do not want to suggest that the choices themselves are understandable. Rather, I want to sketch a philosophical framework that recognizes the truly unintelligible side of irrationality. Moreover, in providing a reading of Willow's prior choices, I do not claim that the prior choices explain or make intelligible Willow's decision to try to destroy the world, though I do think that they are consistent with the latter decision.

I'm Not Your Sidekick

To grow up is to discover what one is unequal to. (Adam Phillips, *Equals*)

We can begin with a basic point about Willow. At the end of the sixth season, Willow is the one core character from the series who has not yet found her place in the world. She is still struggling to define who she is. That fact in itself should make an exploration of her actions and choices interesting, since she has not found a way to be comfortable in the world.

One problem Willow faces is the sheer multiplicity of roles she has played in her life coupled with the diversity of interests she possesses: the computer geek, the practitioner of Wicca, excellent student, and aid to the Slayer. This extravagant range of interests and roles is evidence of the fact that there appears to be no core identity to Willow—nothing that defines her. Willow does, from time to time express her dissatisfaction at a lack of identity and when she does, it tends to be expressed negatively, most famously in her claim that she is not Buffy's sidekick. This claim first surfaced in the Season Four episode "Fear, Itself," in which Buffy and her friends attend a Halloween party where the fear demon Gachnar causes everyone to experience their worst fears. For Willow, her biggest fear is that Buffy thinks of her only as a sidekick. When she offers to cast a guiding spell, Buffy is skeptical:

BUFFY: And how does it work?
WILLOW: It conjures an emissary from the beyond that—lights the way.
BUFFY: Conjuring. Will, let's be realistic here, OK? Your basic spells are usually only fifty-fifty.
WILLOW: (upset) Oh yeah? Well, —so is your face!
BUFFY: What? What does that mean?
WILLOW: I'm not your sidekick!

After stomping off, Willow does try the spell, but it fails and she is attacked by a swarm of lights instead of the one guiding light she tried to conjure. The failure of the spell is due to her emotional confusion and lack of clarity as she tries to decide where the light should lead her. This scene shows two important features of Willow's character: a deep-seated insecurity about being a mere sidekick and the further problem of controlling her emotions. Examples of this insecurity abound, so I will mention only two more. In an argument with Tara in "Tough Love" she worries that Tara might not trust her since Willow has not been "out" as long as Tara, practicing magic as long as Tara, and had not established her "lesbo street cred" before getting into her relationship with Tara. In her "Restless" dream we see the same insecurity surface: her biggest fear is that, deep down, she hasn't changed at all; that beneath all the layers of social roles she has assumed, she is still the nerdy schoolgirl that she was when the show first started.

Willow's dream is certainly worth deeper consideration than I can give it here. For my purposes, it is sufficient to note that it foregrounds Willow's insecurity in relation to every role except for the schoolgirl one, and yet ironically it is that role she fears. We can see the fear, shame, and horror in her face when she is revealed in front of everyone she knows as the same shy, awkward schoolgirl she was at the beginning of the series, as having undergone no development at all. That much of the dream takes place within the context of a production of a play further emphasizes, from within the perspective of her mind, the unreality of all the changes she has undergone. Thus, when Buffy, wondering why Willow is being chased by some unknown monster, states "You must have done something," Willow poignantly responds "I never do anything."

The other feature explicit in the "Fear Itself" sequence quoted above is the problem of emotional control. We get another good example of Willow's problems with emotional control in a scene between Buffy and Willow in the teaser to "Doppelgängland." Willow is floating a pencil, using magic, while she and Buffy are talking. The ability to float the pencil is, she states, a matter of "emotional control," but when the conversation turns to Faith, the pencil becomes a projectile that embeds itself deep into a tree trunk. Willow's belief that Buffy's attachment to Faith jeopardized her own relationship with Buffy and relegated her to a mere supporting role, causes the loss of emotional control. Another significant scene occurs in "Bad Girls" and emphasizes Willow's insecurity in relation to the slayer bond between Buffy and Faith. Rather than join her friends, she sits on her bed, dejected, after Buffy has told her that she and Faith are going out on patrol and that it is too dangerous for Willow to follow. The next day, Willow is still upset enough to avoid Buffy at school and we recognize that one of Willow's greatest fears has been realized in Buffy's choosing a slayer who is her equal over Willow who retreats, at least in her own mind, to an expendable sidekick role. The "sidekick role" insecurity, the insecurity she shows in her relationship with Tara and the issue of emotional control—all are central to Willow's identity and frequently lie at the base of her lack of control when it comes to magic.

Willow Doesn't Live Here Anymore

Anger, then, is only for the engaged; for those with projects that matter. (Adam Phillips, *The Beast in the Nursery*)

At the end of Season Six, we arrived at the conclusion of a character arc for Willow. Throughout Seasons Two and Three, she seemed to emerge from her initial "stupid mousy ways" (Willow's description of herself in "Two To Go") to become a confident young woman. She had been accepted by every college she applied to, represented the "pinnacle of academic achievement at Sunnydale High"("Dopplegängland"), was dating a guitar player in a rock band and, lest we miss the fact that Willow had grown up, lost her virginity the night before High School graduation. Moreover, she'd become a constituent part of the Scooby Gang, enough, indeed, to decide to throw in her lot with fighting evil in Sunnydale rather than go off to a prestigious university. As she puts it in "Choices:"

Actually, this isn't about you. Although I'm fond, don't get me wrong, of you. The other night, getting captured and all, facing off with Faith . . . things just got kind of clear. I mean, you've been fighting evil here for about three years, and I've been helping out some, and now we're supposed to be deciding what we wanna do with our lives and I realized that's what I want to do. Fight evil. Help people. I think it's worth doing, and I don't think you do it 'cause you have to. It's a good fight, Buffy, and I want in.

Despite this apparently strong Willow character development, by the end of Season Six, she has crashed badly. She has become addicted to magic and Tara has left her as a consequence. When she and Tara finally reunited, Willow's happiness was brutally cut short by Tara's senseless murder. Her reaction was to "lose it" to such a degree that she was ready to destroy the world to stop her pain:

> WILLOW: Let me tell you something about Willow. She's a loser. And she always has been. People picked on Willow in junior high school, high school, up until college . . . with her stupid mousy ways and now Willow's a junkie.
> BUFFY: I can help.
> WILLOW: The only thing Willow was ever good for . . . the only thing I had going for me, were the moments—just moments—when Tara would look at me and I was wonderful. And that will never happen again.
> BUFFY: I know this hurts, bad—but Willow, if you let loose with the Magicks now, it'll never end.
> WILLOW: Promise?
> BUFFY: You don't want that.
> WILLOW: Why not?
> BUFFY: Because you'll lose everything. Your friends, your self . . . Willow, if you let this control you, then the world goes away. And all of us with it. There's so much to live for. Will, there's too much—
> WILLOW: Please! This is your pitch? Buffy, you hate it here as much as I do. I'm just more honest about it.

How can the apparently strong Willow that emerged by the end of Season Three be the same Willow that becomes addicted to magic, makes a string of bad decisions and ends up unable to deal with her loss? I do not want to say that there is an answer to that question. Instead, I want to provide a framework for understanding why there can never be an answer.

Building on the strong Willow persona that develops in Season Three (although accompanied by the insecurities manifested in her reaction to Buffy's connection with Faith and her fear of being a mere sidekick), Season Four shows that she, in stark contrast to Buffy, flourishes in a college atmosphere, at least initially. Things go well for her until her boyfriend Oz is attracted to another woman (who, like Oz, is a werewolf). Oz leaves Sunnydale in search of some way to control his werewolf aspect. As a result Willow comes a bit unhinged. As Spike points out in an episode in which Willow shows the stress of the breakup, "she's hanging by a thread" ("Something Blue"). In that episode she turns to both drink and magic in order to make her pain go away. At The Bronze, Buffy, Xander, and Anya discover Willow dancing, trying "to shake and shimmy it off." They also discover that's she's drinking beer. Despite her protestations that it's only lite beer, her friends are worried. Among Willow's statements in this scene we find:

> WILLOW: I've got pain, here—big-time legitimate pain.

> WILLOW: I just can't stand feeling this way. I want it to be over.

> WILLOW: Well, isn't there someway I can just make it go away? Just 'cause I say so? Can't I just make it go 'poof'?

That night, with beer no longer an option, Willow resorts to magic to make the pain go "poof." She casts a spell so that her will might be done, and wishes her heartbreak to go away, but with no result. However, the spell has unexpected consequences as several other wishes Willow makes when angry become reality: Giles becomes blind when Willow says he can't see her pain; Buffy and Spike fall in love when Willow says they should be together, since Buffy's finding Spike is more important than spending time with Willow; Xander becomes a demon magnet when in anger Willow points out his string of relationships with demons. Willow's magic in this episode even catches the attention of the demon D'Hoffryn who proceeds to offer her a chance to become a vengeance demon, but she turns the offer down when she sees the trouble she has caused her friends. At the end of the episode, with the bad effects of her spell reversed, she admits that only seven percent of her inner turmoil has been lifted, but concedes that her getting better will "just take awhile."

In this episode we see Willow turning to magic (but only after beer) to make her pain go "poof." This may be the first time, though certainly not the last, in which we see Willow's impatience cause her to resort to magic. The connection between the use of magic and the use of beer is noteworthy as well since it foreshadows the Season Six connection between magic and addiction. However, the episode also points to the constant Willow self-deprecation, the scars of her "stupid mousy ways," and the fear that she will never escape those ways. It is clear that for all the growth Willow has gone through, she is still capable of letting her past self-image impinge on her current one.

Bored Now

Boredom, I think, protects the individual, makes tolerable for him the impossible experience of waiting for something without knowing what it could be. (Adam Phillips, *On Kissing, Tickling, and Being Bored*)

In "Doppelgängland" the point is made bluntly that there is a connection between a vampire's personality and the "person it was." What are the similarities between Willow and her evil double? One obvious feature: both are "kinda gay," in a phrase Willow uses to describe both Evil Willow in the episode, and herself when she had lost her memory in "Tabula Rasa." However, I think there is a more interesting personality connection:

EVIL WILLOW: This world's no fun.
WILLOW: You noticed that, too?

It is not surprising that Evil Willow experiences Willow's world as "no fun." After all, Willow's world is not one in which vampires hold dominion as they do in Evil Willow's world. In Willow's world, Evil Willow cannot act on her desires; it is not her world. More surprising to the viewer is that Willow finds her own world no fun. The key to understanding the complaint of both Willows can be found in a phrase that Evil Willow is prone to utter: "Bored now." Indeed, this phrase recurs in Season Six's "Seeing Red" when Willow, in full vengeance mode, has finished torturing Warren, the person who shot Tara. Having tortured Warren in various extreme ways, she completes her vengeance on him by uttering a "bored now," and with a mere wave of her hand, signifying both boredom and the use of magic, flays him alive. Now, given that we know there is a connection between Evil Willow's personality and Willow's, the use of the phrase cannot be designed to make us think of just Evil Willow—as if Willow had lost her soul by this point. Instead, it must be the case that Willow *is* bored at that point. Why? More generally, why with all the excitement that Sunnydale has to offer, is Willow *ever* bored? Why is her world no fun? And is there a connection with her insecurity and fear of her "stupid mousy ways?"

Willow, like all of us according to Freud, lives her life under pressure, a psychological "too much." Our attempts to navigate this "too much," to direct it, to tame it, shape the courses of our lives. These attempts are not always the subject of conscious decisions that we make, but rather are informed by the activity of the unconscious, the very source of this "too much." The "supreme fiction" of the unconscious, to use Adam Phillips's description,[3] has to be understood carefully. The temptation to be resisted is to assume that there must be some sort of unconscious rationality—that is, if we could just peer into the unconscious, we could *understand* what it wanted, or to use philosophical jargon, that there is propositional content, intentionality, clear meaning, in unconscious desire. The misunderstanding to resist is that, when all is said and done, we could explain fully why people do the things that they do. In less philosophical terminology, Freud argues that our unconscious desires are not conceptualizable; they are not full-blown thoughts lying just below the surface of our minds waiting for us to know them clearly. That would be to misunderstand the oddness of the notion of the unconscious. Freud, like Plato, wants to leave open the possibility that some of our actions might be inexplicable, not just mistakes.

Denying any explicit conceptual content to the unconscious, we can say that it (and the person along with it) is drawn to some sort of "enigmatic signifier," and, as the name implies, these enigmatic signifiers are opaque to us. We can give such signifiers names, for example, knowledge, happiness, wealth, or drugs, but their content is never something we can grasp. In the technical Freudian sense, an enigmatic signi-

---

[3] Adam Phillips, *Darwin's Worms* (New York: Basic Books, 1999), p. 128. My understanding of the Freudian notion of the unconscious is dependent upon the analysis in Phillips, as well as Jonathan Lear, *Happiness, Death, and the Remainder of Life* (Cambridge, MA: Harvard University Press, 2000) and Eric L. Santner, *On the Psychotheology of Everyday Life* (Chicago: University of Chicago Press, 2001).

fier is a seducer, and its effect is to inscribe on our minds desires that cannot be fulfilled because they can never be understood fully. As Jonathan Lear puts it: "We are, by our natures, susceptible to enigmatic signifiers—oracular utterances, if you will—which we can recognize as having a meaning—indeed, as having a special meaning *for us*—but whose content we do not understand."[4] This fact is important for our purposes because I want to stress the way in which Willow's addictions, to knowledge and magic, are not explicable. They may seem to follow from her history, from her insecurities, but becoming addicted to magic is not something Willow decided to do. She didn't make a mistake one day and suddenly become a magic addict. There is no reason for her to become so addicted and, if that is the case, there is even more reason to think that there is no intelligibility in her decision to destroy the world. In what follows, I will sketch a set of tools that can help us understand why Willow's actions are necessarily unintelligible to her and to us.

Spurty Knowledge

Inhibition at its most minimal, one could say, is a kind of doubleness; and from a psychoanalytic point of view its ultimate referent, its center of gravity, is the forbidden. (Adam Phillips, *Equals*)

In "The Freshman," Willow expresses her excitement about her new experience of college life:

It's just . . . in high school, knowledge was pretty much frowned upon. You really had to work to learn anything. But here, I mean, the energy, the collective intelligence—it's like this force, this penetrating force, I can feel my mind just opening up, you know, letting the place just thrust into it and . . . spurt knowledge . . . into . . . .That sentence ended up in a different place than it started out in.

There are two ways to read this purported explanation for Willow's fascination with college. First, and misleadingly, we could read it as a mere parody, as a joke at the expense of the

---

[4] Lear, *Happiness, Death*, p. 21.

standard understanding of Freud that everything is about sex.
More seriously, though, we could recognize it as a humorous
description of a fundamental Freudian claim: that all desire for
knowledge is the result of a sublimated desire for knowledge
about sex. On this second reading, Willow has said exactly what
she meant—she didn't end up in a place different from where
she started.

What could Willow mean when she says that in high school
one had to work hard to learn anything? Certainly, even a causal
watching of the first three seasons would make us think the
exact opposite. For Willow, in contrast to Buffy and Xander,
learning seems to come very easily. So, the statement cannot
mean what it seems to say. Instead, Willow's statement is making the Freudian point that there is a distinction between the
kind of learning that goes on in high school and knowledge.
This is not to say that everything we learn has to do with sex.
Indeed, there is a term for the sorts of things we learn that are
independent of sexual curiosity: education. Education on
Freud's view is precisely the attempt to make children (and
adults) forget about what most interests them. Our unique
attachments to the world are what education is designed to
erase, and it is those unique attachments that make knowledge
real for us, as opposed to mere rote exercise. But those unique
attachments, Freud teaches, are at root sexual, or at least have
to do with our overwhelming curiosity about sex.[5] Once we
have reached the realm of sex, we have reached the realm of
the unconscious. Now, if the unconscious is not some sort of
subterranean rationality, what is it? How does it form its attachments? Willow's words suggest that the attachments are pre- (or
perhaps proto-) conceptual. That is, what we are attached to is
not so much what we know as what we feel.

Let us return to the fact that Willow feels bored, that her
world is no fun. She is waiting for something and that waiting
plays itself out in her unconscious by attaching to an enigmatic
signifier: knowledge, or in other episodes, magic. Indeed, I suspect that in Willow's mind magic and knowledge may not be all
that different. They seem to form a continuum for her, and just

---

[5] For more on curiosity, Freud, knowledge, and education, see Adam Phillips,
"Learning from Freud," in *Philosophers on Education*, edited by Amélie O.
Rorty (New York: Routledge, 1998), pp. 411–17.

as she excelled at knowing in high school, she comes to excel at magic. Yet her disappointment in what she learned in high school might have, perhaps should have, made her notice that, like knowledge, magic could not provide a fulfillment to her waiting.

To help us think about Willow's actions, I shall make use of a distinction between two sorts of unconscious mental process: "swerve" and "break."[6] Willow exhibits both types of mental behavior. A swerve is our ordinary subconscious activity, the kind that manifests itself in cases of what we popularly call "Freudian slips." Such swerves are attempts to discharge the tension generated by the "too much" of our unconscious mental life, and swerve is informed by the pleasure principle, that mechanism through which we normally attempt to regulate the "too much" of our mental life. A break is something much more severe—not just a redirection, but an actual gap in mental process. Willow's discussion of "spurty knowledge" is an amusing, but realistic, example of swerve. Jonathan Lear points out the deep significance of the notion of swerve: we can never inhabit "the space of reasons" since our actions always mean more than we can know.[7] At its worst, swerve constructs symptoms, phobias (and recall that Willow is "frog-phobic," as mentioned in "Killed by Death" and "What's My Line, Part One"), and other sorts of irrational activities, including, presumably, Willow's own fear of her "stupid mousy ways." It is precisely such unconscious mental swerve that led Willow down the path of magic addiction. Joined to her impatience in the face of obstacles and her deep-seated insecurity about her "stupid mousy ways," magic offered an out. It played the role of an enigmatic signifier that could engage her interest while she played a waiting game, while being bored.

Making the Pain Go "Poof"

So one of the aims of analysis is to free people to do nothing to the future but be interested in it. (Adam Phillips, *The Beast in the Nursery*)

---

[6] Lear, *Happiness, Death*, pp. 114–121.
[7] *Ibid.*, p. 114.

Willow's actions at the end of Season Six are more than yet another attempt to make her life pleasurable. They are an attack on the very idea that life can be pleasurable. Even the pleasure of waiting, of being bored, has lost its reality for Willow. All that is left is destruction, and destruction on a vast scale. This is an extreme example of break. Willow's unconscious mental life can no longer swerve according to the pleasure principle, but instead breaks with her previous mental defenses. Willow's turn to dark magic in an attempt to destroy the world cannot be called a "mistake." It is not analogous to drinking beer to help deal with a broken relationship. Instead, it is much more plausible to read it as simply inexplicable. This makes her actions and situation tragic, but not in Aristotle's sense of the term. In focusing on the dark, irrational depths present in Willow, we are led to see the real and tragic irrational possibilities intrinsic to human nature.

We have seen her psyche disrupt itself. We have seen her regress to a state in which she is not even recognizably Willow: "Willow doesn't live here anymore" ("Grave"). Nonetheless, she does return, but she returns thanks to an external agent, Xander, who provides Willow with an opportunity to regroup after her psychic break. The big point here is that break is responsible for two different sorts of psychic phenomena: traumatic attacks on the psyche and disruptions in psychological trajectories. In Willow's case, we see both types of break. The break that transforms her ordinary swerve symptoms of magic addiction and self-doubt into an attempt to destroy the world is one manifestation of break. One way to think about Willow's actions at the end of Season Six is to recognize that she can no longer be bored. There is nothing left for her to wait for, so she decides to end everything. In short, she has run out of any way to experience pleasure and her "too much" of mental life cannot be redirected via swerve, but attacks the psyche directly. There is, in short, no good reason why Willow's actions should proceed in this way. There is no way to explain why swerve can no longer help Willow.

We see the second type of break at the very end of "Grave." Xander's simple presence to Willow provides her with an opportunity for regrouping. All he does is remind Willow that he has always been there, and he does so by reminding Willow of her shame at breaking a yellow crayon in Kindergarten. This very mundane, even hokey, memory provides Willow an opportunity. It opens up possibilities in the structure of swerve by disrupting mental activity, but not by having the psyche turn upon itself. Willow's "breakdown" at the end of "Grave" is really a *break*down in this second sense of "break." Visibly we see this when her swerve symptoms (including the black hair and black eyes) disappear and she regains an attachment to the world. The second sense of break in play here does not guarantee anything, but at least it might allow Willow to move on.

The reaction of many viewers to the last three episodes of Season Six was understandable, but my argument in this chapter suggests that the reaction was misguided. This reaction took the following form: "We don't recognize Willow in these episodes." I think that response is only half right. It is half right, because our ordinary notion of Willow is one in which Willow would never do the sorts of things she did. It is incomplete as a response, though, because it assumes that we could ever fully understand Willow, that there are no dark currents in her, that we could ever construct a coherent and consistent narrative for Willow. There have always been dark currents in Willow, but she has always managed to swerve when they emerged, to cover them over. This time, her unconscious swerve is helpless in the face of her psyche turning upon itself. Her own psyche disrupts her swerve pattern and propels Willow to decide to destroy the world.

In providing us a character who is outside the scope of rationality in this way, the writers gave us a character who engages in actions that are not pitiable or explicable, who cannot be an Aristotelian tragic hero. This was a very risky move on their part, since they courted alienating viewers who are not comfortable with tragic characters whose mistakes are inexplicable, that is, whose mistakes do not seem like mistakes at all. But, I want to suggest that it was precisely this risk that makes watching these episodes, and thinking about Willow's character development, so valuable philosophically. In Lear's words: ". . . it remains a permanent possibility for human destructiveness to catch us by surprise; for there must be an element in human violence which remains inevitably surd."[8]

---

[8] Lear, "Testing the Limits," p. 181.

You're really enjoying this whole moral superiority thing, aren't you?

Buffy and Ethics

11
Should We Do What Buffy Would Do?

JASON KAWAL

In recent decades there has been a return by many philosophers to forms of ethical theory frequently associated with the ancient Greeks. These theories tend to emphasize moral virtues and good character over moral rules, commandments, or rights, and as such are referred to as 'virtue theories'.[1] They typically tell us that to act rightly, we ought to act as good, virtuous people would act in similar circumstances. Rosalind Hursthouse presents an account of morally right action commonly held by contemporary virtue theorists:

> An action is right if [and only if] it is what a virtuous agent would characteristically (that is, acting in character) do in the circumstances.[2]

Thus, when faced with a moral dilemma we might ask ourselves, "What would the Buddha do?," "What would Jesus do?," or perhaps, "What would Buffy do?" We then try to act as they would; in so doing, we fulfill Hursthouse's definition of a right action—we would act as a virtuous agent would act in the same circumstances.

---

[1] Aristotle is perhaps the best-known philosopher to embrace a form of virtue theory. See especially his *Nicomachean Ethics*, translated by Terence Irwin (Indianapolis: Hackett, 1985).

[2] Rosalind Hursthouse, *On Virtue Ethics* (New York: Oxford University Press, 1999), p. 28.

Here's an example to show how this might work. Suppose you are confronted by an obnoxious driver who dangerously cuts right in front of you, and you're now considering speeding up and flipping off the offender. But you pause and consider what Jesus (or whatever moral exemplar you choose) would do in your situation. You conclude that he would most likely turn the other cheek, and so you decide that you too ought to resist your urge to lash out, and instead let the incident simply pass without further escalation. To do the morally right thing, you try to act in the same way as a morally exemplary person. Notice that you aren't really thinking in terms of strict moral rules or commandments, or what legal rights you have. Instead, you are guiding your behavior by reflecting on the behavior of a good moral person placed in your situation.

In this chapter we'll consider three things. First, we'll look at whether we have good grounds for taking Buffy to be a moral exemplar, someone whom we could establish as a guide to moral behavior. Second, we'll examine certain problems that arise for virtue theories that tell us to try to do what Buffy (or any other moral exemplar) would do, were she in our situation. Finally, we'll consider possible modifications to solve the problems we've raised for virtue theories.

Buffy As Moral Exemplar

So, our first order of business is to consider whether Buffy deserves to be taken as a morally exemplary character, a person whose behavior could serve as a model for our own. What I hope to show in this section is that Buffy holds deep moral commitments that lead her to an ongoing pattern of heroic and saintly actions. As such, we have good grounds to treat Buffy as a moral role model.

Let's begin by distinguishing between heroic and saintly actions, roughly following the distinctions drawn by the philosopher J.O. Urmson.[3] Heroic actions involve a person performing a morally praiseworthy action in a situation where the person must overcome significant fear (or where ordinary people

---

[3] See J.O. Urmson, "Saints and Heroes," in *Essays in Moral Philosophy*, edited by A.I. Melden (Seattle: University of Washington Press, 1958), pp.198–216.

would be likely to feel such fear). Saintly actions involve a person performing a morally praiseworthy action in a situation where the person must significantly sacrifice her own interests or act contrary to her strong natural inclinations. Thus a person who rushes into a burning building to save a child performs a heroic action insofar as her action is morally praiseworthy and she has to overcome significant fear (or potential fear). A person who makes a large charitable donation instead of buying herself a new winter coat to replace her old, thin one performs a saintly action. She does not need to overcome any significant fears to do so, and her immediate well-being is not at stake (thus this is not a heroic action), but she is significantly sacrificing her own interests in a praiseworthy fashion, and thus her action qualifies as saintly.

Let's take a look at Buffy and her actions, then, and see what we find. Obviously, we find heroic actions—*lots* of them. She patrols Sunnydale almost every night, and consistently risks her own life for the benefit of others. Granted, she seems to be able to deal with many of her vampire foes quite easily, but even in these small encounters, there is always the chance of a slight slip, or one wrong move, which could result in her death. And beyond the vampires, she has to overcome a wide range of demons and others where the immediate risk to her own life is tremendous, and often she only hangs on by the slimmest of threads. In "The Gift" she even jumps into what she believes to be a Hell dimension in order to save Dawn and the world—surely this is heroic.

Someone might object that these aren't really heroic actions because Buffy herself usually doesn't seem to get scared. In response, note that heroic actions occur either when the person involved feels significant fear, or when the situation is such that ordinary people would feel such fear (even if the person herself does not). To see why this is so, it might be helpful to distinguish between what we can call pure bravery and will-power bravery. Compare Buffy's actions to those of Xander when fighting evil. Xander seems to feel fear much more frequently—but he is able to take a deep breath, and overcome this fear. Xander has will-power bravery; he feels a great deal of fear, but he has sufficient will-power to continue on, and to act despite his fear. Buffy, on the other hand, generally doesn't seem to feel much fear. It's not that she is blindly unaware of the danger she faces;

she instead is aware of it, but remains calm and collected. This is pure bravery—she doesn't even feel fear where most other people would. Buffy thus performs heroic actions reflecting her pure bravery.

Now what about saintly actions? Here we can again reflect on Buffy's patrols, and other activities. But rather than focusing on the battles she faces, consider what she gives up. When she goes out to patrol not only does she risk her life, she sacrifices her own personal interests and commitments. Dating is almost out of the question, given her need to hide her role as slayer, and her general lack of time; and those romantic relationships she has managed have not ended well. She can't study as much as she might wish—though we must admit that she would not exactly follow in Willow's footsteps here, even given adequate time for such pursuits. She constantly faces detention, and even expulsion during high school as she is associated with strange, violent events. Beyond her role as a slayer, she is forced to leave college and to get a horrible "McJob" in order to provide for Dawn after their mother Joyce dies. She is constantly sacrificing her interests for the sake of others. Dawn recognizes this:

> DAWN: Buffy's never going to be a lawyer or a doctor—anything big.
>
> XANDER: She's a slayer. She saves the whole world. That's way bigger.
>
> DAWN: But that means she's going to have crap jobs her entire life, right? Minimum wage stuff. I mean, I could still grow up to be anything. But for her . . . this is it. ("Doublemeat Palace")[4]

For all that she's the Slayer, Buffy doesn't have it easy. Far from it.

Finally, Buffy's heroic and saintly actions aren't one-time events. It's not as if she just went and saved a kitten from a tree one day and appeared as a hero in the local paper. Instead, her entire life is devoted to protecting others—she risks her life and sacrifices her own interests night after night, year after year.

---

[4] All dialogue quotes from *Buffy the Vampire Slayer* (*BtVS*) are based on unofficial transcripts available at www.studiesinwords.de.

Thus, Buffy lives a morally impressive life with an ongoing pattern of saintly sacrifices and heroic actions. She displays such virtues as compassion, courage, loyalty, justice, and benevolence. So, I propose that Buffy can be taken as a moral exemplar. And this leads us to our next question. Given that Buffy is a moral exemplar, should we do what Buffy would do?

On Doing What Buffy Would Do

Consider the following remarks from Xander, in the midst of a pep talk to Buffy:

> XANDER: Let me tell you something—when it's dark and I'm all alone and I'm scared or freaked out or whatever, I always think "What would Buffy do?" You're my hero. Okay, sometimes when it's dark and I'm all alone I think "What is Buffy wearing?" ("The Freshman")

We'll put aside the second question, interesting though it may be, and focus on the first. Is this really a good guide for Xander's own behavior—should he do what Buffy would do? After all, he lacks the many talents possessed by Buffy as a slayer, and has a different set of commitments. Take a common Sunnydale occurrence (at least for the Scooby Gang)—imagine Xander is confronted by a group of vampires, and asks himself what Buffy would do. Buffy would most likely take advantage of her unique abilities as a slayer and make short work of the vampires. But if we imagine Xander without these abilities, attempting to do the same things, it seems that we'll end up with one dead Xander. Where Buffy could gracefully perform a back flip and stake a vampire, Xander attempting to do the same thing would probably end up flat on his back, perhaps staking himself in the process. So, it's not at all clear that Xander should try to do exactly what Buffy would do.

Perhaps there is a way around this difficulty. Perhaps what we need to do is to imagine what Buffy would do if she were in Xander's situation, but with Xander's abilities—not her own special abilities as a slayer. So, in the case described above, we try to imagine what Buffy would do if she were confronted by vampires while only possessing the talents and abilities of Xander; and we might declare that this is what Xander ought to do. Under these conditions, Buffy would need to find an action that would be within the abilities of Xander, and thus might seem to arrive at an appropriate answer.

So far, so good. This might even give us an appropriate action guide for Xander in the situation described—we'll return to the case shortly. But for now, consider something rather different and trivial: Buffy likes cheese.[5] We aren't given any definitive statement of Xander's tastes, but let's suppose for the moment that he dislikes cheese. Now imagine Xander at a party, feeling nervous, and wondering whether he should eat something. If he asks himself what Buffy would do (even given just his talents), it seems that he would arrive at the answer that he ought to have something off of the cheese plate because Buffy would do this; this answer comes despite the fact that he himself does not like cheese. So, we need a further modification.

Suppose we instead claim that Xander should ask himself "What would Buffy do, if she were to have just my abilities, and also my tastes?" as a guide for his own behavior. Imagine a dreadful dilemma in which both Anya and Joyce are incapacitated and being attacked, and Xander would only be capable of saving one of them. What would Buffy do? Well, if she really could only save one of the two women, we'd expect Buffy to save her mother. But is this really what Xander should do—shouldn't he save Anya (at least while she is his fiancée)?[6] Again, it doesn't seem as if what Buffy would do is what Xander should do, in this case because of their different commitments and relationships. A pattern is starting to emerge.

At this point we can return to the case in which Xander is confronted by a group of vampires. Suppose that Buffy comes up with a plan that would be suitable for her, if she were to have only Xander's abilities. But Buffy is extremely brave, and her plan relies on Xander being similarly brave. And recall—Buffy has pure bravery, but Xander seems to have will-power bravery. Now what if the situation is such that Xander would

---

[5] As reported by Willow to Riley in "The Initiative."

[6] We'll just assume that there aren't further complicating factors. For example, there's not a demon involved who will kill fifty children if Anya lives, but only twenty-five if Joyce lives, or any other elements to the situation which might change our intuitions about what Xander ought to do (or what Buffy ought to do, for that matter).

panic—just for a second—before being able to act as Buffy would (given his abilities), while Buffy's plan relies on Xander having pure bravery, so that even a moment's hesitation will result in failure? That is, it is a finely tuned plan that requires split-second timing, but Xander's character is such that he would hesitate for just a moment (where Buffy herself would not), and that this would cause him to fail. Xander, being Xander, won't always be able to do what Buffy would do. And once again, it doesn't seem as though Xander should try to do what Buffy would do, even given all of the modifications we have made.

We'd now need to make an even stronger modification—and perhaps ask what Buffy would do if she had only Xander's abilities, Xander's tastes, Xander's relationships, and Xander's personality. We could go on and on. But look: once Buffy is given Xander's abilities, tastes, relationships, personality, and all the rest, it seems that we no longer have Buffy—we instead have a carbon copy of Xander! The point here is that as we keep modifying the question, we lose Buffy's identity, and instead end up with her taking on entirely the position of Xander. And once this occurs, we no longer have a guide for Xander, because in our questions we've essentially turned Buffy into Xander.

Here's another way of getting at the same point: Suppose you were to ask yourself (when confronted by some moral dilemma), "What would Buffy do if she were me?" If you keep Buffy as Buffy, it seems that you won't necessarily end up at the right answer for what you should do, because you (I assume) do not have the abilities of the Slayer, her interests, her commitments, her relationships, and so on. We might even suspect that if Buffy were in your situation, she'd ask herself how on earth she ended up in your town, and hop on the next bus back to Sunnydale; she doesn't know your friends or your life. So you might think about the question again, and this time really emphasize the idea of Buffy being *you*—with your relationships, talents, commitments, personality, and all the rest. Now you end up on the other horn of a dilemma—because if you think of what Buffy would do if she were you in this stronger sense, it becomes obvious what she'd do. *She'd do exactly what you would do, because you're imagining what she would do if she were you!* This doesn't help us at all.

So we have an initial problem for virtue theories, at least insofar as these theories tell us to act just as good person (like

Buffy) would act in the same situation. I would now like to briefly develop another problem for these theories, before turning to possible solutions.

Heroism Not Required

The second problem for virtue theories arises when we consider whether we are all morally required to act like Buffy and other saints or heroes. That is, must we always act in the ways a saint would, just to be a morally decent person? Virtue theories would seem to require this; after all, we are told that to act rightly we must act as virtuous people would act in similar circumstances.

The problem comes in when we recognize just how exceptional saints and heroes are. Part of what makes us admire them is precisely that they go beyond what is morally required of them. Consider a doctor who volunteers to travel to a plague-ridden city to help the victims. We admire the doctor, but do we really think that all doctors are morally required to do this? This seems too demanding; or, put another way, it seems that the doctor who does travel to the plague-ridden city is doing something that goes beyond her basic moral duties. It's not that other doctors are failing morally; it's just that the one doctor is going beyond the call of duty. We find the doctor admirable, and praiseworthy, but on the other hand, we don't necessarily think that other doctors who stay home with their families are thereby morally blameworthy.

Philosophers and theologians use the term 'supererogatory' to describe actions, like those of the doctor, which are morally good and praiseworthy, but which are not morally required. Typically, people are to be praised for performing supererogatory actions, but they are not to be blamed for not performing them.[7] Take another example: we might hold that everyone is morally required to give at least some part of their income to charity (if they are suitably employed). But we could also hold that a person who gives away fifty percent of her modest, middle class income to UNICEF is performing a supererogatory action—an action that is morally good, but not required; to give so much goes beyond the call of duty.

---

[7] In making these claims I'm putting aside some technical details that aren't really relevant for our purposes here.

Note also that what is morally required of a person might change based on the obligations that she has taken on, and her natural gifts. Imagine that you, as an ordinary citizen, notice a building on fire, and rush in to rescue a person that you notice yelling for help. This could well be a supererogatory action for you. But if you were a firefighter who had arrived on the scene to fight the fire, saving the person inside might instead be a duty for you. Firefighters and others have special duties and obligations that are not held by ordinary citizens.

Now we can return to Buffy and virtue theories. What I'd like to suggest is that for most of us, doing what Buffy would do would generally be supererogatory—we shouldn't look to Buffy's behavior as a guide to what is morally required of us, contrary to the claims of the virtue theorists. Consider the following exchange between Ben and Giles:[8]

> BEN: She [Buffy] could've killed me.
> GILES: No, she couldn't. And sooner or later Glory will re-emerge and make Buffy pay for that mercy—and the world with her. Buffy even knows that and still she couldn't take a human life. She's a hero, you see. She's not like us. ("The Gift")

Giles recognizes that Buffy, as a hero and a slayer, lives according to different, more demanding standards than normal humans (Giles himself ends up killing Ben in order to prevent Glory from ever re-emerging). Just as what is required of a firefighter, priest, or police officer is often more demanding than what is required of the rest of us, the slayer too has special responsibilities that arise out of her special role and abilities. Beyond this, Buffy seems to perform supererogatory actions—even for a slayer. For us to act morally appropriately, we need not always act as these others do. To the extent that we do so act, we will typically be acting in a supererogatory fashion—going beyond our own moral duties as ordinary non-slayers.

---

[8] A bit of basic background: Ben is a human who shares a body with Glory, a goddess who could more or less destroy the world (if her plans were to work out . . .). By killing Ben, Buffy could destroy Glory.

Buffy As a Watcher (of Sorts)

So, what to do? It doesn't look as if we should try to act exactly like Buffy. As we noted above, this doesn't lead to appropriate actions for *us*. Furthermore, it seems that Buffy, as a slayer, will often be required to perform actions that would be supereroga-tory for ordinary civilians like us—and she might even go beyond the call of duty for slayers. As such, it doesn't seem that we must act exactly like Buffy simply in order to act rightly. On the other hand, Xander and the virtue theorists do seem to be on to something—Buffy is certainly a fine role model. Is there any way that we can still use Buffy as a guide for our behavior?

Here I want to propose a slightly modified form of virtue the-ory, and suggest that we ask ourselves a somewhat different question. Rather than asking "What would Buffy do?," we should ask (roughly) "What would Buffy think *we* should do?" More precisely, I'd suggest that

> A person's action in a given situation is morally right if (and only if) a fully-informed, unimpaired, virtuous observer (like Buffy) would deem the action to be morally right (for this person).

Notice that with this definition of a right action, Buffy could think that Xander should do one thing in a given situation (and deem it to be morally right for him), even if she herself would do something very different. She could recognize that Xander, given his relationships, morally ought to save Anya, even if Buffy herself would save Joyce. Thus, we need not act exactly as some morally good person would act; rather we should try to determine what Buffy (and other virtuous agents) would expect of us, given our own individual abilities and responsibilities, and then act accordingly.

Why do we require the virtuous observer to be "fully-informed" and "unimpaired"? The motivation here is to get the virtuous person's best judgments. If Buffy lacks important infor-mation about a situation, then her judgment might go awry. For example, if she doesn't know how to destroy a particular kind of demon, or if she doesn't know that an apparent friend is really a traitor, she could end up approving of an action that will have disastrous results. So, we need her to be fully-informed about all the details of the situation, so she can take everything into account when deciding what a person ought to do. Further, we want the virtuous observer to be unimpaired in the sense that she is thinking clearly, is not drugged, is not distracted, and so on. Recall when Buffy becomes 'cave-Buffy' in "Beer Bad." Under the influence of drugged beer, Buffy is only capable of making such insightful judgments as "Beer foamy" and "Fire bad." I'm not sure we'd want to trust her judgments about subtle moral dilemmas were she in such a state; as such, we would be wise to require that she not be impaired in this way.

Thus, we can see that a small modification to ordinary virtue theories allows us to avoid the problems that we have discussed, while still allowing us to draw upon moral exemplars in guiding our own behavior. The key point is that we shouldn't try to simply mimic good people—we are each individuals with different abilities, preferences, relationships, and so on; the right action for Buffy might not be right for you or me. But we can still ask ourselves what Buffy would want us to do, given our own talents and commitments. We can imagine an angelic Buffy looking over our shoulders—we can strive to perform actions of which she would morally approve.

On a perhaps more serious note, I hope that a small but significant point arises out of this. Many of us do try to model our lives on those of good people, and many people might ask themselves what Jesus would do in their situation, or what the Buddha would do, and so on. My suggestion is that we shouldn't be asking ourselves these questions—at least, not exactly. Take a final example: presumably Jesus could perform miracles when placed in certain situations we might face. One suspects that things might not work out so well were we to try to perform these ourselves . . . Rather, we should think in terms of what the Buddha (or Jesus—or Buffy) would deem to be morally right for *us* to do in our situation. In this way we can be appropriately guided by the wisdom and goodness of the morally virtuous.[9]

---

[9] Many thanks to James South for all of his efforts in editing this volume. I would also like to thank the following rabid Buffy fans: Steve Eskildsen, Jeremy Fantl, Faye Halpern, Darren Hibbs, Robert Howell, Jennifer Lackey, Matt McGrath, Gerald McGrew, Jay Newhard, Baron Reed, Alanna Webb, Doug Webb, and Thane Weedon.

12

Passion and Action: In and Out of Control

CAROLYN KORSMEYER

The metaphysics of *Buffy the Vampire Slayer (BtVS),* replete with vampires, souls, evil forces, and magical spells, is magnificently discontinuous with both lived reality and contemporary philosophy. Nonetheless, such supernatural conceits dovetail with inescapable practical concerns and perennial philosophical problems. *BtVS* is centrally about what can and cannot be controlled, about force and destiny and choice. Sometimes unruly forces are presented by the world and its circumstances, whether magic, hereditary, or circumstantial; other times they seem to arise within our own minds in the form of strong emotions. The treatment of emotions in *BtVS* covertly links the fanciful fictional world with ongoing philosophical issues concerning the relative power (or the lack thereof) of reason and emotion to determine choice and action.

Philosophy has long held ambivalent views about the emotions. The historically dominant opinion has held that emotions are dangerous forces that are apt to overwhelm the judgment of reason, leading to errors both epistemic and moral. By this analysis, emotions have been interpreted as *passions,* internal forces before which we are literally "passive." On the other hand, emotions seem necessary to motivate action, and despite the presumption that they hinder the exercise of reason, emotions are sometimes capable of an intuitive canniness that guides reason when it falters. Aristotle, for example, observed that without a certain type of anger, one would be unable to perceive when one is unjustly dishonored.[1] Contemporary emotion theory displays similar ambivalence: some theorists emphasize the cognitive role of emotion and its cooperation with reason, while others stress the continuity of human emotion with instinctual animal behaviors.[2]

BtVS manifests parallel ambiguous interpretations of emotions, regarding them as modes of both stupidity and sagacity. Especially in early episodes, emotions are implicitly contrasted with more adult rational control, as Giles repeatedly admonishes Buffy that as the Slayer she has not the license to give in to passion. Buffy herself castigates destructive actions committed "in a moment of blind passion" ("I Only Have Eyes for You"). However, the drama is far from the simple struggle between emotion and reason, and many episodes provide occasions for probing different kinds of affective states, their values, their dangers, and the complexity of their structure. Strong emotions are both portrayed by characters and aroused in the appreciative viewer, though emotive impact for the audience is often mitigated by the comic elements of the series. I shall concentrate on three emotions, skipping the one that might seem most central to the drama: fear. Fear is requisite for a horror-inflected drama, but because the genre requires that it be overcome, the series treats it somewhat more formulaically than it does other emotions such as anger or grief or love. This trio offers for consideration one emotion often linked to animal instinct, one that is entirely human, and one that shares properties with both.

There is philosophical warrant to investigate emotions as they play out in artistic narrative, whether theater, movies, literature, or television. Theories necessarily aim at abstract levels of explanation in order that general parameters and explanatory norms may be formulated. To this end, philosophers analyze prototypical emotions rather than the particular emotion-events

---

[1] Aristotle, *Nicomachean Ethics*, Book IV., Chapter 5, translated by Martin Ostwald (New York: Macmillan, 1962), p. 101.

[2] For contrasting philosophical treatments of emotions see Ronald de Sousa, *The Rationality of Emotions* (Cambridge, MA: MIT Press, 1987); and Paul Griffiths, *What Emotions Really Are* (Chicago: University of Chicago Press, 1997).

that individuals experience in specific circumstances. Psychologists too are unable to study the immense variety of situations in which emotions arise, being bound by the requirements of experimentation, not to mention the ethical standards of human subject review panels. In contrast, emotions portrayed in art have the license to explore the bizarre and singular forms that emotions can take, both insofar as they describe specific characters and as they play out in dramatic circumstances. As a number of theorists—most prominently Martha Nussbaum—have suggested, this aesthetic dimension furnishes opportunities for illuminating particular situations for which general theory only suggests guidelines.[3]

Animal Passions and Emotional Truths

The case against emotions is usually made with strong negative emotions in mind, for these seem to do especially ferocious battle with the rational faculty that ideally guides action. Emotions such as raging anger or paralyzing terror not only interfere with deliberate choice, they have palpable bodily effects, including increased heart rate, trembling, queasiness, and temperature changes—for the "heat of anger" and the "chill of fear" are more than metaphoric. Inability to control bodily aspects of emotions seems the outward symptom of diminished rational power.

The emotions are sometimes linked with appetites, for both involve desire; Plato considered appetites especially dangerous, likening them to wild beasts housed in the body. The metaphor is telling, for appetites and emotions are traits that we share with other animals. Indeed we speak of "animal passions," and the idea that such emotions impair clear reason is captured in that very locution. Kant speaks for the majority when he observes that it is reason that puts us "above nature" and endows human beings with their unique freedom.[4] Because we are not entirely rational creatures, however, the jurisdiction of reason requires constant patrol against rival forces, including emotions.

---

[3] Martha Nussbaum, *Love's Knowledge* (New York: Oxford University Press, 1990). On emotions see her *Upheavals of Thought: The Intelligence of Emotions* (Cambridge: Cambridge University Press, 2001).

[4] Immanuel Kant, *Grounding for the Metaphysics of Morals* (1785), translated by James Ellington (Indianapolis: Hackett, 1999), pp. 49–50.

The connections between emotions and animal nature are by no means limited to philosophy. Many scientists approach the study of emotion from the point of view of evolutionary biology, arguing that emotions perform adaptive functions to protect the organism and the species to which it belongs. Brain studies have shown that parts of the brain that are activated during emotional arousal, such as the amygdala, are shared with other animals. This research has been adopted by philosophers who promote a modular theory of the mind, according to which higher cognitive processes are entirely separate from emotive activation, which proceeds along faster neural pathways and prompts such reactions as flight (for fear), aggression (for anger), related arousal (for sexual jealousy), recoil (for disgust), and so on.[5] But no matter how "animal," emotional paths do not necessarily run counter to reason. Because emotions act as efficient modes of response to urgent situations, their speed and intuitive acuity have a peculiar cognitive power.

However, they also can run amok. We speak of being "in the grip of fear," "mad with grief," "blinded by love," and so on. In *BtVS* metaphors become literal, for magic spells induce emotions and people can transform into animals. Being "beside oneself" with emotion fits neatly with the capacity of magic to wreak havoc that the person in his or her ordinary mind would never attempt.

Anger: The Beast Within

Ira furor brevis est, says Horace: "Anger is a short madness." This statement sums up the idea that emotions can put one out of one's mind, overwhelming the balance of reason. Because anger typically leads to action, this brief madness can be a dangerous interval of irrational destruction. Anger combined with love is especially potent, for emotions typically occur in clusters rather than singly. In "Bewitched, Bothered, and Bewildered" Xander, angered and hurt by Cordelia's rejection, seeks redress by asking Amy to put Cordelia under a spell that will make her love him. But Amy is an amateur at witchcraft, and the spell goes comically wrong: every female but Cordelia becomes

---

[5] Griffiths, *What Emotions Really Are.*

obsessed with Xander. The ties between love and anger—in the guise of jealousy and possessive rage—are brought out in the murderous displays of normally pacific people such as Willow and Joyce Summers. In "Something Blue" Willow, her witchcraft growing more adept than she realizes, wreaks her own destruction by accidentally casting spells through the power of her anger. Here the intensity of her emotions—a combination of hurt, frustration, and exasperation—culminates in her every irate whim being satisfied. In the process she blinds Giles and causes Spike and Buffy (who hate each other at that point) to become engaged. Anger and hurt at social rejection are also sources of the nasty antics of the invisible Marcie in "Out of Mind, Out of Sight." One could say that the destructive and thoughtless power of anger is displayed in these promiscuous displays of temper, made dramatic—and also funny—by the fact that they assume magic form.

Anger is the emotion of aggression, and aggression without reason is brute danger. Oz, who in his human form is the least irascible of characters, transforms monthly into a predatory werewolf. Even after he has brought his lycanthropy under control, jealousy prompted by anger at rival Tara and love for Willow is able to tip him back into werewolf form ("New Moon Rising"). The figure of the human turned animal vividly captures the picture of anger and aggression as brutish elements of the emotional range, a suggestion also developed with Xander's plunge into hyenahood in "The Pack." This theme seems especially apt for the male of the species; as Faith says, "Every man has a beast in him" ("Beauty and the Beasts"). Emotional forces apparently work on supernatural beings as well: strong passions are triggers that cause vampires to assume their demon faces.

However, despite the fact that it can be a violent emotion that clouds judgment and moral deliberation, anger is not always bad. Not even Plato thought so; in the *Republic* he lauds what he calls the "spirited element" (often interpreted as a variety of anger), which imbues a person with energy and direction and which is the natural ally of reason in the governance of the just soul.[6] Thus while anger can send one out of control, judi-

---

[6] Plato, *Republic*, Book IV 439d–441a, translated by G.M.A. Grube (Indianapolis: Hackett, 1974), pp. 103–04.

ciously cultivated it can also hone one's focus and energize efforts to enhance effectiveness. When Kendra, the disciplined Slayer, criticizes Buffy for indulging in emotions rather than being guided by reason, the latter replies, "My emotions give me power" ("What's My Line?, Part Two"). She teases Kendra into seeing this as she goads her into fighting ("That would be anger you're feeling"). Practical anger is put to use later when a faltering Kendra is incensed that Patrice of the Order of Taraka has torn her only blouse. Anger also rouses an unconfident Buffy to defeat the punk vampire Sunday on the Sunnydale campus ("The Freshman"). Both these arousals are treated rather humorously, as the damage that prompts anger is relatively trivial (a torn shirt, a broken umbrella that was Buffy's Class Protector award); but these small incidents are just the goads needed for the good fight to triumph.

Dramatically speaking, doses of anger also humanize characters whose rational control sometimes overgoverns their characters. Giles, the figure most devoted to reason and discipline, occasionally indulges in bursts of temper both sympathetic and hilarious. He feels the burden of his youthful wild past and is habitually on guard against the resurgence of his old "Ripper" self, which sometimes surfaces, as when he threatens Principal Snyder on Buffy's behalf. When he barks in exasperation at Xander for cracking jokes at a desperate moment, this lapse in manners succinctly portrays his extreme anxiety. When he castigates Willow for interfering with nature and raising Buffy from the dead, his subdued fury indicates the depth and intensity of his concern ("After Life"). And on the hilarious front we have Giles transformed into a lumbering demon in "A New Man," gradually losing grip on his rational control as his voice roughens and he reports to Spike how good it feels. Catching sight of the hated Maggie Walsh, he leaps from the car and menacingly frolics after her, a deeply satisfying indulgence that human-Giles would never permit himself.

Grief

While anger is a serious and sometimes terrible emotion, it is also capable of comic treatment. Such is not the case with grief, an emotion quite closed to comedy. Grief is probably a uniquely human emotion requiring the resources of language and propositional understanding for its full manifestation. It has many forms and can be harbored for years in quiet. But its first stages include shock and wild reaction, and in this aspect it is one of the hardest emotions to bring under control. Probably the most extreme caution regarding grief was recommended by the Stoics, who understood all emotions to be judgments about the value of events and circumstances—judgments that are more than likely to be incorrect. Strict determinists, Stoics held the view that we are incapable of effecting meaningful changes in the world outside ourselves, and so emotions are just so much wasted energy. Epictetus offers counsel that sounds at first heartless:

> In the case of everything attractive or useful or that you are fond of, remember to say just what sort of thing it is, beginning with the least little things. If you are fond of a jug, say "I am fond of a jug!" For then when it is broken you will not be upset. If you kiss your child or your wife, say that you are kissing a human being; for when it dies you will not be upset.[7]

Grief is the emotion that acknowledges irreversible loss, and not to feel it seems virtually impossible, even wrong. And yet there is wisdom in his advice as well, for unlike anger or fear or love, which are capable of motivating action to effect positive ends, grief is never, ever able to bring about its desperate desire.

Grief includes the terrible wish that events not have happened the way they did, and it can prompt fruitless fantasies of turning back time. Therefore this emotion is especially consonant with drama that harbors the possibility of foreordained fate. But not even magic can stave off death, though we see Dawn pitifully entering zombie territory to try to resurrect her mother, and Willow (twice) trying to raise the dead. But while she succeeds with Buffy's death, which is interpreted as the result of dark magic rather than a fall off a hundred-foot tower (Slayers are tough), even she cannot undo the damage of a bullet to Tara.

In terms of the expression of grief, the show has tried several devices, including the noisy rampage of Willow at the con-

---

[7] Epictetus, *The Handbook of Epictetus*, translated by Nicholas P. White (Indianapolis: Hackett, 1983), p. 12.

clusion of Season Six and Buffy's spell of catatonia at guilt and grief when Glory takes Dawn—portrayed as an example of strong emotion becoming utterly dysfunctional. Surely the most moving depiction of the shock of immediate grief was displayed in "The Body" after Buffy discovered her mother dead and silently, numbly walked through the house, at one point collapsing to the floor and vomiting as if her very body rejected what had happened. Grief is the gateway to despair, and the series skirts a dangerous edge of its own genre precisely because the possibility of lightening emotional weight by means of comic elements is foreclosed.

Love: Heart, Soul, and Chip

Anger and grief are examples of passions that some philosophers have warned against, at least in their extreme forms. But there is far more to learn about emotions than the circumstances of their warrant or control. As Aristotle may have been the first to point out, emotional disposition is a constituent of character; but it is also the case that "character" in the fictional and dramatic sense can reveal something about the nature of emotions themselves.

Love is so complex that some theorists try to simplify the phenomenon by breaking it down into types: romantic love, lust, friendship, parental affection, and so on. The brand of love that comes with the warning label is, predictably, romantic love with its ties to lust and attendant loss of rational control. Other varieties of love can (literally) save the world, as we have seen in two season finales, "The Gift" and "Grave." Despite the subtleties and distinctions among different aspects of love, the various components of this emotion are very difficult to disentangle, and many of them seem to require one another. Romantic love includes eroticism, but does it not also require friendship or respect in some degree? The reverse may also be the case; Xander's steadfast friendship for Willow has an early erotic aspect. Can there be love even of the divine without eroticism? (Many have puzzled over the language of Saint Teresa; it seems there are only so many ways to be transported.) Elements of love appear to be grounded in the body. ("Love isn't brains, children," Spike admonishes Angel and Buffy in "Lovers Walk." "It's blood. Blood screaming inside you to work its will.") At the same time, love—even sexual love—far exceeds biological response mechanisms, involving elaborate cognitive assessments.

The complexities of love can be seen in virtually all the different relationships among the characters that populate *BtVS*, but two stand out for their extreme qualities: Anya's love for Xander, and Spike's love for Buffy. Both characters are demons in some part, though for most of the show Anya's powers are lost and Spike's diminished by the chip implanted in his head. And both are obsessively devoted to the objects of their desire. But in terms of their dramatic conviction, they could not be more different. Spike's love is persuasive, absorbing, and rendered sympathetically even in its extreme perversity. Anya's is a love we are told about but rarely feel. This is not a matter of acting but of the conception of the characters and the very way their emotional profiles are drawn. And because of this dramatic feature, these two characters illuminate something about the structure of love itself, at least the species of love that is romantic.

Romantic love is an emotion that requires a singular object—that is, there can be only one at a time. This is, admittedly, a "romantic" concept itself—the idea that a lover is devoted to one and only one person, forsaking all others. But it does describe an emotion deeply inscribed in societies with monogamous ideals and in the literature and art they produce. As some theorists put it, this kind of emotion is not "fungible," that is, no substitute object of the emotion, no matter how similar, can replace the object of love.[8] (By comparison, if one fears spiders, just about any spider can serve as the object of fear.) But here is a complication: While true love requires the love of one and only one other, loving *only* in this singular fashion is incoherent both dramatically and in actual fact. Without a wider and more robust scope of affection somewhere in one's character and experience, non-fungible love is not credible.

This foundation for love is what Anya lacks. Evidently her thousand-year stretch as a vengeance demon so distorted her character with habitual anger that it drove out her propensities for affection. While she is friendly with the Scoobies and shows growing fondness for Giles, she really isn't adept with human relations at all. Her character is wonderfully comic in

---

[8] On fungibility see de Sousa, *Rationality of Emotions*, pp. 98, 261–62.

this dimension, but it severely truncates her emotional register. Though she weeps over Joyce Summers's death, her expression of confusion at the fact of death is neither consistent with other elements of her personality nor entirely convincing. Xander's devotion to her is portrayed as a bit of a puzzle to his friends, and this is because really it is a mystery why someone with his far greater depth of character would be drawn to such a creature. "I finally get love, Xander, I really do!" she declares at their abortive wedding ("Hell's Bells"). But Xander, tormented by an insidious vision of his future as an abusive husband and the weight of his unhappy family history, deeply loves but cannot marry.

In contrast to Anya, Spike's love is grounded in an intense, messy, and psychologically believable history of painful collisions with love and desire and hate. His human past is not so distant, and we learn something about his early life as an aspiring poet, social failure, and rejected lover. He evidently once knew something of comradery with his former vampire friends, and even at his most wicked, he was obsessively in love with the loony Drusilla. (As the Judge says of them in "Surprise": "You two stink of humanity. You share affection and jealousy.")

The chip implanted in his head forces Spike to change his predatory habits. He can no longer bite humans and has to resort to drippy leftovers from the local butcher shops for nourishment. His propensity for violence can only be exercised against demons, and so he is drawn to the company of the Slayer and her friends. He is a lonely figure, and while he professes to prefer solitude, as his character gradually changes he is obviously capable of hurt feelings when left out of the gang. The effects of his chip are far more interesting than the restoration of Angel's soul, for while the sudden infusion of a soul visits a weight of guilt for the bloody career of Angelus, the transformation is so abrupt that we see merely a metamorphosis from evil to good. But Spike blunders through his emotional change, often comically (his swagger is meliorated with mishaps and undignified "Ows"), and it is clear that he is not always prepared for his own feelings. By the time he awakens to his passion for Buffy, he has acquired the foundation for a genuinely convincing—if disquieting—attachment. Spike's love, for all its obsessiveness and perversity and kinkiness, is disturbingly recognizable. In short, it would seem that although romantic love demands that we love only one person, forsaking all others, we may not properly be said to love truly if one person is all that we are capable of loving.

Emotions and Aesthetic Response

The varied portrayal of emotions in this series signals an unexpected aesthetic depth in a show that might at first seem relatively fluffy entertainment. Some of these emotions are painful and intensely presented, and combined with the metaphysics of destiny presumed by the drama, *BtVS* shares elements of plot device with classic tragedy. Despite this feature, the show is leavened with comedy, and this adds a final complexity to the emotions portrayed in the series.

I have been discussing the emotions of the characters, but emotional arousal on the part of the audience is one of the chief enjoyments of *BtVS*. (Noël Carroll goes so far as to call emotions "the cement that keeps audiences connected to the mass artworks that they consume"—including television.)[9] The form of a television serial puts certain restraints on the arousal and catharsis of emotion in comparison with a stand-alone work such as a play, for often emotional crises are not resolved for a week or two. Indeed serial art perhaps places more demands on a certain type of memory than do other art forms.[10] Equally important is the mixture of high emotional arousal and comedy in *BtVS*. Comedy, especially the sort that inspires actual laughter, is commonly understood to be a killer of emotions. "Laughter has no greater foe than emotion," declared Henri Bergson.[11] Whether mirth itself ought to count as an emotion is

---

[9] Noël Carroll, *A Philosophy of Mass Art* (Oxford: Clarendon Press, 1998), p. 248.

[10] Alexander Nehamas, "Serious Watching," in *The Interpretive Turn: Philosophy, Science, Culture*, edited by David R. Hiley, James F. Bohman, and Richard Shusterman (Ithaca: Cornell University Press, 1991), pp. 260–281. For a variety of views about the role of emotions in appreciation, see *Emotion and the Arts*, edited by Mette Hjort and Sue Laver (New York: Oxford University Press, 1997).

[11] Henri Bergson, *Laughter: An Essay on the Meaning of the Comic*, translated by Claudesley Brereton and Fred Rothwell (New York: Macmillan, 1911), p. 4; see also John Morreall, *Taking Laughter Seriously: Comedy, Tragedy, and Religion* (Albany: State University of New York Press, 1983).

a subject beyond my scope here, but certainly insofar as comedy is a buffer for serious emotions, it is cleverly used in this series to blunt the temptation to make the show carry more weight than it is able to.

Precisely because emotions can present themselves psychologically as forces that overtake the judgment of reason, an aesthetic response that is strongly emotional often prompts a retrospective disclaimer, for example that an episode that moved one to furtive tears was "merely manipulative." Comedy can be used both to temper emotional extremes aroused in the audience and to curb any aesthetic excess the plot is inclined towards. Therefore, it is critically important that a show like this keep its wit; too much sobriety fighting the forces of evil becomes tiresome.[12] (This is the major aesthetic difference between Chris Carter's magnetically clever *X-Files* and his leaden *Millennium*—or for that matter between the first seven seasons of *The X-Files* and the last two.)

High drama and mitigating comedy are cleverly mingled in the best of the *BtVS* episodes. Buffy is late saving the world on one occasion because she was grounded. "If the apocalypse comes, beep me!" runs a famous line used in a trailer. During a sober exchange when Joyce Summers reminds Angel of the gap in age between him and Buffy—in terms that any concerned mother might invoke—Angel broodingly replies, "I'm old enough to be her ancestor." This unexpected line, which could be a quip except for the manner of delivery, flatly acknowledges the real reason the relationship is doomed. Remarkably (contra Bergson) it does not diminish the poignancy of the scene, though it does remind us of the fantasy element of the genre. Sometimes humor simultaneously shapes audience response and keeps the emotions portrayed in the show from becoming overblown, such as we saw with Giles's unexpected, contagious, and dramatically brilliant fit of giggles at an intense moment in "Grave." Perhaps the most notably judicious comic touch appears at the end of Season Five after Buffy's sacrificial plunge off a tower to keep a hell dimension from swallowing us whole. We end with a

---

[12] Steve Wilson, "Laugh, Spawn of Hell, Laugh," in *Reading the Vampire Slayer: An Unofficial Critical Companion to Buffy and Angel*, edited by Roz Kaveney (London: Tauris Parke, 2001), pp. 78–97.

shot of her gravestone with the deadpan epitaph: "She saved the world a lot." Buffy may have saved the world, but it is the comic touch that saves the show for another season and the audience from emotional overkill.

13

Buffy in the Buff: A Slayer's Solution to Aristotle's Love Paradox

MELISSA M. MILAVEC and SHARON M. KAYE

. . . erotic love tends to be an excess of friendship.
— ARISTOTLE (*NE* 1171a11–12)[1]

Aristotle captures both the triumph and the tragedy of erotic love in this single, cryptic remark. On the one hand, erotic love is a form of friendship and friendship is one of the most valuable of all human goods. On the other hand, erotic love tends toward excess, which is the great enemy of a happy life.

The contradictory nature of erotic love gives rise to a paradox, painfully familiar to anyone who has lain awake heartsick at night. Do we choose erotic love, or does it choose us? In other words, is erotic love something that human beings deliberately seek out, or does it take hold of us unawares? Upon reflection, the answer is not clear. It seems that erotic love must be chosen, since the actions that lead to it are voluntary. At the same time, however, it seems that erotic love must not be chosen, since the reasons for choosing it never quite add up.

Despite this puzzle, or perhaps because of it, contemporary culture shows no shortage of interest in erotic love. *Buffy the*

---

[1] Throughout this chapter, we use the abbreviation *NE* for Aristotle's *Nicomachean Ethics*. The numbers following the abbreviation refer to marginal page numbers that are the same in any edition of this work. We used the translation by Terence Irwin (Indianapolis: Hackett, 1985).

Vampire Slayer (BtVS) owes much of its popularity to making erotic love a dominant theme. At first glance, it is a soap opera, complete with classic heartthrob actors and sexual tension. Nevertheless, the supernatural premise of the series enables it to explore the nature of human relationships at a deeper level.

In this chapter, we wish to draw a connection between Aristotle and *BtVS*. Aristotle's analysis of friendship provides a useful framework for analyzing Buffy's love life, while at the same time, Buffy's love life suggests a solution to Aristotle's love paradox.

The Aristotelian Framework

According to Aristotle, there are three levels of friendship. The lowest form, "utility friendship," is a relationship based on mutual benefit, irrespective of whether or not the two parties especially enjoy each other. Utility friendships are deliberately chosen for specific reasons. Aristotle provides the examples of fellow travelers, business partners, and soldiers seeking advantage in war (*NE* 1160a16). In each of these cases, the individuals establish a relationship in order to accomplish a conscious goal.

The next level is "pleasure friendship," a relationship based on mutual enjoyment, regardless of whether or not either party is especially beneficial to the other. Pleasure friendships are driven by subconscious needs and desires over which human beings have little control. Aristotle provides the examples of dining clubs and religious cults (*NE* 1160a19). In each of these cases, the members get together to indulge passions and escape the toil of everyday life.

Finally, the highest level, "complete friendship," includes both utility and pleasure but does not exist for the sake of either. In a complete friendship, each party values the other for his or her own sake. Complete friendship is rare. In fact, Aristotle is hard-pressed for examples. We argue, however, that Buffy's relationships with Riley, Spike, and Angel illustrate each of the three levels of friendship, respectively.

Riley and Utility Friendship

Although Riley is not a supernatural character, his involvement in the Initiative takes him beyond his upbringing as a "corn-fed

Iowa boy" ("Doomed"). Through the Initiative, Professor Walsh plots to take over the world, choosing Riley as her protégé because he is so good at following orders. She implants a chip in Riley's chest to enhance his obedient nature to the point of robotics. Riley's deadly mission is to deliver the world from stupidity, emotion, and weakness ("Primeval"). With Buffy's help, Riley survives this incident, but it reveals the defect in his character that becomes the defect in his relationship with Buffy. On the surface, Buffy and Riley are a perfect match. They share the same goal, fighting evil, and they accomplish this together. Yet Riley is "Mister Joe Sensible" ("New Moon Rising"), and Buffy comes to reject the logic he embodies.

Buffy realizes that it is beneficial to spend time with Riley while patrolling the streets and cemeteries of Sunnydale. Even from the beginning, however, Buffy acknowledges that when she is with Riley, she feels "like something's missing" ("Something Blue"). As Buffy and Riley grow closer physically, they also become emotionally distant and detached. This is symbolized in "Where the Wild Things Are," when poltergeists temporarily magnify the psychic distance between Buffy and Riley. Despite being wrapped in Riley's embrace, Buffy feels completely disconnected, telling Riley, "you're too far away from me. You . . . have to . . . keep touching me."

In "Buffy vs. Dracula," we learn the reason for the distance between the two. Being a slayer, Buffy is deeply connected to the supernatural world. This fills her with needs and desires that Riley will never understand. As one *BtVS* scholar observes, it is obvious "that she is not fully satisfied by Riley. While he lies in bed sleeping (likely in post-coital bliss), she sneaks out to patrol. Only after hunting and slaying a vamp can she snuggle in Riley's arms and fall asleep."[2] Buffy's far-away gaze is not lost on Riley. Although Riley loves Buffy, he feels emotionally isolated from her and concludes, "she doesn't love me" ("The Replacement").

The problem is that Buffy deliberately chooses Riley with a particular goal in mind: to have a "normal" boyfriend ("Doomed"). He is a utility friend for her. Utility friendships are

---

[2] Anne Millard Daugherty, "Just A Girl: Buffy As Icon," in *Reading the Vampire Slayer: An Unofficial Critical Companion to Buffy and Angel*, edited by Roz Kaveney (New York: Tauris Parke, 2001), p. 161.

not ideally suited for erotic love because of the strict rationality on which they are built. This becomes clear when the problem with Riley is echoed in a series of episodes concerning robots.

In "I Was Made to Love You," Buffy's former schoolmate Warren creates the robot April to be his girlfriend. He programs her to say and do everything he wants, exactly as he wants it. Buffy accuses Warren of creating April for the purpose of having a convenient sex object. Warren's goal, however, is more idealistic: "I made her to love me. I mean, she cares about what I care about, and she wants to be with me. She listens to me and supports me. I didn't make a toy. I made a girlfriend."

Since Warren is successful in making April exactly according to his desired specifications, he believes that he will love her in return. In the process of interacting with April, however, Warren discovers that he does not love her. While acknowledging that she is perfect, he says, "I don't know, I . . . I guess it was too easy. And predictable. You know, she got boring. She was exactly what I wanted, and I didn't want her."

In "Intervention," the enterprising vampire Spike learns the same lesson. Since Buffy rejects Spike's expressions of love and refuses to have a relationship with him, Spike forces Warren to create a robot exactly like Buffy, except programmed to love him. He reasons that "weird love's better than no love . . . better than the real thing." When Spike sleeps with the Buffybot, however, he finds the experience disconcerting:

SPIKE: You're mine, Buffy.
BUFFYBOT: Should I start this program over?
SPIKE: Shh! No programs. Don't use that word. Just be Buffy.

Since Spike's goal is to have a cooperative Buffy that will return his affection, and since the Buffybot meets this criterion exactly, it would be rational for him to love her - program and all. Yet Spike does not love the Buffybot. Realizing that Buffy's feelings cannot be programmed, Spike, like Warren, concludes that "a robot is predictable. Boring" ("Bargaining, Part One").

Because Riley and Buffy do not connect emotionally, their relationship is essentially robotic. Spike hints at this in "Into the Woods," when he tells Riley, "the girl needs some monster in her man . . . and that's not in your nature." Foreshadowing his own experience with the Buffybot, Spike goes on to say, "sometimes I envy you so much it chokes me. And sometimes I think I got the better deal. To be that close to her and not have her. To be all alone even when you're holding her. Feeling her, feeling her beneath you. Surrounding you. The scent . . . No, you got the better deal." Spike soon discovers that this is not true. If we compare the relationship between Spike and the Buffybot to the relationship between Riley and the real Buffy, we can see that neither got the better deal. Thwarted with passionlessness, Spike and Riley got the *same* deal.

Buffy and Riley demonstrate the friendship of utility based on rationality. Their relationship makes sense and they are a great benefit to one another. In fact, their breakup is genuinely heart-wrenching. First Buffy decides to let Riley go, and then she convinces herself that she could try harder to love him. She is too late to catch Riley, however, and this is just as well. Erotic love cannot survive on reason alone.

Spike and Pleasure Friendship

Buffy and Spike tumble into a relationship aptly described through Angel's voiceover from "Passion": "Passion. It lies in all of us. Sleeping. Waiting. And though unwanted [and] unbidden, it will stir, open its jaws, and howl. It speaks to us. Guides us. Passion rules us all. And we obey."

When Spike first comes to Sunnydale, Buffy never imagines that she will ever have any positive feelings toward him. In fact, Buffy despises Spike and her goal is to kill him. When the Initiative plants a chip in Spike's head that prevents him from harming people, she only grudgingly agrees to spare his life. Things are different, however, after Buffy dies and the Scooby Gang brings her back from the grave. Feeling as though she is going through the motions of slaying and sleepwalking through life, Buffy turns to Spike in a moment of need. Although Buffy knows that she is being seduced by darkness, "giving in to it [and] going totally wild" helps her to cope with the misery of being back in the world ("Smashed").

Buffy reveals her subconscious desire to be with Spike when she sings, "this isn't real, but I just want to feel" ("Once More, With Feeling"). Yet she denies it and tries her best to make it go away. She reasons with him: "you don't . . . have a soul! . . . You can't feel anything real! I could never . . . be your girl." She reasons with herself: "He's everything I hate. He's everything that I'm supposed to be against." All of this reasoning, however, cannot keep Buffy away from the secret she shares with Spike in the shadows ("Dead Things").

Spike is irresistible to Buffy because he is a monster: monsters are evil, evil is dangerous, and danger is exciting. He is exactly the opposite of relaxing, reliable Riley. Spike is the only one who knows that "Buffy likes it rough" ("The Weight of the World"). He can give her what she likes because he likes it too. So, if Buffy and Spike enjoy each other's company so much, then why not carry on?

The problem is that the very danger that Buffy enjoys in the relationship makes it wrong. It is significant that Buffy finds herself completely unable to tell her friends about her new lover. She cannot tell them because she is ashamed of herself for putting them, as well as herself and her entire life's work, at risk. Buffy knows that "to act on want can be wrong" ("Surprise"). Since sleeping with Spike is counterproductive to her most cherished goals, it is a strictly irrational affair.

After sleeping with Spike many times, Buffy finally comes to her senses in "As You Were":

BUFFY: It's over.
SPIKE: I've memorized this tune, luv. Think I have the sheet music. Doesn't change what you want.
BUFFY: I know that. I do want you. Being with you makes things simpler. For a little while.
SPIKE: I don't call five hours straight a little while.
BUFFY: I'm using you. I can't love you. I'm just being weak and selfish . . .
SPIKE: Really not complaining here.
BUFFY: . . . and it's killing me.

Buffy realizes that Spike is nothing but a pleasure friend for her. Pleasure friendships are not ideally suited for erotic love because they are driven by needs and desires over which one has little control.

While the relationship clearly has a negative effect on Buffy, it seems to have a positive effect on Spike. Over the years, his goal has been to kill Buffy. In "Out of My Mind," however, he becomes aware of his subconscious desires for her through a dream. Being around Buffy gradually makes Spike vulnerable and sympathetic. The viewer is inclined to believe Spike when he says to Buffy: "something happened to me. The way I feel about you. . . . It's real" ("Entropy"). Two *BtVS* scholars assert that "Spike, motivated by his erotic love for Buffy, has *cultivated* a soul, suggesting a materialist rather than metaphysical conception of human ethics: his goodness is built, not given."[3]

If Spike is capable of transformation, then why does Buffy refuse to give him a chance? The answer to this question emerges in a frank exchange between Buffy and Spike in "Seeing Red":

SPIKE: . . . you love me.
BUFFY: No. I don't.
SPIKE: Why do you keep lying to yourself?
BUFFY: I'm not saying I don't have feelings for you. I do. But it's not love. I could never trust you enough for it to become that.
SPIKE: Trust is for old marrieds, Buffy. Great love is wild and passionate and dangerous. It burns and consumes.
BUFFY: Until there's nothing left. That kind of love doesn't last.

The appeal of the relationship is the excitement, and the excitement is premised on danger. When the danger is gone, so is the appeal. Buffy has put herself in the twisted position of valuing darkness in someone. Carrying on with the relationship would mean actually rooting *against* Spike's improvement.

Buffy and Spike demonstrate the friendship of pleasure based on irrationality. The two share a strong chemistry. In fact, it seems it might be possible for them to start all over again under different circumstances. Buffy is wise, however, to terminate the relationship as it stands. Erotic love cannot survive on passion alone.

---

[3] See Brian Wall and Michael Zryd, "Vampire Dialectics: Knowledge, Institutions, and Labour," in *Reading the Vampire Slayer*, pp. 62–63.

Angel and Complete Friendship

So far, we have seen why Aristotle's first two levels of friendship are less than ideal as bases for erotic love: utility friendship disregards emotion, and pleasure friendship disregards reason. In Aristotle's philosophy, reason and emotion are the two operative forces in the soul. Given reason's orientation toward utility and emotion's orientation toward pleasure, it is difficult to see how Aristotle can successfully develop a third way of valuing another human being.

After Aristotle, however, medieval philosophers began to wonder whether there are not just two but three operative forces in the soul. St. Augustine was the first to identify the missing component as the will. In one of his philosophical dialogues, Augustine asks his friend Evodius, "Do you have a will?" When Evodius has difficulty answering, Augustine proves to him that he does have a will by arguing that he would not be able to demonstrate good will toward others if he did not.[4] Although Augustine never combined his idea with Aristotle's, later medieval philosophers did. William of Ockham was the strongest will theorist of the Middle Ages. Explaining how the will fits into an Aristotelian account of the soul, he writes that the will "commands the inferior powers, including reason, . . . [and] moderates one's passions."[5] Since the will has power over both reason and passion, it need not value things for the sake of utility or pleasure. The will is free to value things for their own sakes. It therefore provides a basis for complete friendship.

Buffy's relationship with Angel demonstrates complete friendship. Angel is the most complicated character of all because he shifts between the natural and the supernatural world. Like Riley, he has a soul; like Spike, he is a vampire. During the times when Angel is in full possession of his soul, his relationship with Buffy is both beneficial and enjoyable. Angel helps Buffy accomplish her goal of protecting Sunnydale, and Buffy provides Angel with inspiration to make amends for the evil deeds he committed in the past. Far from being bored

---

[4] See Augustine's treatise, *On Free Choice of the Will*, translated by Anna S. Benjamin and L.H. Hackstaff (New York: Macmillan, 1964), pp. 23–25.
[5] William of Ockham, *Opera Theologica* I, edited by G. Gál *et al.* (St. Bonaventure: The Franciscan Institute, 1967), p. 278.

with Angel through all of this, Buffy worries that *he* might be bored with *her*. Angel confirms, however, that there is no need to worry: "Buffy, you could never be . . . boring, not even if you tried" ("Helpless").

Despite the fact that the relationship includes both utility and pleasure, it does not exist for the sake of these things. This is evident because their love persists through extraordinary circumstances that deprive them of the benefit and enjoyment they share. In "The Prom," it becomes clear that the gypsy curse, set to annihilate Angel's soul whenever he experiences a moment of perfect happiness, is the ultimate test for a relationship. It prevents Buffy and Angel from having sex and other normal things like dresser drawers ("because that's what couples do, they have drawers"). Buffy and Angel both indicate on a number of occasions that they are willing to give up the things other couples have if it means that they can be together. Each is willing to sacrifice anything. At the same time, however, neither is ultimately willing to let the other make these sacrifices. They part at the end of Season Three because they value each other for their own sakes.

Complete friendships are rare because valuing someone else for his or her own sake is extremely difficult. As Aristotle puts it, complete friendship requires virtue. For Aristotle, virtue is found in strength of character, and for William of Ockham, strength of character is found in willpower. Buffy and Angel are two individuals of rare willpower. This is symbolized on the series through fighting.

As a vampire slayer, Buffy is essentially a fighter. Even among slayers, however, Buffy is famous for her power. This suggests that her power is not just a function of the physical and mental abilities that destiny bestows upon the chosen ones. Buffy has inner strength all her own. After defeating the king of vampires, Dracula himself, Buffy is still "chock full of free will" ("Buffy vs. Dracula").

As a result of his dual nature, Angel is also a fighter. His vampire nature causes him to desire the blood of the innocent, while his human soul causes him terrible anguish over this desire. In "Amends," Angel musters the strength to kill himself. Buffy prevents him, however, insisting that "strong is fighting! It's hard, and it's painful, and it's every day. It's what we have to do. And we can do it together."

In "Something Blue," Buffy intuitively recognizes that the love she seeks goes beyond what most people settle for: ". . . I have to get away from that bad boy thing. There's no good there. . . . But I can't help thinking—isn't that where the fire comes from? Can a nice, safe relationship be that intense? . . . part of me believes that real love and passion have to go hand in hand with pain and fighting." Note that Buffy says this prior to her relationship with Spike. She has not yet learned that the pain and fighting of real love do not come from the "bad boy thing." They come from the difficulty involved in valuing the other person for his or her own sake.

It is natural for human beings to value themselves for their own sakes. This is why Aristotle says that being in a complete friendship is like having another self (*NE* 1166a30). In the *Angel* crossover episode "I Will Remember You," Buffy and Angel experience this in a striking way.

> BUFFY: I don't know—I just know that when you're around, whether I see you or not, I feel you—inside—and it throws me.
>
> ANGEL: Throws me, too.

Separating is difficult because they are part of each other. As Aristotle says, "nothing is as proper to friends as living together" (*NE* 1157b20). What is unusual about Angel and Buffy is that their love endures despite their separation, showing that erotic love survives when two people value each other for their own sakes.

The Paradox Revisited

We are now in a position to revisit Aristotle's love paradox. Is erotic love chosen or not? Buffy's relationship with Riley demonstrates the problem with conceiving of erotic love as a choice. When you choose, you have some goal in mind, and when you have some goal in mind, you are not valuing the other person for his or her own sake. You end up with a utility friendship, defective in its stultifying rationality. At the same time, if we think of erotic love as something that chooses us, we run into the opposite problem, demonstrated by Buffy's relationship with Spike. When you have no choice, you lose control, and when you lose control, you cannot value the other person for his or her own sake. You end up with a pleasure friendship, defective in its frightening irrationality. By giving us only two options, the paradox suggests that erotic love is altogether incompatible with valuing others for their own sakes.

In his bleaker moments, Aristotle seems to indicate that erotic love is limited to the first and second levels of friendship. We need not draw this conclusion, however, if it is possible for erotic lovers to value each other for their own sakes. Buffy's relationship with Angel suggests that the will makes this possible. The will solves the paradox because it is arational, meaning that it is neither strictly rational nor strictly irrational. Willing is a choice insofar as it is in one's control, but it is not a choice insofar as it is not undertaken with some further goal in mind. The other person becomes an end in himself or herself. This is the perfect love that Buffy and Angel would achieve were they not beset with impossible obstacles (including the writers' prerogative to milk the forbidden love formula for all it's worth).

It might be objected that Aristotle's account of the soul without the will is more realistic. After all, Buffy and Angel are only fictional characters, and even they fail to achieve the perfect love. If reason and emotion are sufficient to explain human relationships in real life, then there is no need to posit the will. William of Ockham should be the first to admit this since he is the namesake of the principle of simplicity known as Ockham's Razor. According to Ockham's Razor, one should always choose the simpler theory. Aristotle's theory is simpler because it explains erotic love without the will.

In answer to this objection, we concede that we are hopeless romantics. It may be true that erotic love can be explained without the will, but erotic love cannot reach the ideal of complete friendship without the will. If one loves another either for a reason or due to passion, then one does not love that other for his or her own sake but rather for the sake of something else. Those who want to believe in the possibility of perfect love are therefore justified in rejecting the simpler theory.

Erotic Love and Friendship

If what we have argued is correct, then erotic love can achieve Aristotle's third level of friendship. In order to be complete, erotic love must be neither rationally chosen nor irrationally caused but rather arationally willed. Thus, *BtVS* solves Aristotle's love paradox by recognizing three powers in the soul: reason, emotion, and the will.

If erotic love is this complicated in theory, it must be mind-boggling in practice. No wonder it slays even the Slayer herself. As Spike often says, "Ain't love grand?"[6]

---

[6] We wish to thank Earl Spurgin of John Carroll University and Peter Alward of the University of Lethbridge for critical comments on earlier drafts of this chapter.

14

A Kantian Analysis of Moral Judgment in *Buffy the Vampire Slayer*

SCOTT R. STROUD

Buffy the Vampire Slayer (BtVS) has been an extremely interesting member of the current resurgence of occult/mythic shows populating television programming. Unlike *Charmed, Sabrina the Teenage Witch, Witchblade,* and other such shows, *BtVS* mixes in demonic escapades with more than a touch of humor. Indeed, within this show of "the blonde girl who strikes back" is a narrative that holds seemingly limitless opportunities for philosophical analysis. As fans of the show know, Buffy Summers is one of the latest in a long line of "slayers," chosen ones who protect humanity from the evil forces of the demonic underworld. Mix in other characterological aspects, and what one has in Buffy is a vigilante hero with a scrunchy—a seemingly ordinary teenager who is charged with an extraordinary task of protecting the community from demons and its own ignorance.

What kind of moral system could be brought to bear on this show to highlight some of the tensions and dimensions of Buffy's struggle against evil? While it seems obvious to many, how can one philosophically enunciate the reasons *why* the "evil" forces should be resisted and fought with the level of violence Buffy so often displays? We can use the thought of the German enlightenment philosopher Immanuel Kant to analyze the various levels of moral judgment within this epic story of good vs. evil vs. teenage impulses. What is unique about Kant's thought is that it provides a fairly sophisticated way of looking at the process of how individuals morally judge the intentions behind their own actions, and how systems of agents (that is, a community) can judge the actions of agents within that system. Kant's overall thought on morality involves an emphasis on rationality, but more importantly, on a correct ordering and balancing of interests, capabilities, and actions. Such a balance is often sought on the individual level in *BtVS* as well as in the community level of Sunnydale.

Kant on Moral Virtue and Right

To discuss Kant on moral judgment and right action, it is best that we start briefly at the beginning—the rational agent. For Kant, a rational agent has the ability to freely choose the inner maxims or principles on which she acts (inner freedom) and the external freedom to choose how she is going to physically act in the surrounding environment (outer freedom).[1] The first type of freedom, inner freedom, deals with the maxims that one can choose. It is this choosing of guiding rules to order and govern one's actions that Kant finds as lying within the realm of virtue— while others cannot detect or enforce certain maxim choices in the will of others, one can deduce through rational thought *what* would be the virtuous (moral) maxim for one to adopt in certain situations. Thus, Kant holds that humans and their duties (of virtue) are commanded by one fundamental categorical imperative—one should *"act only in accordance with that maxim through which you can at the same time will that it become a universal law."*[2] This version of the "moral law" is often referred to as the Formula of Universal Law (FUL), as Kant also provides other versions of this law—one is also commanded by the Formula of Humanity as an End in Itself (FHE), *"So act that you use humanity, whether in your own person or in the person of any other, always at the same time as an end, never merely as a means."*[3] While the other variations of this

---

[1] Immanuel Kant, *Metaphysics of Morals* in *Practical Philosophy*, translated and edited by Mary J. Gregor (Cambridge: Cambridge University Press, 1996).
[2] Immanuel Kant, *Groundwork of the Metaphysics of Morals* in *Practical Philosophy*, p. 4: 421.
[3] Ibid., p. 4: 429.

moral law need not be discussed in this inquiry, these two versions of it are extremely important in that they define key aspects of a virtuous person's decisions concerning what maxims to adopt in determining his or her actions—maxims must be universalizable by a community of agents (and still be able to function), and maxims must respect the intrinsic value of rational agents not as mere tools, but instead as having value beyond any use one can put them to. Thus, one who acts based upon a principle stemming from these two iterations of the moral law is one who is *virtuous* in his or her willing of guiding maxims.

Concerning external freedom, Kant finds that humans (being equally free and valuable agents) should respect the outer freedom of others. Thus, he postulates the "Universal Principle of Right," which indicates, "Any action is *right* if it can coexist with everyone's freedom in accordance with a universal law, or if on its maxim the freedom of choice of each can coexist with everyone's freedom in accordance with a universal law."[4] Thus, in a community of agents, Kant finds that a state of "right" is that state where equal agents act in such a way as to preserve and promote the freedom of outer action for all. For this reason, a system of agents, usually personified in terms of representative officials (politicians, police officers, and the like), is justified in using coercion against non-rightful actions. Kant's reasoning is fairly simple in this matter—an action that hinders another action that is hindering the freedom of others is an action that maintains or creates a state of right (that is, one that sustains the freedom of all to act). An example may be helpful: if one agent sets to murdering other agents (thereby depriving them of their freedom to act), state actions that hinder that action (murder) would be actions that increase the freedom of all. In other words, the freedom of the murdering agent is not true freedom as it infringes on the freedom of other equal agents—true freedom of action comes about in a state of equal action and reaction among the components of a system. In terms of a community of rational beings, a state of freedom is engendered when the equal agents have the power to bind others equally.

For Kant, moral judgment takes two fundamental turns with this description of the freedom of agents. Judgments can be

---

[4] Kant, *Metaphysics of Morals*, p. 6: 230.

made about maxims that guide individual choices (inner freedom) and judgments can be made about actions of an agent that
affect others (outer freedom). Simply put, Kant would allow
enforcement and coercion in regard to correcting and preventing harmful external actions, but he can only hope that each
individual tries to act from maxims that stem from the moral law,
and not from their desires and inclinations (fear, self-love, greed,
etc.). Let us now look at moral judgment on the individual level,
dealing specifically with inner struggles of characters to will
from the moral law (in choosing their maxims), and on the systemic level, in which character actions are judged and reacted to
based upon their conformity (or lack thereof) to a state of right
among agents.

Moral Judgment on the Individual Level

Many of the individuals in *BtVS* are caught in the struggle that
Kant finds intrinsic to human nature—that of their "good" side
battling for control against their "bad" side. In more specific
terms, it is their rational nature as moral beings that struggles to
determine their actions from moral motives (that is, the thought
of the moral law itself), whereas contrary forces are being
exerted from their natural side, namely their desires, aversions,
and wants (grouped under the term "inclination"). What distinguishes humans from all other (non-rational) creatures is that
they have the ability to determine their motives from the natural
world (through these inclinations), or they can struggle toward
what one *ought* to do (determine their actions from the idea of
the moral law). Thus, judgment concerning whether one is acting morally or not comes from examining this tension that
seems to be an inherent part of human will.

Buffy finds herself in such a position throughout the history
of the show. While providing every example of such a struggle
would be unnecessary, it will be useful to examine her moral
judgments in the most recent seasons. One theme of Seasons
Five and Six has been the Slayer's reluctance to be a slayer.
Instead, she wishes for a normal life, a normal college experience, and normal experiences at her places of work. Even when
she is forced to find gainful employment in such episodes as

"Doublemeat Palace," Buffy seems to attract the forces of evil from all directions. The result is that her normal boring life is perpetually wrecked. What eventually brings her back to her duty as the Slayer? A Kantian analysis would be that it is her recognition of her powers and capacities as the Slayer, and how she is duty bound by such a position to protect the community. While there are some problematic matters to this reading, such as the issue of whether Buffy had a choice in becoming the Slayer, the alternative decision is clear—if Buffy shirks her duties as the Slayer, she will be acting on maxims that privilege her inclinations and desires, and not her rational side. For instance, if Buffy retreats from the role of the Slayer, the results will be disastrous for the community—innocent lives will perish because of her abdication of duty, and one can say that she is not willing to treat others as ends in themselves. By valuing her contingent wants and desires over the safety of others, Buffy would be making a fundamental moral judgment about her maxims that Kant would find to be reprehensible.

This theme of a moral judgment of one's determining drives plays a large role in Season Four, where the character of Oz is developed. His place as Willow's significant other is ultimately destroyed by his inability to control his natural side, personified in his werewolf form. In this form, Oz has sex with another werewolf, Veruca, and acts in such a way that he even suspects himself of certain gruesome murders the Scooby Gang is trying to solve. Here we have a case of the natural side, exemplified by the inclinations and cravings of animalistic desire, overcoming the rational side of human nature; instead of a balanced control of the inclinations, they are running wild in Oz's case. The lesson of this character is not that it is wise to avoid relationships with singers of bands who are also werewolves, but instead that the moral judgments about what an individual is to will should stem from their rational nature. Part and parcel of this nature, for Kant, is a human's ability to motivate himself to act from the intrinsic respect that other humans are due and to act on maxims that others could conceivably act upon too.

At the end of Season Five, Buffy is faced with a monumental choice. Her sister is found to be the "key" that will unlock multiple hell dimensions. A goddess, Glory, wishes to use Dawn (killing her in the process) to wreak havoc on Sunnydale. Buffy and the Scooby Gang stage a valiant fight against Glory and her

minions, but at the last moment Buffy sacrifices her life in place
of Dawn's to save not only her sister, but her friends as well.
What can be made of this situation? One could speculate that
Buffy did this action to defeat Glory, but that does not seem
supported by the feelings that Buffy has for her comrades and
her sister. Instead, it is safer to read this situation as being in line
with Kant's Formula of Humanity (FHE)—in order to act in such
a way as to respect (preserve and promote) the intrinsic value
of her friends and family as rational beings, Buffy *had* to act in
the way she did. If she adopted any maxim that was not in line
with FHE, such as one that led her to try to protect Dawn but
then acknowledge failure when Dawn dies, she would be necessarily writing one or more of her friends "off." Buffy knew that
it was either she or Dawn who was going to take the literal fall;
given that scenario, Buffy seemed to act in contradiction to her
natural inclinations (of survival, self-preservation) and altruistically saved the lives of her sister and her friends. What was at
issue here is whether Buffy could muster the strength to let her
will be determined by such a high moral ideal as FHE instead of
the very powerful natural feelings that were pulling at her as a
human. At the conclusion of Season Five, she judges that her
moral duty is to sacrifice herself to save Dawn, and she does just
that—luckily for *BtVS*'s fan base, Season Six begins by negating
the physical act of deathly sacrifice.

In "Bargaining, Parts One and Two," the Scooby Gang is
found in a dismal state without the Slayer. Willow and the others eventually set out to magically resurrect Buffy, but are inter-
rupted at the conclusion of the spell by a gang of marauding
demon bikers (literal Hell's Angels?). Buffy claws her way up
through the coffin and the dirt and is eventually reintegrated in
the Scooby Gang. A few episodes later, in the musical narrative
of "Once More, with Feeling," a tonally inclined demon forces
everyone in Sunnydale to communicate in a musical fashion. In
this episode, Buffy reveals to her friends that she was in what
can only be called heaven and the resurrecting party (her
friends) took her from heaven. She vocalizes that she lacks
direction, and that she was dragged from a heavenly repose into
a demon-filled world of being buried alive beneath Sunnydale.
Again, Buffy is faced with a fundamental choice between satisfying her inclinations or fulfilling her moral duty to protect the
citizens of Sunnydale as the Slayer. One choice involves her

determining her will from her inclinations, and the other involves her acting in the face of some inclinations to uphold the ideal of FHE. She eventually judges that the maxim to follow is the latter, and she ends up working as a construction worker, a burger-flipper, and as the Slayer in order to provide for her sister and to protect her friends and community.

Moral Judgment on the Systemic Level

While the maxims that a person acts upon are often buried deep inside their mind, Kant finds that agents can judge other agents quite well in terms of the actions they perform. Thus, judgment in *BtVS* also relates to the systemic level of creating a community of agents that exist in a state of right. This state of right involves the ability of agents to exercise equal freedom compared to any other agent. No one agent is allowed to use her external freedom of action in such a way as to preclude others from also using their freedom of external action. A state of right is created when equal agents act in such a way as to not harm the capability of other agents to act. In *BtVS*, this type of analysis gives strength to the systemic judgment about demons and vampires being bad and non-desirable. Instead of slaying them because it is her job (a rather mindless justification), Buffy is authorized in her role as Slayer to curtail the freedom of demons (often with brutal force) because they act in such a way as to radically harm the external freedom of agents in the community of Sunnydale. If the demonic forces were content to play kitten poker and hang around like Spike's floppy-eared friend Clem, Buffy would lack any type of warrant to slay them and to prevent any of their actions. She would not be able to discern if their maxims were moral or not, and their actions would be in the same league as that of ordinary human agents—not harming the ability of others to be free agents in their actions. The story, however, is different; the demonic forces seem to love wreaking havoc and revel in killing innocent humans. These types of actions destroy a state of right in the overall community of Sunnydale—the demons and vampires are reducing the capability of other agents to act by killing them, eating them, and destroying their property.

With the demonic element *acting* in such a harmful way, Kant would say the systemic judgments that authorize the coercion of these demonic elements are allowable. What is interesting to problematize, however, is the role of the Slayer. It seems that Buffy has been given this power and responsibility out of the blue, and with no procedural sanction by the political system representing the citizens of Sunnydale. While Kant would agree that the demons and vampires could be controlled or even killed to create a state of right, it is unclear that he would approve of such a divine force implementing the creation of the state of right in the community. What if Buffy lost control and "turned to the darkside" like fellow Slayer Faith in Season Three? The lack of any type of control over the Slayer and her use of her power seems to be a problem waiting to happen. Fortunately for the world, the Watchers and the Council have managed to minimize such abuses, and Buffy has turned out to be a conscientious Slayer. As the main character, Buffy seems fated to be good and in control; however, the worry is still there—does the Slayer answer to anyone?

Perhaps such a worry of powerful individuals effectively being let loose on their own (even with a nagging mentor such as Giles) would lead one to hope for the community to take measures to coerce the demonic elements into line. Such measures seemed to be the goal of the Initiative. In Season Four, Buffy eventually finds out that her Psychology teaching assistant, Riley, is part of a government unit that tracks, destroys, and captures demons. The main research efforts of this group are lead by Dr. Maggie Walsh, Buffy's Psychology professor. It eventually comes to light that Walsh is building a hybrid *Übermensch* out of human, demon, and mechanical parts. "Adam," as he is called, eventually goes haywire and kills Dr. Walsh and many others before being destroyed by the Scooby Gang. What this lesson teaches is that no matter how it is done, concentrating too much power in the form of a single person carries intrinsic risks to the community that he or she is supposed to be protecting. Adam hardly contributed to the creation of a state of right among the citizens of Sunnydale; instead, he used demon forces to kill and terrorize, necessitating further coercion to bring his external freedom in line with the freedom of others.

Threats to this state of right that the community of Sunnydale so longs for come not only from demonic angles, but also from the human sector. In Season Six, episodes such as "Flooded" and "Life Serial" develop the pubescent evil of Jonathan, Warren, and Andrew, three intelligent and geeky human teenagers. They decide one day that they will rule Sunnydale and destroy the Slayer; through magic, trickery, and deceit they manage to come close to this goal. Eventually their plans are thwarted, but not before they damage Sunnydale, kill Tara, and almost slay the Slayer (the last two actions were the work of Warren). This element of *BtVS* illustrates that demons and humans can both be harmful elements within a community if their external freedom is used in such a way as to limit the freedom of others. The message of the evil human trio is that any agent can act in such a way as to destroy a state of right among equal agents, whether they are human or demon. The most important thing for a community of agents such as Sunnydale, however, is that the equal rational agents all be protected in their ability to act freely, and consequently, to develop as agents and as end-setting beings. If only the demonic elements could adapt to this set of simple moral rules, the town of Sunnydale would be much improved. Thankfully for the anxious viewers, this peaceful, yet boring, situation is not the case.

Following the Moral Law

In his later work on religion,[5] Kant speculates that the fundamental choice any rational agent has in terms of determining her will is the choice of following the maxim of the moral law or the maxim of self-love. For Kant, radical evil ultimately boils down to eschewing the rational demands of other intrinsically valuable agents and following merely the maxim of satisfying your own desires. This reading of evil goes a long way in uniting the individual moral judgment of the demonic forces in Sunnydale and in the condemnation of their external actions—the reason *why* they act in such a way as to infringe on the freedom of other agents is that they make the fundamental choice to value their inclinations and desires over the intrinsic value that other agents are due. At first glance, it is hard to see how an apparently innocuous hierarchy reversal turns rational agents (the demons appear very rational in terms of setting and achieving ends) into

---

[5] Immanuel Kant, *Religion within the Boundaries of Mere Reason*, translated by Allen W. Wood and George Di Giovanni (Cambridge: Cambridge University Press, 2001).

murderous and harmful destroyers of community. This reversal, however, is the root of evil insofar as it is the degree to which an agent privileges his own inclinations over the value of other agents that results in the various degrees of evil action. Whether it is telling lies or killing innocents, the basis of such behavior must be some sort of fundamental privileging of one's own wishes over limiting obligations to others. While Kant does not think a rational agent will adopt a maxim of self-sacrifice and denial of her own inclinations (indeed such a being would be not be fully rational), he does speak against the total surrender to one's natural, inclination based side in terms of how one judges the actions and maxims one is to adopt. The demonic forces on *BtVS* are *harmful* because they act in such a way as to infringe on the freedom of others; they are *evil* primarily because they guide their actions based solely on the subordination of the moral law (that is, treating others as ends in themselves and universalizing one's maxims) to the pursuit of their own natural inclinations. These inclinations are idiosyncratic, and if solely pursued at the expense of duties to others, become harmful in leading to a system of agents in which innocents are harmed or killed. *BtVS* allows for an excellent case study of how individual moral judgment of appropriate maxims/principles and systemic judgment of non-permitted actions can be seen as complementary aspects of the moral enterprise. The Kantian vision of morality is a system of individual agents pursuing their own goals without harming the ability of other agents to pursue their goals; the ideal version of this plan also involves individual agents continuously struggling to order their lives and their actions through maxims based not in inclination, but instead in the moral law. It is such a system that Buffy fights for, and it follows that her inner battle also revolves around controlling the urges and desires that are part of the very makeup of human nature.

That's the kind of wooly-headed thinking that leads to being eaten

Religion and Politics in the Buffyverse

15

Brownskirts: Fascism, Christianity, and the Eternal Demon

NEAL KING

What if Buffy came out as Slayer rather than toiled in secrecy? How fascist would her Buffyverse be? *Fascism* is a mass struggle to renew a nation by forging a superior citizen in the crucible of war.[1] Such a movement features spectacular celebration of its combat and heroes, aggression against a racially inferior foe, and authority derived from an ancient order. The Buffyverse already sports these philosophical and symbolic elements of fascism, but lacks the national movement and focus on the state that would bolster Buffy's death-squad patrolling. This chapter recounts its proto-fascist elements and then imagines a world in which folk could join the Slayer's battles, in a fascist national movement, to keep their race pure. Why not squads of brownskirts, parading their power to cleanse the world; patrolling by night to mock, beat, and kill the demonic? *Buffy the Vampire Slayer* (*BtVS*) could develop an army of death-dealing youth and a fascist state in that case. It need only build upon the philosophical elements that it already has.

I take the trouble to imagine a fascist Buffyverse for two reasons. First, I remain baffled by scholarly assessments of the Buffy's civilian "Scooby" gang as a liberal, anti-authoritarian,

---

[1] See, for instance, Roger Eatwell, *Fascism: A History* (New York: Penguin, 1995); Umberto Eco "Ur-Fascism," in *New York Review of Books* (22 June 22 1995), pp. 12–16; Ian Kershaw, *Hitler, 1889–1936 Hubris* (New York: Norton, 1999), and *Hitler: 1936–1945 Nemesis* (2000).

easy-going bunch.[2] Do they not kill on sight, wisecracking as
they go, with no obvious guilt about their incremental genocide?
Second, I have never understood how the fact of the demon
world remains so secret. Though I do not look for realism in a
show about vampires and werewolves, neither do I understand
why characters who lose loved ones to these predators make no
public fuss. The government knows, hence the Initiative. High
school kids sort of know, hence "The Prom" and "Graduation
Day, Part Two." In "The Harvest," Giles explains that "People
have a tendency to rationalize what they can and forget what
they can't." Though I try to take such entertainment on its own
terms, I must observe that this is a bit of a stretch given the ease
with which characters go so far as to *join Buffy's gang* once
merely told the truth (Xander and Willow, Cordelia, Oz, Tara,
and Riley). This odd general ignorance of the obvious is part of
what one film critic calls the "idiot plot," in which many characters must be stupid for the story to progress. The thin plot
device allows *BtVS* the convenience of somewhat normal
teenage life for Buffy (student, daughter, girlfriend, purveyor of
Doublemeat) who thus cannot blossom into the hero around
whom a fascist movement would rally. I will suspend that mass
disbelief to demonstrate the ease with which one could turn
BtVS into fascist propaganda.[3]

---

[2] See, for instance, Robert Breton and Lindsey McMaster "Dissing the Age of
MOO: Initiatives, Alternatives, and Rationality" *Slayage* 1, www.slayage.tv
(January 2001); Daniel A. Clark and P. Andrew Miller, "Buffy, the Scooby Gang,
and Monstrous Authority: *BtVS* and the Subversion of Authority," *Slayage* 3
(June 2001); Tanya Krzywinska, "Hubble-Bubble, Herbs, and Grimoires:
Magic, Manicheans, and Witchcraft in *Buffy*," in: *Fighting the Forces: What's at
Stake in Buffy the Vampire Slayer*, edited by Rhonda V. Wilcox and David
Lavery (New York: Rowman and Littlefield, 2002), pp. 178–194; Mary Alice
Money, "The Undemonization of Supporting Characters in *Buffy*," pp. 98–107
in: *Fighting the Forces*; Zoe-Jane Playden, "'What You Are, What's to Come':
Feminisms, Citizenship, and the Divine," in *Reading the Vampire Slayer: An
Unofficial Critical Companion to Buffy and Angel*, edited by Roz Kaveney
(New York: Tauris Parke, 2001), pp. 120–147; Brian Wall and Michael Zryd,
"Vampire Dialectics: Knowledge, Institutions, and Labour," in: *Reading the
Vampire Slayer*, pp. 53–77; and Rhonda V. Wilcox "'Who Died and Made her
Boss?' Patterns of Mortality in *Buffy*," in *Fighting the Forces,* pp. 3–17.
[3] Paul Verhoeven's 1997 movie *Starship Troopers* offers sarcastic fascism,
replete with inhuman enemies and military choreography taken from Leni
Reifenstahl's *Triumph of the Will*.

Let me note, however, that I love this television show and never tire of the exploits of the young women at the center: Willow and Buffy. I like their smart-alecky abuse of vampires, demons, and venal young men; and I would like to see more empowerment of the heroic pair to do violence. The climax of Season Six, in which Willow tortures to death the young man who has shot her girlfriend, provided a satisfaction rarely afforded by this show—a mixture of thrill at rough justice done and dread for Willow's soul. A scene in which a young lesbian flays a woman-hater offers much to a world in which men prey upon those whom they find attractive. I state this now to forestall misinterpretation. I write not to denounce a pop-culture vision of young women empowered in battle, nor to plead for pacifism in the Buffyverse. To the contrary, I want a different distribution of the bloodshed and defend this ethic in my conclusion.

The quasi-fascist philosophy that justifies Buffy's slaying concerns me in my next discussion. I will outline the show's cosmology and by doing so set up my imaginary Buffyverse, just to make my point about the show's potential for fascism. I conclude with a better solution to this problem, one that stretches credulity less and eliminates the show's nasty streak of racism. The important characteristics of the existing Buffyverse that prime it for fascism include elements of a Manichean racism (tempered by an Augustinian division of the world's evils), adherence to primal and state authority, and formation of citizenship in ritual combat. I consider these in turn.

The Demon Question

BtVS is merrily racist. The Slayer destroys demons, and their undead half-breeds the vampires, pretty much on sight (unless she finds some other use for them). While many of these amount to separate species, such creatures as vampires and vengeance demons operate more as distinct races: made of human flesh, able to interact as people, enjoying sex with humans, even receiving transfusions from them ("Graduation Day"), altered mainly by the occupation of human bodies by demon souls and powers.[4] Certainly the Master sees vampires

---

[4] According to Giles, in "The Harvest," the first vampire was "a human form possessed—infected—by the demon's soul." Vampires reproduce by combin-

this way (in "The Wish"): "Undeniably we are the world's supe-rior race." Real-world fascist propaganda referred to Jews, Blacks, and Gypsies both as other species *and* as other races, acknowledging the fluid (and historically mutable) nature of the distinction. Such propaganda recognized the human appearance of those hated groups but considered them corrupt and often wondered whether those "dirty" races had souls.[5] So it is on *BtVS*, that the others slaughtered by the Slayer amount to a demonic array of evil, some savage in disposition, others well-spoken and attractive, but all of them vile unless graced with human souls.

Buffy allows some of these creatures to live, and tolerates an edge-of-town tavern that caters to them. But they are fodder nonetheless, and have no rights in her eyes. Those with human souls, on the other hand, merit due process. "Being a Slayer doesn't give me a license to kill," says Buffy in "Villains," as friends debate the lynching of a murderous young man. Lest this sound like nonsense, she clarifies: "Warren's human. . . . the human world has its own rules for dealing with people like him." Likewise, in "Bad Girls," Buffy lectures the errant Slayer Faith that "being a Slayer is not the same as being a killer."

Faith, human blood on her hands after a misguided staking, retorts that "We're warriors, we're built to kill."

"To kill *demons*!" Buffy cries. "But that doesn't mean that we get to pass judgment on people, like we're better than every-body else." Buffy draws the line plainly, between a race with legal rights and the lower orders controlled by summary execu-tion. Three years later ("Dead Things"), Buffy comes to believe

---

ing their blood with that of humans, forming new vampires out of the mix-tures of demon soul and human flesh. Later, in "Angel," Giles observes that any vampire is "demon at the core."

[5] Authored by committee, the show does not police its technical usage; and, like racist propagandists, the characters mix the terms. Willow and Giles quote ancient texts to describe demonkind sometimes as races and sometimes as species. In the field of biology, ability to produce viable offspring works as a conventional marker of shared species. Racial groups can interbreed; and whether humans and vampires can do the same we do not know, at least not as of early Season Seven. They can enjoy sex with and transfuse each other, however, suggesting strongly that only racial difference divides them. This would mean that Buffy's Slayage amounts to racial genocide (a series of "hate crimes," in current parlance).

that she has made Faith's blunder—killed a young woman by accident. Stricken, she beats a vampire in frustration and walks to the police station to turn herself in, just as Faith eventually did to atone for her crime (in "Sanctuary," from the first season of the spin-off *Angel*). Vampires—mongrel mixtures of human flesh with demon souls—lack human souls. Buffy kills them to protect every pure-blooded human she can.

Other analysts of the show argue that *BtVS* avoids the Manichean demonization so crucial to fascism. In fact, the show directs such hatred toward its fictive demons and mongrel vampires, such that Buffy can slaughter enemies without killing people.[6] Demons are fodder for the simple moral mechanics central to a fascist philosophy. Humans can be touched, reformed, made useful again (so the stories of Willow, Faith, Jonathan, and other human villains teach us); but vampires do evil without conscience and deserve to die. Killed mostly on sight, vampires turn to ash like death-camp victims. Demons tend to meet the same fate, even though some of them seem kindly enough (and we never learn what becomes of their corpses).

Does the fact of nicer demons muddle a fascist philosophy? Nazi propaganda warned that many Jews were pleasant in public settings but untrustworthy just the same, prone to unholy feasts in private. The sweetest demon on *BtVS* plays cards for kittens ("Life Serial"), with clear implication of foul intent (a crime against the innocent mirroring those in the anti-Semitic blood libel). There are among vampires only two who challenge the show's dichotomy between the human and the demon.

That vampires Angel and Spike find intermittent redemption, upon either losing their ability to kill humans (Spike) or regaining their human souls (Angel and Spike), merely updates the Manichean philosophy to an Augustinian split between kinds of evil. In his influential *Confessions*, Augustine (who had by this

---

[6] Mani (216–277 C.E.) proposed that evil inhered in the natural world, a principle of darkness in eternal battle with the principle of light—a Devil opposed to the one God. In his cosmology, the bodies of humans are foul products of demonic mating, just as vampires spring from the unholy union of demon and human in *BtVS*. Indeed, all matter, especially flesh, is tainted by this evil. Mani was branded a heretic (albeit a hugely influential one) by early Christians uncomfortable with the notion of such a powerful devil. After all, why would God in His mercy create such a dark lord?

time begun to alter his own Manichean worldview), divided the
world's ills into *natural* evils such as disease and disaster, and
moral evils chosen by humans. This plays out in *BtVS* as the difference between those with demon souls (who include most
vampires) who cannot do other than evil, and those with human
souls who can choose to be bad and who therefore can be
talked back into choosing good. The latter group includes Faith
in Season Three, Ben in Season Five, Willow and the trio of men
in Season Six. Buffy cannot kill these evildoers. The former
group, however, includes the many vampires and demons cut
down for any challenge to Buffy.

Buffy defines the dirty races in Augustinian terms, by presence or absence of a human soul (vampires have demon souls
unless magically bequeathed their human ones again, as in the
cases of Angel and Spike). When Angel has one, he is like a
man with a choice to do good. Lacking one he becomes the
evil Angelus, feared and hunted. Spike goes six seasons without a human soul and so never becomes more than a reluctant
ally or love-struck hero of the moment. Though restrained
mechanically from following his blood-sucking impulses (this
vampire appetite is another element of the anti-Jewish blood
libel), Spike cannot be trusted. Xander calls him an "evil, soulless thing" ("Entropy"), and Buffy remains disgusted with him,
prone to violence when even mildly annoyed. That Buffy takes
Spike as a lover in shame-ridden trysts does no more to rewrite
our racist scenario than does her tolerance of the demon tavern at the edge of town. White slave owners notoriously
exploited slaves whom they found appealing, and survivors of
the Nazi camps tell us of guards obsessed with the "dirty" sexuality of the very Jews they sent to the ovens. Representing just
that "dark" and "dirty," Spike appeals to Buffy for perhaps the
same reason that violence does. Regardless, lacking a human
soul, he cannot be trusted. "I know you never loved me," he
says in "The Gift," "I know that I'm a monster. But you treat
me like a man." A year later ("Seeing Red"), frustrated by unre-
quited love, Spike tries to rape Buffy, confirming the wisdom
of her refusal to open her heart. She feels no need to kill hob-
bled vampires, and even finds them attractive in a way that disgusts herself and her friends; but Buffy retains her racist
worldview throughout. Demon males may be attractive but are
demon nonetheless.

That the nature of the soul rather than full membership in the master race becomes the Slayer's criteria for respect suggests the modern nature of the show. A human soul seems to work as a conscience, allowing contemplation of one's crime and thus guilt. Human-souled killers such as Willow, Faith, and Angel suffer remorse and so affirm the authority of the law over them. Spike, however, so long as a demon soul drives him, can do "good" only in his love-struck self interest. Untrustworthy, he does evil all the while (see "As You Were" in Season Six for this lesson). Modern criminal justice profits little from the deaths of criminals with genuine conscience, and Buffy seems to draw the same disciplinary (and Augustinian) distinction.[7]

The Slayer's Authority

Is Buffy the most fascist character on the show? Others have argued that both the short-lived grassroots crusade Mothers Opposed to the Occult (MOO), and the military-psychology experiment The Initiative, seem more fascist than Buffy's gang of friends, because they are well-organized, authoritarian movements to wipe out evil.[8] Let's consider them in turn. MOO ("Gingerbread") is a group of Sunnydale parents caught in a moral panic over child-murder, who err by trying to kill humans rather than demons for crimes (they sentence Wiccans Amy and Willow, as well as Slayer Buffy, to the stake). Giles defeats them by breaking the demon's spell that holds them in thrall. Like Buffy's psychotic break in "Normal Again," the episode's human aggression owes more to dark magic than to the usual dynamics

---

[7] For a Foucaultian analysis of law enforcement on *BtVS*, see Martin Bunicki and Anthony Emms "Buffy the Vampire Disciplinarian: Institutional Excess and the New Economy of Power," *Slayage* 5 (December 2001). This analysis also suggests why Buffy allows the demon tavern to operate. The joint allows demons to spread news of her activities and so prompts demons to consider her presence, thus allowing her a measure of control over them. Far from being anti-authoritarian, Buffy exercises an insidious power over the races around her.

[8] Of both organizations, Robert Breton and Lindsey McMaster argue that, "as a result of a mechanized approach, adult rationalism leads to a kind of suburban fascism." See "Dissing the Age of MOO: Initiatives, Alternatives, and Rationality" *Slayage* 1. On the Initiative, see also Wall and Zryd, "Vampire Dialectics," cited above.

of the Buffyverse, however. It is a fluke and does not recur. Of more concern is the military force behind the Initiative, which endures in some form for at least three seasons, is entirely created by humans, and poses more threats to Buffy and her friends.

The Initiative might seem to provide the true fascism against which Buffy stands in contrast. Its state authority, medical experiments, and fetishization of all things martial lend it a Nazi edge. And its twisted progeny Adam aspires to create a new, powerful "race" of cyborgs under his command ("Primeval"). Nevertheless, the contrast between Buffy and the soldiers is not so clear. Consider that the Initiative does good, disarming Spike and, presumably, other evildoers. Buffy benefits by their work, appreciates their trained comradeship, and works with this organization until an insane commander attacks her in jealousy. The hyper-rational, organized nature of the Initiative poses no problem for Buffy.

Buffy rejects the operation because its commanders upset a primal order between demon, human, and machine by mixing them all in the psychotic cyborg Adam. As mystic Ethan Rayne (in "A New Man") observes of the Initiative's scientists, "This new outfit, it's blundering in a place where it doesn't belong. It's throwing the worlds out of balance."[9] The leader of the Initiative yields to temptation to do evil, creates monstrous Adam, and dies for it. Only when imperiled by this leader does Buffy recoil from the organization. She retreats further when the soldiers abuse men with human souls (Riley and Oz, in "New Moon Rising"). A werewolf, Oz retains his soul and thus may not be used like a member of a lower order. Once this corrupt admin-

---

[9] Though *BtVS* uses them interchangeably, two notable uses of the terms "race" and "species" arise over the course of Adam's rampage, suggesting that *race* remains an allegorical theme. In "Where the Wild Things Are," Giles teaches that, "As a rule, demons have no empathy for any of the species other than their own. In fact, most think of vampires as abominations, mixing with human blood and all." He guesses that the manipulative cyborg Adam has urged this camaraderie among separate kinds. To this, Tara replies, "So he's, um, bridging the gap between the races?" Willow gives the punchline: "Huh, like Martin Luther King." Later, in "Primeval," Adam reveals his laboratory experiment: "This is where it all happens, where the new race begins." Against the show's preference for the pure-blooded, Adam would populate the earth with cyborg mixtures of demon, human, and machine. Buffy rips his heart out.

istration is out of the way, however, all is righted; and, midway through Season Six ("As You Were"), Buffy is anxious to cooperate with the military again. Buffy and members of the Initiative hunt, capture, interrogate, abuse, and kill demons at will. All take pleasure in their work and even find in combat an aphrodisiac (for example, "Where the Wild Things Are"). Buffy draws the line between good and evil differently than the Initiative members do (she in terms of the nature of their souls, and they at the human/demon boundary). But the rarity of a human-souled demon renders this a moot point through most of the action.

Buffy's preference for community-level vigilantism to military force is based not upon a rejection of authority per se. She derives her own license as Slayer from primal forces (the Powers That Be, and That Which They Serve, as described in the *Angel* episode "I Will Remember You") that impel her to slay but also keep her in check with rules that she respects; and she maintains the authority of the police in matters between humans. Though *BtVS* rarely engages state issues, it implicitly affirms state authority when it does and removes only the corrupt from their seats of power. Bound to her calling, Buffy never questions the racist logic that distinguishes killing from slaying, or that bars Willow from using magic to solve all of her problems. When, in Season Six ("Villains"), Willow does begin to kill people, Buffy warns, "There are limits to what we can do. There should be. Willow doesn't want to believe that. And now she's messing with forces that want to hurt her, all of us." The balance requires defense, to preserve the privileges of the human race. Buffy fights to the death for humankind and respects the limits placed upon her.

Analysts have complimented *BtVS* for its cheery rejection of local authorities from the battlefields of the demonic: Buffy ducks teachers and her principal, dynamites the (demonic) mayor, runs from police, turns against the Initiative, and scorns the Council of Watchers when she feels hampered or abused by them. However, we should not take this for a rejection of institutional authority *per se*. In her more mundane pursuits, Buffy never stands up to college professors, high school teachers, or even her burger-joint manager or parents, at least beyond adolescent sneaking. Buffy shifts strategies and relations to authority as she needs in order to do her work. She claims moral authority (by force in "Checkpoint," and with a death threat to anyone who disobeys in "The Gift") as her calling demands. What remains throughout is her own authorized mission to protect her race in combat with the demonic, and submission to police in matters of human crime. The show has its authoritarian cake and eats it too as Buffy spites a few stuffy Watchers but otherwise heeds her ancient calling with a smart-ass vengeance. The good citizen, she is duty-bound.

The New Young Woman

BtVS spends much of the first seasons contrasting Buffy and Willow, bonded in virtue, to Cordelia and the dim-witted boys around them. The former defend their kind; the latter float through a narcissistic haze of parties, clothes, and petty status. Like a good fascist hero, Buffy eschews the decadence of an idle life. Called into service by a primeval order, wielding ancient weaponry, often excited by conflict, and ready to give all to redeem her world, Buffy cuts a proto-fascist figure even in the absence of the nationalist movement that would render the show truly fascist. The hero is messianic, saving the world by victory in bloody combat, giving her body to the land and the pureblooded folk whom she's called to defend.

The show also contrasts Buffy to her bookish friends. Buffy neglects her own education to pursue her more physical calling (and quits college, twice: once when her mother falls ill, and a second time—in "Life Serial"—when an hour in a sociology class convinces her that she cannot keep up). Willow and Giles, meanwhile, lean upon millennia of learning as well as their own investigative skills. In "Checkpoint," Buffy—armed with a broadsword and fresh from combat—tells the Council of Watchers that she has power because she is a warrior rather than a feeble scholar with a meaningless life. Never a strong student, Buffy seems to feel more at home with weapons than with books in hand. This valorization of the dynamic over the ruminative characterizes fascism, with its celebration of physical purity and combat. Few episodes end without a kickboxing match, and Buffy tends to choose physical force as she makes plans.

Duty-bound and dynamic, Buffy will also sacrifice self for

land. Though, at a young age ("Prophecy Girl"), her fear of death leads her to quit for a day, Buffy soon takes up her cross again. Moved by Willow's fear of rampaging vampires, Buffy accepts her duty to give her life to the war, and literally puts a cross—that great Christian symbol of agonizing blood sacrifice and redemption—back around her neck. After dying and rising again, Buffy slays her opponent. The show, deeply Christian, rehearses this messianic plot several times. Buffy has, by the end of the sixth season, given her life to defeat evil, and been reborn, twice. Xander the loving carpenter offers his own life to bring salvation in "Grave," Angel took the plunge in "Becoming, Part Two," and evil Drusilla found rebirth through the blood on a Christian altar in "What's My Line, Part Two." Shuttling saviors and devils between Heaven and Hell, offering apocalypses out of the Book of *Revelation*, the Buffyverse sports a Christian citizenship in which sacrifice of the young redeems a world lost to the sins of Sodom.

The blood sacrifice usually comes through combat. Those kickboxing matches, the chases, the standoffs and skill with weaponry, all mark the Slayer and her pals as good citizens of a spiritually renewed society. We see the most dramatic shift, of course, in the young women and girls. Long ignored as combatants and saviors by the traditions on which *BtVS* draws, they blossom into warriors and messiahs. They wield magic, act as seers, defend themselves, and defeat evil with their hands. This inspiring view of empowered young women—made possible by the economic advancement of women and their accompanying feminist movement—allows *BtVS* a sense of genuine *renewal*, the sort that fascism celebrates in its quest to build a great society. Buffy is the New Woman, called from a life of bourgeois bliss and second-class status to save her world.

Thus empowered, Buffy and her friends set to work in a loosely-organized gang. Though the secrecy with which they work prevents the show from entering the realm of fascism, the "Scooby" gang looks a lot like the brownshirts who wandered 1930s Germany looking for Jews to savage, or the neo-Nazis who stalk Western cities today, looking for immigrants and Blacks. Armed with the ancient weapons fetishized by skinheads (rarely modern or smacking of science: bats and clubs that beat, or knives and arrows that slice), they savor their hand-to-hand combat to the point of sexual charge.

We glimpse a more public, wartime Buffyverse at the end of Season Three, as high-school graduation approaches and youngsters heed a call to defend their world from demonic invasion. In "Choices," Willow has survived a brush with death and offers a speech out of a recruitment film:

> The other night, being captured and all, facing off with Faith [the turncoat Slayer], things just kind of got clear. I mean, you've been fighting evil here for three years, and I've helped some, and now we're supposed to decide what we want to do with our lives. And I just realized that's what I want to do—fight evil, help people. I mean, I—I think it's worth doing. And I don't think you do it because you have to. It's a good fight, Buffy, and I want in.

Buffy is moved and welcomes Willow to the struggle. Eventually, most of their graduating class wants in as well. In "Prom Night" those classmates acknowledge Buffy's status as Slayer with a gift (to the "Class Protector"), noting that "We don't talk about it, but it's no secret that Sunnydale High isn't really like other high schools. A lot of weird stuff happens here."

Later, in "Graduation Day, Part Two," the veil of secrecy cloaking the demon world and the Slayer's struggle shreds. Buffy calls her classmates to battle.

> BUFFY: Get everyone. I'm Ready.
> WILLOW: Ready for what?
> BUFFY: War.

Scores of kids, anxious to do their part for their land, robe up for graduation. They produce explosives, pack medieval weaponry and flame throwers beneath their gowns, and prepare for combat. A man ascending to demon godhood even offers a rabble-rousing speech before the battle, with words and images right out of a Nazi propaganda film. The camera pans over rows of determined faces in the graduating crowd, as the speaker urges pride in the face of conflict:

> It's been a long road getting here—for you, for Sunnydale. There's been achievement, joy, good times. And there's been grief; there's

been loss. Some people who should be here today aren't. But we are . . . Today is about change. Graduation doesn't just mean that your circumstances change. It means you do. You ascend to a higher level. Nothing will ever be the same.

Within minutes, inspired by their calling and sense of communal power, the graduates rise to battle throngs of vampires and a demon serpent, with Buffy in command and Xander in fine military form. Fiery arrows fly, bodies collide, and kids taste the blood and glory of war. This is the new citizenship of a proto-fascist world: masses of volunteers, happy to give their lives in battle with the demon Other, proud of their physical strength, military discipline, anxious to ascend and renew their land.

From such a spectacle, absent mass insanity to wipe their memories, a larger crusade would likely spring. Why the graduation battle does not start a war we never know. The plot point dangles without explanation.

Brownskirts

Suppose we picked up that thread, however, and imagined where this show might tend but for this curious lack of interest among its background characters. Widespread acknowledgment of what many citizens appear already to know could free the (otherwise useless) Council of Watchers to publicize the work of the Slayer. Her celebrity would allow them to build a larger team, on a national scale. With enough people watching our graveyards, mortuaries, and edge-of-town taverns, a final solution to the demon problem would present itself quickly, and hopes for a healthy nation might grow. Her handlers could burnish the Slayer's image with those low-angle tracking "hero" shots (as they are known to Hollywood artists) often used in the show's credit sequences, which themselves offer glimpses of a fascist publicity machine. Would not thousands of young girls swept up in wartime enthusiasm adopt this new womanhood: nice clothes, a determined stance, bloodied weapon in hand? Fascism dearly loves its newsreels, billboards, and parades of stylish heroism. Imagine the sheer spectacle of a world crawling with death squads, worshipping physical fitness, clean dress, disciplined patrolling, the vitality of youth, and the purity of race in service to their society. *BtVS* would make a fine fascism indeed. The combination of racist demonization, traditional authority, and renewed citizenship through combat needs only the sense of national purpose to blossom into fascism.

Buffy's moral philosophy ascribes the worst evil to the soulless, and calls its characters to combat, rehearsing a fantasy of subhuman Others beyond the reach of social tenets—ideal fodder for blood sacrifice. At its center a well-dressed, dutiful young Aryan, keen to save her world, patrols the town, part of a teenage death squad. This group finds members of the subaltern races and sends them up in puffs of death-camp smoke. Would Hitler's minions not smile at the humor?

Against Fascism

How might we undo the quasi-fascist knots into which this series has been tied? Three approaches come to mind. First, an episode of *Angel* ("Hero") projects fascism onto a race of intolerant demons and blows them up, rejecting "fascism" with a murderous vengeance but retaining the Manichean moral blindness. Humanist in the worst way, this tactic allows anti-fascists to project evil and the taste for violence onto some Others rather than recognize such impulses in themselves.[10]

Second, we might do away with the Slayer altogether and ban her killing work. Why do we need such violence, after all? We need it because the slayage allows *BtVS* to harness the moral and visceral force of blood sacrifice. The show maintains a strong religious character in this sense. Ritual rehearsal, on the public stage, of the deaths of our enemies as well as our own, lends meaning to our lives and draws us together. Stories of sacrifice and loss, invested with supernatural significance, give import to our communities and inspire in us selflessness and trust. Religion does this best when the blood sacrifice that it celebrates is most vivid, as in wartime. When presented in a moving fashion, media violence can generate the *solidarity* (pride in group membership and willingness to contribute to communal welfare) that sustains a society. Far from anti-social swill, media

---

[10] For an extended discussion, see Kriss Ravetto, *The Unmaking of Fascist Aesthetics* (Minneapolis: University of Minnesota Press, 2001).

[11] On media violence in civil religion, see Carolyn Marvin and David Ingle, *Blood Sacrifice and the Nation: Totem Rituals and the American Flag* (Cambridge: Cambridge University Press, 1999).

violence can knit groups tighter by investing their suffering with meaning and turning grief into calls to action.[11] Removing it from *BtVS* would defang the show and sap its moral force. I like that Buffy slays. The issue is whether she may kill.

The third anti-fascist option remains my favorite. I say let Buffy sacrifice whom she will without so much racist angst, be they bad boys, errant Gods, anyone demonic or human, whose deaths can make us jump in our chairs and teach us moral lessons. Only with a sense of humankind as the master race does one view the killing of demons as trivial, routine, or even terribly different from the execution of humans (that "slaying" vs. "killing" distinction that Buffy draws). I vote to replace the chauvinism but preserve the ritual sacrifice at the heart of Buffy's heroism by directing the female aggression along more ethical and less biological lines. The recent death of misogynist Warren at Willow's hands ("Villains") was too long in coming for my taste, though it was great when at last it occurred. By the logic of the show, Willow must suffer for her crime;[12] but I hope that she hasn't killed her last evil boy. I say remove the racism and make a Buffyverse that finds genuine evil within humankind (especially mankind) rather than projecting it outward onto the demonic. Put to rest the incipient fascism that threatens to turn this inspiring vision of empowered women into one of patrolling brownskirts serving a master race. Let us repair the Augustinian split between the natural and the moral evil, drop the wall between the human and the demonic, find the sin within as well as without, and let justice reign. Let malicious young men run and hide, for this would be a Buffyverse with genuine chocolaty goodness.

---

[12] See her partially flayed, as if in poetic justice, in "Same Time, Same Place."

16

Prophecy Girl and The Powers That Be: The Philosophy of Religion in the Buffyverse

WENDY LOVE ANDERSON

Making "Amends"

ETHAN: We used to be friends, Ripper. When did all that fall apart?

GILES: The same time you started to worship Chaos.

ETHAN: Oh, religious intolerance. ("A New Man")

Buffy the Vampire Slayer's third-season episode, "Amends," written and directed by series creator Joss Whedon, generated terrific controversy within the show's fan community when it first aired in December 1998. "Amends" features the ensouled vampire Angel being overwhelmed by horrific visions of his past victims until he finally plants himself outside on Christmas Eve to await sunrise and inevitable death. As Buffy pleads with him to reconsider, unseasonable snow begins to fall in the Southern California town of Sunnydale, miraculously obscuring the rising sun and preserving Angel's (un)life. The episode ends with a montage of characters marveling at the snow while the camera pans past a theater marquee reading "PRAY." Fans were baffled by what they perceived as a pro-Christian message or a hokey plot device. After all, *BtVS* was centered around an irreverent take on the genre of horror, up to and including those moralized endings in which the evil or naughty are killed while the good (however traumatized) survive.[1] While *BtVS* had borrowed the use of crosses and holy water from standard horror/vampire mythology, it had left their relation to Christianity or any other official religion quite deliberately unanswered. "Amends" seemed to throw this pattern off, and Whedon finally responded in the show's official Internet forum, "The Bronze": "Was it God? Well, I'm an atheist, but it's hard to ignore the idea of a 'Christmas miracle' here. . . . The fact is, the Christian mythos has a powerful fascination to me, and it bleeds into my storytelling."[2]

Longtime *BtVS* and *Angel* fans have little doubt that "the Christian mythos has a powerful fascination" for Whedon. Some have even tried to claim that both shows' heroes are Christ figures, thanks to their self-sacrificial habits and occasional trips to hell and back.[3] On the other hand, "Amends" is not much of a victory for organized religion, "PRAY" notwithstanding (Whedon claimed that the marquee message was "an unintentional coincidence"). None of Buffy's friends attend church or synagogue services during the episode; instead, they work together, in what one jokes is a display of "Hanukkah spirit," to trace Angel's visions to a group of evil eyeless priests complete with chanting and runic tattoos. These "Harbingers of Death," described by a prophecy that Buffy cheerfully compares to supermarket tabloids, do more than kill Christmas trees growing above their underground hideout; they also summon the self-proclaimed "First Evil, beyond sin, beyond death" who is trying to convince Angel to kill Buffy. Hanukkah jokes and Christmas trees aside, the only unmistakable evocation of the Judeo-Christian tradition comes in a flashback when one of Angel's victims begins reciting *Psalm* 23, quite ineffectively, just before his death.

What's going on with *BtVS*'s use of religion? Obviously, Buffy and company move in a world that is not easily secularized:

---

[1] See for example the treatment of Buffy's "anti-authoritarianism" and how it "is a kind of anti-horror . . . it openly mocks the underlying morality [of horror movies]" in David Graber, "Rebel Without A God," *In These Times* (27 December 1998).

[2] Joss Whedon, "The Bronze" (Cf. the Bronze VIP Posting Board Archives, www.cise.ufl.edu/cgi-bin/cgiwrap/hsiao/buffy/get-archive?date=19981215) (15 December 1998). Post edited to regularize capitalization and spelling.

[3] See "Pastor Steve's Buffy Page," www.mtcnet.net/~bierly/buffy.htm.

quite apart from their use of crosses and holy water to repel vampires, the so-called Scooby Gang and their spun-off compatriots at Angel Investigations routinely encounter cults, worshippers and devotees of exotic gods, concrete manifestations of those gods' power, effective religious artifacts, or accurate prophetic writings. What is striking about the Buffyverse conception of religion is how regularly and frequently it is *demonized*, in both the literal and figurative sense of the term. As in "Amends," the heroes and antiheroes of the Buffyverse scorn religious observance and ritual, while their (usually demonic, but definitely evil) opponents cling to it. Buffy has no trouble using holy water, crosses, prophecies, her friends' spellcasting abilities, or even miracles to her own advantage in the fight against vampires and demons. She does not, however, feel compelled to pray as a result, much less attribute her success to any of the deities she may have invoked. The snowfall in "Amends," like Angel's unexpected return from Hell several episodes earlier, is entirely unasked-for and unexpected; the handful of genuine, unattributed miracles throughout *BtVS* and *Angel* point out the extreme rarity of such inexplicable events. Most religious activity in the Buffyverse signals the presence of demons or other forces of evil. However, this evil is usually defeated not by miracles, but by the forces of self-reliance and friendship.

New Religious Movements, Hellmouth-Style

> "Don't Forget! Winter Solstice Hanukkah Christmas Kwanzaa & Gurnenthar's Ascendance Are Coming!" (Sign at the Magic Box, "Into The Woods")

The religions of the Buffyverse are overwhelmingly demonic; as such, it comes as no surprise that most religiously motivated characters turn out to be Buffy's opponents. Buffy's first-season adversary is the Master, a vampire trapped in an abandoned church who heads the "Order of Aurelius," regularly quotes some sort of scriptures, and performs liturgical readings from Aurelius's prophetic writings. He seeks to restore the dominion of the "Old Ones," the demons who existed before the creation of mankind, by opening the Hellmouth located in Sunnydale. This inversion of Christianity becomes even stronger when the

Master is joined by a vampire child identified as "the Anointed One." Eventually, Buffy fights the Master directly and is drowned, but her friends show up in time to revive her, allowing her to defeat the Master and close the partially opened Hellmouth; the remnants of the Order of Aurelius are eliminated early in Season Two. But the Buffyverse features a wide variety of other religions; in the first season alone, there is the borderline case of Catherine Madison's invocation of "Corsheth" during witchcraft, the questionable Christianity of serial-killer-turned-vampire Andrew Borba (who quotes from the Apocalypse of John and rants about sin and judgment), and the Masai "Primals" and their zookeeper follower who operate in some way analogous to "demon possession." More positive religious role models only appear briefly: there are the fifteenth-century Italian monks who bind the demon Moloch (although their religious affiliation may be incidental to their actions, since Giles and Jenny manage to do the same) and a monk named "Brother Luca something" who forwards Jenny a verse from *Isaiah* containing vital information about Buffy's fate, but he never reappears. Religion—whether identifiably based on real-world beliefs, identifiably demonic, or both—seems either to support or (much more rarely) fight against the forces of evil.

Even in seasons without overarching religion-related plots, Buffy and the Scoobies constantly find themselves battling against demonic cults and sects ranging from the (human) worshippers of the demon Machida to the (demonic) Sisterhood of Jhe to the vengeful "spirit warrior" Hus of the native Chumash people. The Chumash raise an interesting point, since they are an historically real Native American people; in fact, Mission Santa Barbara—the town on which Sunnydale is based—was founded largely in order to Christianize them. In "Pangs," Hus's first act after killing his academic captor is to head for a church and slaughter the resident priest, who is identified as having connections to the (closed) mission. Sometimes, then, the religions of the Buffyverse straddle the line between reality and fantasy, but usually at the expense of religion. We learn in passing that Rasputin was both a "member of an obscure religious sect" and a vampire. Vampires have their crusading Saint Vigeous, mimicking the destruction wrought by the medieval Crusades. Giles's ex-companion Ethan Rayne keeps returning to Sunnydale to work mischief and ally with demons precisely because he worships the Roman chaos god Janus.[4] Demons invoked as "Götter" in German are shown to have been behind centuries of witchcraft persecutions in "Gingerbread."

A more contemporary example is the "Family Home" in "Anne," which is obviously based on a fundamentalist Christian ministry: Buffy tries to infiltrate it by asserting that "I woke up, and I looked in the mirror, and I thought, hey, what's with all the sin? . . . I'm dirty. I'm, I'm bad, with the sex and the envy and that, that loud music us kids listen to nowadays." She encounters the home's operator, Ken, and his latest victim, Lily, at a "ceremonial pool" (the shooting script carefully does *not* call it a baptismal font) where he is encouraging her to "wash away the past . . . the sin and the pain and the uncertainty." Of course, this being the Buffyverse, the pool turns out to be a portal to a demon dimension where humans are forced to spend their lives in industrial labor while their identities are destroyed. Ken—now revealed as a demon—helpfully identifies it as "hell" and tells Lily that she's "been heading here all your life." Then Buffy saves the day by leading a slave rebellion during which she poses atop a platform holding a hammer and sickle before killing Ken. Marx's famous definition of religion as "the opiate of the masses" is clearly at issue here.[5]

The category of religion is simultaneously a metaphor for human evil and a quasi-historical source *of* human evil throughout the Buffyverse. Even dead religions remain dangerous, since

---

[4] In "Halloween," Rayne's first appearance, Giles identifies Janus as "the Roman god of chaos." More precisely, Janus seems to have been the Etruscan god of chaos, while the Romans demoted him to the lesser role of boundary deity. One could also cite the extent to which, for instance, the fifth-season Knights of Byzantium are clearly based on medieval crusaders and evoke the Fourth Crusade (1198–1204), in which Catholic forces—at the behest of their Venetian travel agents—fought their fellow Christians in the Byzantine Empire.

[5] Joss Whedon's remarks in "The Bronze" forum about "Anne" are rather entertaining: "The hammer and sickle were not intentional, but I too noticed the imagery when I saw them and was most pleased. The sickle, by the bye, is actually an African weapon called a HUNGA MUNGA and I am terribly in love with it. In times of excitement I am known to shout HUNGA MUNGA in an irritating fashion. And to sing the *Internationale*" (3 October 1998). Post edited to regularize punctuation and spelling. For a discussion of Marxist imagery in *BtVS* see James B. South, "'All Torment, Trouble, Wonder, and Amazement Inhabits Here': The Vicissitudes of Technology in *Buffy the Vampire Slayer*," in *Journal of American and Comparative Cultures* 24 (2001), pp. 93–102.

their artifacts and knowledge can be used for evil by uncon-
nected individuals. Whatever Josephus du Lac's "religious sect"
was (apparently Catholic, as he was "excommunicated by the
Vatican"), it produced a book "said to contain rituals and spells
that reap unspeakable evil," and when Spike uses the du Lac
Cross to decode the book, he summons the demon Eligor to
restore Drusilla's strength ("What's My Line?, Part Two"). The
Egyptian cult of the Sobekites left transmogrification spells
which allow the hellgod Glorificus to turn a cobra into a giant
serpentine ally ("Shadow"). There is a particularly telling
moment in one scene of this episode: the giant snake slithers
through an empty church and a crucifix looks sadly down on
it with absolutely no effect. Eventually, however, Buffy overcomes the snake with help ˋfrom Giles and a makeshift
weapon. Even when religious knowledge or religious objects
are used in the fight *against* evil, as in Buffy's final confrontation with Glorificus, the Slayer and her allies must ultimately
rely on their own abilities and their bonds with one another.
This theme has been reiterated in every *BtVS* season finale to
date, and most recently in Season Six: Willow, who has been
consumed by vengeance and dark magic, decides to end the
world by raising a "Satanic temple" and unleashing the powerful "she-demon" Proserpexa. "No magic or supernatural
force can stop her," Giles warns, but it turns out that she can
be—and is—defeated by Xander's obstinate and entirely
unmagical refusal to stop loving her ("Grave"). It is not
insignificant that Buffy and her friends are called "the Scooby
Gang" in several episodes. The original *Scooby-Doo* cartoon
featured a band of teenagers who constantly found themselves
in seemingly supernatural explanations; in every episode, the
"meddling kids" eventually discovered one or more human villains with inventive tricks instead. Buffy and company may be
dealing with "real" supernatural entities, but the teenagers still
triumph over the forces of quasi-darkness through self-
reliance, research, friendship, and a healthy dose of luck.
Religion is not necessary.

Religion and the Regular Character

BUFFY: I gave Riley the day off. . . . I'm sure he'll come over
    later looking for a little . . . Bible study.

> JOYCE: Well, good. I mean just as long as the two of you are
> spending some quality time with . . . the Lord. ("Into the
> Woods")

What about the forces of good? Of *BtVS*'s regular characters, it
is difficult to find many who qualify as "religious" by even the
most lenient standards. Most of them exhibit very little interest
in religion. Buffy, their leader, occasionally mocks organized
religion—along with nearly everything else—but focuses on
saving her family, friends, and the world, not necessarily in that
order. She refers to slayerhood as a "sacred duty, yadda yadda
yadda" ("Surprise") and jokes with her mother about "Bible
study," that is, sex with boyfriend Riley ("Into The Woods"). In
"Triangle," after Buffy and Riley break up, Buffy asks a nun
about entering a convent, but her goal is clearly "the whole
abjuring the company of men," and she uneasily asks "do you
have to be, like, super-religious?" She does not seem to have
any clearly articulated vision of an ideal world beyond survival,
security, and happiness. Even her sixth-season revelation that
she was torn from heaven means only she was "warm, and
loved, and finished, complete" ("After Life"); a later episode
("Normal Again") equates this "heaven" with a delusional,
demon-induced world in which Buffy is a psychiatric patient.
On the whole, Buffy's attitude towards most religious beliefs
and practices is pretty well summed up in a single exchange:

> GIRL: Have you accepted Jesus Christ as your personal savior?
> BUFFY: Uh, you know, I meant to and then I just got really
> busy. ("The Freshman")

Buffy's dependence on friends, family, and ultimately her own
inner strength is what the show truly emphasizes. When
Angelus taunts that he has stripped away her friends, weapons,
and hope, she tells him that she still has "me" ("Becoming, Part
Two"); when the First Slayer challenges her in a dream, she
responds, "I am not alone . . . Now give me back my friends"
("Restless"). These, not religious crises or affirmations, are
Buffy's moments of triumph.

Most of Buffy's friends and allies have equally little to do
with religion, and the deviations from this norm are telling.
Anya, the on-and-off vengeance demon, only uses religious lan-

guage in her efforts to invoke the "Lower Being" D'Hoffryn. Spike, Buffy's sometime vampire lover, enters the Buffyverse as an iconoclast: after hoisting the Anointed One into the sunlight and destroying the vampiric religion which began with the Master, he announces: "From now on, we're gonna have a little less ritual, and a little more fun around here."[6] Elsewhere, his attitude toward religion is remarkably like Buffy's: for instance, he uses the du Lac Cross but makes fun of the resultant ritual ("What's My Line?, Part Two"). Giles is a slightly more complicated case: one could argue that the Council of Watchers borders on a religion, but Giles has begun to question the Council's agenda by the end of the first season and decisively breaks from it in the third-season episode "Helpless." As for more conventional religions, it is Giles who finds Sunnydale's forty-three churches "excessive" ("What's My Line?, Part Two"), and his handful of magical invocations throughout the series are relatively deity-free and involve no apparent sense of continued obligation. In fact, the Buffyverse's only connection between magic and religious practice comes from Willow's annoyed response to her mother's accusations of witchcraft in "Gingerbread": "I worship Beelzebub. I do his bidding. Do you see any goats around? No, because I sacrificed them!"

Willow probably has the best-explored religious identity of any regular character in the Buffyverse, but this is not saying much. She identifies herself as Jewish through Season Five, but this only motivates her to resist traditional Christmas celebrations in various seasons and to worry about her father's reaction when she nails crosses to her walls to keep out vampires in "Innocence." By the fourth season, she is identifying alternatively as "witch" and "Wiccan," but she ignores Tara's concerns

---

[6] Stacey Abbott argues that the iconoclastic Spike is a "modern vampire," by comparison to the traditionally-minded Master and his first-season acolytes, and that *Buffy* "has, with each season of the television series, gradually disembedded itself from these traditions in order to create a modern vampire and slayer, both independent and self reliant," in part by "highlighting the physical over the spiritual." However, Abbott does not examine the extent to which the category of religion plays a role in the transformation from vampire-legend tradition to modernity. See "A Little Less Ritual and a Little More Fun: The Modern Vampire in *Buffy the Vampire Slayer*," *Slayage* 3, www.slayage.com (June 2001).

about Wiccan attitudes towards resurrection in "Forever," along with the latter's cautions about the proper use of magic in Season Six. Many of Willow's spells invoke gods and goddesses, but these invocations seem purely instrumental, and they are most prominent in Season Six, as she (temporarily) becomes a force of apocalyptic evil. Tara's religious beliefs apparently do influence her actions, but it seems significant that both the character and the audience spend more than a season after Tara's introduction—that is, until "Family"—suspecting her of being some sort of demon. The only known churchgoer among Buffy's friends or acquaintances is Riley, although he is not otherwise given to discussing or practicing religion; he is initially controlled by the Initiative, then succumbs to the temptation of paid vampiric bloodletters. The ill-fated Jenny Calendar initially identifies herself as a "technopagan," asserting that "the divine exists in cyberspace same as out here," but she considers bone-castings and email to be equally valid information sources ("Prophecy Girl"). It is interesting to realize that Tara and Jenny both wind up dead, while Buffy's less religious friends continue to thrive. Once again, Buffyverse religious characters are somewhat ineffectual at best and demonic or evil at worst.

The title character of *Angel*, who started on *BtVS*, supposedly "has a thing for convents" ("Dear Boy"). However, it manifests only during his evil vampire phase; Angel seems relatively uninterested in religion while he possesses a soul. The cross he gives Buffy in "Welcome to the Hellmouth" seems to be purely for defense against vampires. When Cordelia, another *BtVS* crossover character, tries to describe her vision of a demon-worshipping cult and explains that its disciples are killing one another over how to worship it, he responds, deadpan: "This is why personally I rarely go to church" ("Dear Boy"). Angel's own message of hope and his soul-saving mission certainly bear affinities to religious projects, but he disclaims any connection, emphasizing the same messages of self-reliance and friendship highlighted on *BtVS*:

ANGEL: You're at a crossroads, I know. It's either go for the easy fix and wait for the consequences, or take the hard road and go with faith.
RACHEL: Oh, God. You're not from that freaky church on Sunset, are you?

ANGEL: In yourself. That kind of faith. ("In The Dark")

Angel's second-season epiphany puts him even further away from anything we could identify as religion: "In the greater scheme or the big picture, nothing we do matters. There's no grand plan, no big win . . . all that matters is what we do, cause that's all there is. What we do now, today."[7] He redefines his mission in the most secular terms imaginable: "I fought for so long, for redemption, for a reward, finally just to beat the other guy, but I never got it. . . . I want to help because I don't think people should suffer as they do" ("Epiphany"). Cordelia is equally skeptical about organized religion; she responds to a shroud dyed with virgins' blood by complaining that this has nothing to do with purity. "This is all about dominance, buddy. You can bet if someone ordered a male body part for religious sacrifice, the world would be atheist like *that*" ("The Shroud of Rahmon"). *Angel*'s other regular and recurring characters tend to be interested in religion only insofar as they are demons, vampires, or contributing to the cause of evil; Darla, Angel's recurring adversary in the second season, accuses him of "probably flogging himself in a church somewhere" ("Redefinition") and claims—in one of the show's most memorable lines—that "God doesn't want you, but I still do" ("Dear Boy"). Angel does not respond.

Religious Truths: Prophecies, Powers, and the Plural of "Apocalypse"

ANGEL: Don't believe everything you're foretold. ("To Shanshu in L.A.")

At first, prophecies in the Buffyverse might seem to be an exception to the rule that religion is anti-demonic and not terribly effective at best, demonic and evil at worst. As Wesley Wyndham-Pryce points out in the *Angel* episode "To Shanshu in L.A.," the definition of prophecy is indeed that "it came from on high." Prophecies certainly play a larger role in the lives of Buffyverse regulars (especially on first-season *BtVS* and on

---

[7] For more on this theme, see Chapter 18 in this volume.

Angel) than other religious symbols or objects. Yet they, too, are connected implicitly and explicitly to demons, and are routinely evaded or circumvented. In the first season of *BtVS*, the Slayer manages to fulfill the letter but not the spirit of an infallible prophecy that climaxes in her death. She stops the "preordained massacre" in "The Harvest" before it has reached epic proportions, allows the Anointed One to "lead her into Hell" precisely because she wants to locate the Master, and dies at the Master's hands only to be resurrected minutes later by Xander's CPR ("Prophecy Girl"). Before he kills Buffy, the Master taunts her, pointing out that "prophecies are tricky creatures. They don't tell you everything." When he encounters her later, however, he is shocked: "You were destined to die! It was written!" Buffy counters, "What can I say? I flunked the written" ("Prophecy Girl"). Prophecies drop out of the main *BtVS* storyline after this: Buffy's own prophetic dreams become rare after Season Two, and characters with prophetic abilities are usually possessed by demons, insane, or both (for example, Drusilla, or Tara in "The Gift"). In "A New Man," even the Initiative is able to deal with the fore-ordained raising of the demon prince Barvain. Prophecy has obviously lost its sacred cachet. Over on *Angel*, assorted prophecies continue to play a major role in the storyline, but Angel and his friends frequently circumvent them; in *Angel* Season Three alone, translation difficulties and the forgeries of time-traveling demons combined to ensure that everyone who tried to rely on prophecies was betrayed.

Another apparently religious category which rapidly lost power on *BtVS* is "apocalypse," a term with strongly Judeo-Christian connotations but which simply implies the end of the world in Buffyverse terms. It first turns up at the end of the show's two-part pilot, when Buffy summarizes events as "We averted the apocalypse. I give us points for that" ("The Harvest"). Xander and Willow are shocked that nobody else remembers the previous night's events, but this is only the beginning of the multiplication of apocalypses on *BtVS*. In "Never Kill a Boy on the First Date," Buffy blithely tells Giles, "If the apocalypse comes, beep me." Jenny Calendar describes the Master's rising as an "apocalypse" twice in "Prophecy Girl." At various points during the show's run, Buffy's encounters with Angelus and Acathla, the Sisterhood of Jhe, the Mayor, the Vahrall demons, and Glory are all described as apocalypses. In

Season Four, Riley complains that "I suddenly find myself need-ing to know the plural of 'apocalypse'" ("A New Man"), but Buffy and company have an even calmer reaction to the Vahrall menace:

> GILES: It's the end of the world.
> BUFFY, WILLOW, XANDER: Again?
> GILES: It's, ah, the earthquake—that symbol—yes.
> BUFFY: I *told* you. I—I said "end of the world" and you're, like, "pooh-pooh, southern California, pooh-pooh."
> GILES: I'm so very sorry. My contrition completely dwarfs the impending apocalypse.
> WILLOW: No, I—it can't be. We've done this already.
> GILES: It's the end of the world. Everyone dies. It's rather important, really. ("Doomed")

By Season Five, Willow's vengeful trip into dark magic is jok-ingly called "an apocalypse" by Glory ("Tough Love"), Anya can observe that "usually, when there's an apocalypse, I skedaddle" ("The Gift"), and Buffy can ask Giles: "This is how many apoc-alypses for us now?" ("The Gift"). "Apocalypse" is a more rou-tine event in the Buffyverse than plumbing repairs or passport renewal; there is often no religious imagery involved, and cer-tainly no sense of a successful divine (or demonic) plan.

It's difficult to say precisely who or what governs the Buffyverse, or what its fundamental religious truths might be. As we might expect, the powers of evil get a more thorough intro-duction than their opposites; in fact, from all accounts, evil came first. In "The Harvest," *BtVS*'s second episode, Giles explains that the world "did not begin as a paradise" but as a "hell" for demons. After the demons "lost their purchase on this reality, the way was made for mortal animals, for man." There is no hint of creation—much less a Creator—here, and human beings do not seem to occupy an especially privileged position. In "Amends," Buffy finds herself battling "the First Evil" for Angel's soul and sanity. This "First"—another confirmation, should we need it, that evil precedes good—is represented by a group of priests and can apparently take on any human form it chooses. It tells Buffy "I'm not a demon" and adds that it is "Beyond sin, beyond death . . . I am everywhere. Every being, every thought, every drop of hate." In short, the First Evil is not only a First

Mover; it is also omnipresent and extremely powerful. Buffy, typically, is not interested in the theological implications, saying, "All right, I get it, you're evil." Still, it is interesting that Whedon chose to write the show's only morally absolute force as neither human nor demon. Pure evil is often demonic, but it has a human face as well; Hell and Earth are equated in Giles's creation narrative ("The Harvest") and again when Angel discovers that Wolfram and Hart's "Home Office," the source of much of the evil he battles, is in fact located in his own dimension and his own city of L.A. ("Reprise"). In Season Six, Buffy's human adversary Warren does more damage to her friends than any previous enemy except perhaps Angelus ("Seeing Red"), and her human friend Willow does her best to end the world ("Grave").

In contrast to this plethora of options, any supernatural forces of good other than Buffy, Angel, and their companions and fellow Slayers are entirely absent from *BtVS*.[8] On *Angel*, the Powers That Be are not only inscrutable and impersonal, but also unapproachable, and the "channels" by which Angel approaches them tend to undercut their authority. In *Angel*'s first season, the mysterious Oracles have human foibles and are killed by the "warrior of the underworld" Vocah. In later seasons, Angel Investigations' connections to the Powers grow less and less imposing: the demon Krevlornswath and his karaoke-linked aura-reading abilities, the cheerful demonic pop-culture maven Skip, the unseen and spectacularly unhelpful Conduit, even Cordelia herself. The joke becomes obvious in "Loyalty," when Wesley seeks clarification about a prophecy from a *loa*— presumably the West African spirit—who manifests in a giant plastic hamburger at a fast-food drive-through window. Even Cordelia's visions are unreliable; it turns out that the "celestial pipeline" through which they are transmitted can be "hacked" ("That Vision Thing") and that they have been slowly destroying her human brain tissue. In order for her to continue with the visions, she becomes part demon ("Birthday"). The Powers are certainly powerful, but their ethical status vis-à-vis humanity is extremely muddled, and it is frequently unclear whether they are unequivocally forces of good.

---

[8] Whistler, in "Becoming, Parts One and Two" is a demon charged with maintaining the balance between good and evil.

Whatever the Powers and the First Evil "are," they are not easily reducible to any recognized religion. Vampires fear crosses—Whedon has explained that this came from established vampire mythology[9]—but the Trinity is cleverly edited out of a Latin exorcism ritual and replaced by "God" ("I've Got You Under My Skin"). Meanwhile "God," like Little Red Riding Hood and James Bond, is also a legitimate Halloween costume option ("Fear, Itself"). Sometimes, in fact, Buffyverse religious truths seem aimed at debunking traditional Judeo-Christian expectations. In "The Harvest," Giles dismisses accounts of a primordial Golden Age or Eden as "popular mythology." There is a definite reduction of metaphysics to physics in the later seasons of *BtVS* and *Angel*, as the afterlife becomes more and more malleable while representatives of assorted higher and lower powers are found in their own "pocket dimensions." In "After Life," Buffy simply equates "theology and dimensions." As in *Angel*'s demon dimension Pylea, where the theocracy's "sacred texts" become the basis for dimension-crossing equations, religion can often be reduced to either human actions or pseudo-science. It is not much of a basis for moral action, and no "sensible" person in the Buffyverse seems inclined to treat it as such.

Note to Self: Religion Freaky

As we have seen, the outward manifestations of Buffyverse religion can almost always be reduced to the demonic. The show's most irreverent and skeptical characters, humans and demons alike, are heroes and antiheroes; its villains are usually the most religious. Religious texts and artifacts are occasionally useful for fighting demons, but they can equally well draw human beings over to the side of evil. In the rare moments when Buffy and her friends are *not* fighting demons, neither religious belief nor religious practice plays a major role in their lives. Ultimately, then,

---

[9] See Joss Whedon, "The Bronze," (www.cise.ufl.edu/cgi-bin/cgiwrap/hsiao/buffy/get-archive?date=20000418) (18 April 2000): "Aggg! Stupid crosses! They were in the stories, okay, and we hadda use 'em and now I'm always worried, how do I explain crosses working on all vampires, maybe no one will notice and I can just NOT MENTION IT!!! . . . Actually, during my little rant I came up with the answer. It isn't the person who reviles the sy[m]bol of the Christian God, it's the demon that possesses them. Whew! It's cool. We're cool."

the moral center of the Buffyverse and the source for ethical behavior is neither demonic nor divine, but human. Since "Amends," the closest thing *BtVS* has had to a "Christian" episode is probably "Grave," the finale to a remarkably religion-free Season Six, in which Willow attempts to end the world with help from Satanists and demons but is foiled by the unconditional love of her friend Xander. Not only does Xander explicitly call himself a "carpenter" in the process, but the montage of characters realizing that the world has not ended is accompanied by a musical setting of the "Prayer of St. Francis," and the shooting script points out that Willow and Xander's climactic scene takes place on the same bluff above Sunnydale where Buffy confronted Angel in "Amends." But fan reaction to "Grave" centered around character issues, so that Whedon found himself called upon to explain Tara's death and Spike's transformation rather than Xander's momentary imitation of Christ. In contrast to the questioning of religious motives that accompanied "Amends," most *BtVS* fans quickly concluded that the religious imagery in "Grave" was simply a storytelling technique. This contrast suggests just how effective *BtVS* and *Angel* have been at reducing religion to a secondary issue, well behind the interpersonal relationships which lie at the heart of both shows. The Buffyverse, with its plethora of religious beliefs and practices, is far from secularized, but it is also far from sacralized. Or, as Buffy puts it much more succinctly in the second-season episode "What's My Line?, Part One": "Note to self: religion freaky."

17

Justifying the Means: Punishment in the Buffyverse

JACOB M. HELD

Consider the myriad of instances in *Buffy the Vampire Slayer* (*BtVS*) where punishment is doled out. There are vengeance demons who dish out punishment at the self-declared victim's request. Angel is "inflicted" with a soul. Spike has an electronic chip implanted in his brain. Many demons and villains are slain for their evil ways, or the potential threat they pose society. Faith is in prison. The list could go on and on. These examples are enough, however, to point out that *BtVS* repeatedly deals with the issue of punishment and attempts to illustrate the pros and cons of different approaches to justifying it.

Traditionally there have been two main schools of thought regarding punishment: retributivism and utilitarianism.[1] A retributivist maintains that punishment is justified only when meted out to the guilty in proportion to their criminal transgression: "Punishment should be given only when it is deserved and only to the extent that it is deserved."[2] The guilty are punished because they deserve to be; their punishment is what their crime requires. If asked why crimes require punishment at all, retribu-

---

[1] I am aware there are other schools of thought on punishment, such as restitution theories. The length of this paper precludes an exhaustive discussion of every theory of punishment. I have therefore decided to discuss only the two main schools of thought on this subject.

[2] Jacques Thiroux, *Ethics: Theory and Practice*, sixth edition (Upper Saddle River: Prentice-Hall, 1998), p. 133.

tivists have many answers available. Punishment may be said to re-establish the balance of morality that is disturbed when a wrong is committed, or it re-establishes the burden of self-restraint necessary for society to function, which is removed when a criminal commits a crime thereby giving the criminal an unfair advantage over those who obey the law.[3] Robert Nozick maintains that punishment connects the wrongdoer to proper values in such a way that these values as values have a significant effect on her life.[4] For this essay it will be sufficient to describe a retributive theory of punishment as one that maintains that punishment is only justified in so far as it is meted out to a guilty person for the sole reason that they deserve it. The important thing to recognize is that the consequences of the punishment are irrelevant in determining whether or not the punishment is justified.

By contrast, a utilitarian, or consequentialist, theory justifies punishment solely by the consequences derived from it. As such utilitarianism looks to the future whereas retributivism looks to the past. When justifying punishment the utilitarian asks three basic questions: 1) Will the wrongdoer be deterred from further offenses? 2) Will others be deterred from committing similar crimes? 3) Will society be protected from the criminal? If these three questions can be answered in the affirmative, then the punishment is justified.[5] In designating a utilitarian theory greatest happiness need not be the end goal. Theories of this sort justify punishment in so far as they promote a particular end, whatever that end may be.

Both theories have attractive and unattractive aspects. Retributivism must address its inflexibility, its disregard for consequences, and most importantly the feasibility of determining the severity of punishment based on the vague notion of desert. Utilitarianism, on the other hand, can discuss its justification in terms of prevention and deterrence, which are more easily mea-

---

[3] Since this last position justifies punishment based on its beneficial consequences, the re-establishment of self-restraint, it is questionable whether it is retributivist in the proper, non-consequentialistic sense.

[4] Robert Nozick, "Retributive Punishment," in *Readings in Philosophy of Law*, edited by John Arthur and William H. Shaw (Engelwood Cliffs: Prentice-Hall, 1984), p. 201.

[5] Thiroux, *Ethics: Theory and Practice*, p. 136.

sured than desert. However, basing punishment solely on consequences requires that one address foreseeable problems of untoward practices such as the prosecution of the innocent in order to "send a message" to would-be transgressors. The utilitarian must be able to answer the question, "Can one punish an innocent if it will deter crime or save lives?" Utilitarianism needs a way out of answering a frightening "yes."[6]

This essay will present both views and demonstrate the merits of a utilitarian view over a retributivist position, using three main examples from *BtVS*. First, we will examine the nature of vengeance demons and how their sense of justice illustrates the arbitrary, relative, and subjective nature of determining what one's just desert is. Retributivism, based as it is on a theory of just desert, must address this issue if it is to remain a tenable position. Second, we will discuss Angel and Spike to demonstrate the benefits of deterrence rather than desert as a goal of punishment. Finally, we will discuss the problem of punishing the innocent from a utilitarian perspective using the killing of Ben/Glory by Giles. This survey will support the claim that retributivism is an untenable position. In addition, we will see that utilitarian theories of punishment are best able to provide the state with the means towards its end of securing freedom for the populace as well as adjudicating between alternatives in hard cases.

Halfrek Prefers the Title "Justice Demon"

In "Older and Far Away," Halfrek, Anya's former colleague, is referred to as a "vengeance demon." She responds that she prefers the term "justice demon." Apparently she thinks that what we perceive to be vengeance is better construed as justice. What a vengeance demon portions out, then, is not revenge but moral punishment based on desert. As a result, one may wonder how a vengeance demon, or retributivist, determines what somebody's just desert is. If a retributivist maintains that punishment is justified as the meting out of desert, then she must be able to determine what a criminal's desert is by: a) showing how

---

[6] Notice this sentiment presumes that consequences alone do not justify a theory of punishment.

this desert is proportionate to the crime; b) why the determination of desert is not relativistic; and c) how meting out desert can be justified regardless of consequences (particularly in cases wherein the punishment creates additional harm). We will address each of these questions in order.

Assuming that punishments are justified in so far as they mete out desert there is the key problem of establishing a hierarchy of deserts. For example, how does one determine what a thief deserves and what a murderer deserves? Clearly, on the retributivist view one deserves a harsher penalty than the other, but how much harsher? Robert Nozick has suggested an equation for the determination of desert: one's desert is the product of culpability (r) and severity of offense (H), represented as 'r × H.' However, there is a problem in quantifying the severity of criminal offenses and culpability. Although Nozick suggests that culpability can be represented as a scale from 1 (full responsibility) to 0 (no responsibility) the intermittent values are not determined, and are probably indeterminable. The determination of the degree of the severity of offenses is plagued with the same difficulty. Although there are other suggestions for the determination of desert, they are all subject to the same difficulty. For example, one may be able to create a scale of offenses whereby they are ranked from least to most harmful. One also may be able to do the same with punishments, for example, a scale consisting of fines, community service, and prison terms. If one lines these two scales up one to one, there then seems to be a system of determining desert. But the question remains: how do we determine that the least harmful offense deserves, for example, a fifty-dollar fine and the worst crime deserves death? How do we determine what a criminal deserves in an objective manner, irrespective of societal norms and personal value judgments? The retributivist position relies on our ability to justify a correspondence between offense and desert, and a clear exposition of this correlation.

One possible view holds that a criminal should have imposed on him an amount of suffering equal to that he has imposed on his victims. This is the motivation behind Angel's Gypsy curse. The Gypsies restored Angel's soul in order that he might suffer the guilt consequent on his murdering and torturing, just as the victims' families must suffer for their loss. Although in Angel's case this seems to be appropriate, and it seems to have done a good job of causing him suffering, how can we determine how much suffering is enough? Angel's victims suffer a brief amount of torment or pain and the victim's family suffers a loss, but their wounds heal over time. Even if wounds don't heal, the victim's family will be dead in fifty or so years anyway so their suffering is limited. Angel, by contrast, theoretically could live indefinitely; his suffering would then be of a greater magnitude than the suffering he created. Of course this discussion assumes suffering can be measured and that is a big assumption.

Another suggestion for determining deserved punishment, known as *lex talionis*, recommends "an eye for an eye." This position maintains that the criminal must suffer the same hardship that the victim suffered. Such a view is clearly untenable. Do we rape a rapist, kidnap a kidnapper's child,[7] or steal from a thief? Obviously not.[8]

An additional problem in determining desert is the inherent subjective nature of such a determination. Consider Halfrek and Anya. As a vengeance demon, Anya chose to punish boyfriends, fiancées, and husbands. Her self-determined mission was to vindicate and avenge scorned women. The scorned woman determined what the ex-boyfriend deserved in terms of punishment and indicated this to Anya via a wish.[9] Halfrek by contrast chooses to avenge children by punishing their neglectful, abusive parents. Again, the person scorned determined the punishment and communicated it to Halfrek via a wish. Clearly there can be no objectivity in these cases, but are circumstances in our universe really any different? Some retributivist theories suggest that desert ought to be the result of democratic processes; such a process, though, could result in relativistic results.[10] After all, it is apparent that desert, severity of crime, and proportionate

---

[7] Holtz's abduction of Conner can be seen as a case of *lex talionis*, since it supposedly repays Angel for murdering Holtz's family.

[8] For an extended discussion of *lex talionis* and its inherent problems see, Russ Shafer-Landau, "Retributivism and Desert," *Philosophical Quarterly* 81(2000), pp. 189–214.

[9] Good examples of this principle in the series include Anya herself in "Entropy" (when she attempts to get revenge on Xander for leaving her at the altar) and Cordelia's wish in "The Wish."

[10] Shafer-Landau, "Retributivism and Desert," p.198.

punishment are affected by societal norms. In practice we are in no position to determine objectively the moral desert of a crime: people, societies, and governments will always disagree. In the end one's desert is what society determines that desert to be. In Iran thieves deserve to have their hands cut off; in the U.S. some murderers deserve to die. Who can adjudicate between disputes and say who is right and who is wrong? *Ultimately an appeal to desert is an appeal to our reactions to criminal activity.* We desire to see the criminal punished. Moreover, the determination of who counts as a criminal is determined by our own societal norms. For example, marijuana possession deserves criminal punishment in the U.S., but not in the Netherlands. Such an example demonstrates that crime is a geographic and political notion: when desert and crime go hand in hand, the specter of relativism looms. Desert simply is a concept too vague to have any objective and effective meaning in the context of punishment.

Although it cannot be discussed here, I contend that if one goes through the history of law, one will notice that the harshest punishments are enacted against those things that threaten the social fabric the most. As a good example of this phenomenon, consider the case of the criminalization of adultery in societies that rely on practices of primogeniture or general inheritance. In such societies violations against necessary constituents of social cohesion are considered the most despicable ones. If this example supports my claim, then desert is socially determined and relativistic. In essence, it is being determined based on the deleterious effects of the action. Thus it turns out to be possible to reduce retributivist claims of this nature to utilitarian/consequentialist bases.

Angel, Spike, and Oz: The Case for Deterrence

There is a major problem in attempting to demonstrate the merits of deterrence relative to retribution in justifications of punishment. I cannot appeal to the greater benefits derived from deterrence over retribution, since whether consequences are a legitimate source of justification is the very question at hand. Accordingly, the method I will use is to appeal to the role of the state and the good of the person. Although it is contestable, I maintain that the role of the state is the securing of goods for individuals that promote their freedom or the exercise of their abilities within limits, but that do not impinge on the liberties of others. What goods are necessary for the promotion of a person's freedom or well being can be defined only by a theory of human nature.[11] However, any basic theory of liberalism[12] comports closely enough with my view of the state such that we can maintain that the state's role is the securing of the freedom and liberty of the individual. Of course, theories differ in describing how this is to be done in practice, but that is an issue we can avoid here.

Once we have determined that the role of the state is to provide for the security of the citizenry and the promotion of their freedom, the role of the legal system must be to provide the means for the state to do so. Thus, the legal system is concerned with consequences, namely, with whether the state is providing what it is that it is the state's role to provide. Punishment becomes merely a means among others for securing these goods. As such we must see whether or not retributivism or utilitarianism provides the best means for securing these ends.

Retributivism is obviously at a disadvantage. Since this theory of punishment is consequence neutral, by definition it is not concerned with whether punishment assists in securing the citizenry or providing necessary goods for the realization of freedom. As far as punishment is concerned, the consequences in question, are the prevention and deterrence of criminal activity, and, arguably, the rehabilitation of the offender. Retributivism, however, is satisfied if those who deserve punishment are punished, regardless of whether such punishments prevent further criminal activity. If retributivism were concerned with these issues, it would no longer be retributivism, but utilitarianism.

---

[11] For our purposes we merely need consider goods such as security and free self-determination within limits respecting others' ability to equal self-determination.

[12] Liberalism is to be understood as a political conception containing a specification of certain basic rights, an assignment of priority to these rights, and the delineation of measures required in order assure that the individual has adequate means to make effective use of these rights, liberties and opportunities. See John Rawls, *Political Liberalism* (New York: Columbia University Press, 1993).

Utilitarianism is suited perfectly to deal with the problem of deterrence and prevention, both of which are necessary functions of the state in providing the services for which it is designed.

Since the state is designed to provide security and freedom to the citizenry, and the legal system provides a means to this via a system of rewards and punishments, a punishment can be justified in so far as it provides for the securing of security and freedom for the citizenry. Thus a punishment that fails to do so would be unjustified. Nonetheless, a problem remains: is *any* punishment justified provided it secures more desirable consequences than other available punishments? In other words, can we punish the innocent if the consequences outweigh the small disutility created? Let's look at the cases of Angel and Spike.

Angel and Spike are more similar than many people recognize.[13] Both are vampires and neither is able to do evil towards human beings. Angel is prevented by his conscience, or the possession of a soul. Spike is prevented by an electronic chip imbedded in his brain. Both Angel and Spike have had a punishment imposed on them. Angel's punishment was imposed for the purpose of desert. The Gypsies only wanted Angel to feel the suffering that they felt. Spike's chip was implanted for the sole purpose of prevention or deterrence. Desert was no issue, the Initiative wanted to prevent Spike from harming other human beings. Now if the state is to provide for security and freedom, which method works better?

Angel's punishment had the unforeseen benefit of causing him to desire redemption and pursue this through good works. On a retributivist account his punishment is not justified because of this fact, but it is a felicitous side effect. Spike's punishment, by contrast, prevents any further wrongdoing to humans. As such, Spike's punishment is guaranteed to secure the ends of the state whereas Angel's punishment only does so contingently and as an unforeseen consequence of meting out his just desert. After all, it's possible that giving Angel his just desert wouldn't

---

[13] The similarities between Angel's soul and Spike's chip are striking. Both are in a sense social constructs imposed on the subject and coercing him to fall in line with societal norms. Angel's is imposed through moral education and Spike's is imposed through science. In essence Spike's chip is a material soul, or conscience.

prevent him from doing further harms, since it is easy to imagine cases where punishing someone according to desert has no beneficial consequences and may even lead to deleterious effects. If such is the case, then the punishment has failed to secure what the state requires to be secured, namely, security and freedom. In this context it is worth remembering that even with a soul Angel allowed Drusilla and Darla to slaughter several Wolfram and Hart employees.

Spike and Oz present similar cases in terms of prevention. Each is "punished" for the preventative effect the punishment guarantees. Oz, who has done nothing wrong, is arguably justifiably imprisoned every full moon to prevent him from committing acts of violence. Spike has a chip implanted in him to prevent further acts of violence. But these two cases raise a frightening issue. Neither can willingly cause harm. It is not a choice; it is forced upon them by the state, which has antecedently determined right and wrong. Oz is innocent and punished solely for the beneficial consequences of deterrence. Spike is preemptively punished, much like Alex in Anthony Burgess's *A Clockwork Orange*. If we allow that the state may use any means necessary to secure the ends it deems fit, then we may also be allowing for a totalitarian state.

Utilitarian theorists have many responses to these problems and I will mention what I take to be the two strongest. First a utilitarian can maintain that the end of punishment is the securing of human rights and the prevention of violations of these rights. So defined, punishments that circumvent human rights cannot be allowed. If freedom to choose between good and evil, that is, self-determination, is a human right, then Spike and Alex type punishments are unjustified, since they contradict the very ends to which they are directed. So too, Oz's right to freedom on the night of a full moon may be outweighed by everybody else's right not to be viciously mauled while walking home from school. This introduction of rights talk allows for adjudication between competing claims, but only so long as there is a recognizable hierarchy of rights. Second, a utilitarian can suggest that the punishment of innocents merely for beneficial results will lead to worse effects than only punishing guilty criminals. On such a position if a citizen recognizes that he may be punished for a crime even if he does not commit it, the law ceases to be a deterrent. There remains no motivation to refrain from committing a crime. As such, the punishing of innocents would have to be secret, and this would require a massive governmental "conspiracy." In the end it can be argued that since punishing only the guilty is more beneficial than punishing the innocent, it is better to only punish the guilty.[14] The point here is that there are ways to amend a utilitarian view of punishment to guarantee that the state is limited in its abilities to punish in accordance with our conceptions of human rights and what human beings require. Now that we have assessed the pros and cons of both sides, it would benefit us to test out each theory on a truly hard case: Ben/Glory.[15]

Buffy Should've Killed Ben

In "The Gift" Buffy is faced with the decision whether or not to kill Ben, a human whom Glory requires in order to manifest herself. Glory is a God planning to open up a portal that will collapse all worlds together, thereby destroying the earth and all of humanity. Buffy is afforded the opportunity to kill Ben, whose body is an occasional vessel for Glory, thereby effectively killing Glory herself. Ben, though, is innocent and did not choose to have Glory manifest herself through him. As a slayer, Buffy cannot kill an innocent since an innocent does not deserve death, or punishment, even if such punishment will secure the safety and well being of the entire planet. Buffy as representative of the state's coercive ability to punish must decide whether to punish based on desert or consequences. In short, Buffy represents the retributivist view when she refuses to kill Ben because she recognizes that he does not deserve punishment. Adopting the position of the state, Buffy is given the opportunity to punish an innocent in order to procure the security and freedom of

---

[14] For discussions on this topic see: Russ Shafer-Landau, "The Failure of Retributivism," *Philosophical Studies* 82 (1996), pp. 289–316; Richard B. Brandt, "The Utilitarian Theory of Criminal Punishment," *Readings in Philosophy of Law*, edited by John Arthur and William H. Shaw, (Englewood Cliffs: Prentice-Hall, 1984), pp.189–194.

[15] A discussion of rehabilitation would be fitting here, were it not the case that space is limited. However, as could be anticipated from previous argumentation, utilitarian views will be better able to address issues of rehabilitation whereas retributivist views will be unconcerned with such a discussion.

the world's population. However, the results are irrelevant to her. She simply reasons that Ben is innocent and so should not be killed. By way of explaining her decision, Giles points out that Buffy is a hero and thus could not kill Ben even though she was aware of the dire consequences. Giles, though, takes the utilitarian view and makes short shrift of Ben, strangling him to death. It seems as though we are to view Buffy as heroic—truly valiant and noble—whereas Giles is somehow less than heroic—merely human. Thus he does the dirty, and perhaps unnecessary, work of killing Ben.

This interpretation of Buffy's situation would favor a retributivist view. However, my contention is that we should admonish Buffy and maintain that if she truly wants to protect the welfare of the people, that is, if her goal is the security and freedom of all people, then this goal dictates that she should kill Ben. Glory will inevitably manifest herself again, and the next time Buffy may not be able to stop her. The only way to guarantee a positive outcome is to kill Ben. Yes, it is unfair to kill an innocent. Yes, it seems repugnant and brutal. But if it saves the universe, then we need to overcome our disgust and do what only Giles was strong enough to do: kill Ben.[16] As Giles himself notes, ". . . I've sworn to protect this sorry world, and sometimes that means saying and doing . . . what other people can't. What they shouldn't have to" ("The Gift").

This hard case points out the difficulties inherent in providing a justification for punishment. Given our conception of the state, punishment should prevent crime and deter criminals, and would-be criminals, from criminal acts. But in what does the happy medium lie between a strong secure state and a police state that punishes the innocent and circumvents freedom for one's own good? The retributivist position has a clear answer: regardless of consequence, punishment is only justified in so far as it is meted out to those who deserve it. There is a sense of respect afforded all individuals and to use them as a means to the end of the state is to violate this respect. Such a view has

---

[16] The other interesting case is whether they should have killed Dawn. Giles suggests that it will be necessary once the ceremony to open the portal begins. Buffy refuses to even consider killing her sister. In the end her refusal to kill Dawn and her desire to protect the world are what lead to her sacrificing herself.

some plausibility since it is in line with our sentimentalities. But a hard case like Ben, or even the possible evil of Angel, shows that consequences are a factor that the state must take into account if it is to do the job it is designed to do. Retributivism prevents supposed injustices such as the killing of Ben, but it relies on untenable presuppositions, and disregards relevant considerations.

We also can ask about the role of the state in the relationship between the state and the individual. This question can be answered through science and theories of human nature, through democratic efforts to determine the limits of the state as proposed by the governed, and through many other checks and balances in place to secure the rights and the freedom a human being requires. Since we can determine the role of the state, we can determine its end and choose the most effective means to attain that end. Punishment is justified as one such device in so far as it secures that end. If we reflectively maintain that this is the role of punishment, then we can guarantee that violations of human rights will be kept to at least a minimum. I will not say they will be eliminated. I consider the killing of Ben an affront to his freedom and his rights. But at the same time, I think Giles was justified in killing Ben and I should only hope that were Giles not there, someone else would have been strong enough to do the same. Utilitarian equations for maximizing whatever end is proposed are always fallible or troublesome, but whether to trade one life for six billion has an obvious answer.

18

No Big Win: Themes of Sacrifice, Salvation, and Redemption

GREGORY J. SAKAL

Life is difficult.
— M. Scott Peck, *The Road Less Traveled*

The hardest thing in this world is to live in it.
— Buffy Summers ("The Gift")

The terms "Sacrifice," "Salvation," and "Redemption" when applied to *Buffy the Vampire Slayer (BtVS)* and *Angel* might, to someone not familiar with either series, be taken to indicate that both these shows have a religious overlay to them, perhaps even Christian. Despite a few arguably Christian overtones (vampires vulnerable to sacred symbols, for example), this is most decidedly not the case.

It might further seem incredible that these two genre shows, whose apparent subject matter is sheer fantasy, could possibly explore issues so profound and fundamental to the human experience. Yet, it is precisely the genre of myth and fantasy that gives itself so perfectly to the exploration of these themes, whether or not specific religious beliefs are involved. Myth and legend are *meta*-themes that draw us out from the realities of "everyday life." While the definition of "everyday life" changes from one generation to the next, myth and legend provide a continuity to the human experience from age to age that "real life" cannot.

Because mythological themes transcend time and place, they become an effective vehicle for the presentation and exploration of the universal challenges that have confronted all people everywhere through time. This has, after all, been the function of myth and legend through history. One contemporary example, J.R.R. Tolkien's epic fantasy, *The Lord of the Rings*, continues to attract successive generations of readers who are sufficiently inspired by the work to plow through its better than one thousand pages. Despite its underpinnings of English rural life, the broad themes that it explores, set out against a backdrop of mythic history, continue to have universal appeal.

Monsters, vampires, demons, dark forces and those that worship them; heroes, sages, and wise councils, are all common to the legends and mythology of many cultures. Within the context of postmodern life, *BtVS* synthesizes a reality in which all these things work together to make perfect sense. Like the mythologies of past civilizations, the players here are just plain folk, pulled from the fabric of "normal" life, and thrown into the eternal struggle between good and evil. Unlike the academic or theological discourse that would be the usual venue for this kind of inquiry, the synthesis of mythic themes with the daily lives of the inhabitants of the Buffyverse provides a much more immediate and meaningful encounter.

We will begin this exploration by carefully defining the terms "Sacrifice," "Redemption," and "Salvation." This will help us to place the discussion in a broader context than their usual religious connotations might allow. The nature of vampires and how they relate to their human counterparts will provide a good opportunity for a brief examination of the nature and purpose of evil, and the part that both good and evil play in the overall balance of things. This will inform an in-depth character analysis of Xander and Spike, human and vampire, by which I will show that, while it might be tempting to assume that good belongs wholly to one species, and evil to the other, or that redemption is something which only humanity can attain, this is most definitely not the case. Moreover, we shall see that regardless of the path taken, sacrifice is an important part of the journey, and the journey itself is as important as the destination.

On Sacrifice and Salvation

What, exactly, are we talking about here? The word "sacrifice" for example, evokes the image of a pagan ritual in which some living thing, human or animal, is killed for the purpose of satisfying some hungry deity. The Christian church has loaded this word with many layers of interpretation. The most pertinent to the present discussion is that sacrifice is the conscious obedience of humankind to the will of God. Taken for its Latin roots, the word means literally "To make holy." For the present purpose at least, we might even say that it means "To consecrate to a higher purpose." So, Buffy gives up much of what life would be like for an attractive, talented young woman to dedicate herself to saving the world. Angel gives up the notion that he might somehow recover the kind of existence that he never had as a living man, as he seeks redemption from over two centuries of wanton cruelty and malice.

Like "sacrifice," the word "salvation" has Christian overtones. So does the word "redemption." However, it is important to distinguish between the theological definitions of these terms within the Christian tradition, and the broader meaning that these words have taken on in secular culture, outside of any specific religious belief. Taken together in the context of the Buffyverse, "salvation" might be thought of as a process by which individuals, with the help of a "Greater Power" (in *Angel*, the "Powers that Be"), turn from living only for the self to the exclusion of the needs of others, to a life by which all of humanity is helped to suffer less. Redemption, then, is the state of having recovered, (or better perhaps, rediscovered) in the eyes of this Greater Power, this higher purpose for which one's life was originally intended, thus bringing oneself into "right relationship" with the those Powers.

The character of Cordelia Chase, present from Season One of *BtVS*, provides a very clear example of the transition into this state of right relationship. Over the first three seasons of *BtVS*, we watch Cordelia grow from a selfish, self-centered, bigoted rich girl who had everything, who believed she didn't need anything from anybody, to someone reduced to having to work for a living because her parents lost all their money to the I.R.S. Cordelia is only able to attend her senior prom through the charity of Xander Harris, a rejected boyfriend, who secretly pays the remainder of what Cordelia owes for her evening gown ("The Prom").

In Season One of *Angel*, we find Cordelia living in abject poverty, a state from which she is lifted, again through the charity of others, to become an integral part of Angel's team, battling evil, and helping the helpless. By Season Three of *Angel*, she has come a long way indeed, when she recognizes her former self in the person of Lilah Morgan, a member of the demonic law firm, Wolfram and Hart. In a confrontation with Cordelia, Lilah defiantly states, "So, you know me." to which Cordelia replies, "Know you? I *was* you, except with better shoes" ("Billy"). Cordelia has clearly come a long way on the path towards redemption through her selfless helping of others. However, as part of this transformation, she finds herself succumbing to the cumulative destructive effects of visions that she was never meant to have. Having dedicated herself to this work, she refuses to give it up, even when offered an opportunity to have a life of glamour and stardom, to which she has always aspired ("Birthday"). At this point, she realizes that she has come too far along this path to turn back, and becomes willing to give up something she has always desired, leaving behind the person she once was to fully embrace the person she has become.

Cordelia's sacrifice in this instance touches on another element that must not go unexplored in this discussion: the path to redemption does not become easier through time, or its trials any easier to bear. On the contrary, life becomes more difficult, and the loss and pain all the greater.

The Nature of Vampires

The nature of vampires in the Buffyverse is often ambiguous. Buffy tells old flame Billy Fordham, who seeks to become a vampire in the hope of fending off his pending death from brain cancer, that when someone changes from living to un-dead, no part of who they were remains. Instead, a demon tenants itself in the body, and takes over the mind and memories of the former human occupant. To quote Buffy, "You die. And a demon sets up shop in your old house. It walks and talks and remembers your life but it's not you" ("Lie to Me").

However, Angel provides a less cut-and-dried account of what happens. As Angel, he remembers every evil deed he committed while he was without soul. He feels accountable for the deeds of his "evil twin," and seeks redemption through the self-less helping of others. During his brief reprise as the soulless Angelus, he remembers everything (with great contempt) about his life as Angel. So, it would seem that, according to Angel at least, the divide between the living and the undead is not as clear as Buffy might have led us to believe. It might be more accurate to observe that as a vampire, the darkest aspects of who that person once was come to the fore and are given free rein.

An interchange with Darla, the vampire who turned the young man Liam into the un-dead Angelus, reveals the more subtle aspects of conversion. Angelus has just slaughtered his entire family, mostly out of resentment towards his father, to whom as Liam, he could never be good enough. With bodies strewn about, Angelus sits at his father's table with a glass of wine, reflecting on what he has done, thinking that he's made an end of the struggle with his father once and for all. Darla, telling him that this wasn't the end of anything, but more of a beginning says, "What we once were informs all that we have become. The same love will infect our hearts—even if they no longer beat. Simple death won't change that" ("The Prodigal"). The human Liam had an unfinished agenda with his father. Once relieved of his soul, his anger and resentment could manifest themselves unfettered by any moral considerations. Clearly, there is much that continues on in the transition from human to vampire. Were it a simple tenancy arrangement, whereby a random demon occupies a converted human body, then the continuing agenda of that person's life would not be a factor.

Spike is a vampire with a complicated past that we learn about mostly through flashback. As human we see William as a sensitive but weak-willed romantic: inept, insecure, and clumsy in his attempts to win the heart of someone who considers herself his social better. When Drusilla makes him a vampire, he renames himself "Spike," and becomes a reckless adventurer whose violence seems less informed by sheer malice and revenge (as in the case of Angelus), than by a need to rebel against his weak and foppish human counterpart. He tells Buffy, "Getting killed made me feel really alive for the very first time.

I was through living by society's rules. Decided to make a few of my own" ("Fool for Love"). While it is true that he enjoys murder and mayhem, his actions appear to grow more out of a passion for his existence, as contrasted with the willful cruelty of Angelus that has no other purpose than a desire to harm.

Thus, in The Buffyverse, the vampire manifests the dark, or shadow-side of the human. Liam was a "a drunken, whoring layabout" ("Amends") whose main pleasures in life were drinking and women. As the vampire Angelus, this total obsession with the pleasures of the flesh turns to wanton cruelty and destruction for its own sake. It also gives way to his violent homicidal riff in which he kills his family. Both his human and vampire personas exhibit extreme behavior, without focus or purpose, and without any regard for the needs of others.

Similarly, William as human was needy, sensitive, and inept. As Spike, the vampire, he becomes adventurous, violent, and passionate—everything, in fact, that he was unable to be as human. Both Angelus and Spike manifest a rebellion against all they perceived to be holding them back as human beings. Spike is fighting off his former persona as an effete gentleman. Angelus has no such history to fall back on and is instead consumed with anger towards his father.

Both characters appear to be on a path towards some kind of redemption, although with different motivation. Angel, in his intense relationship with Buffy, attempts to recover the human life that he never had. The escape clause in the Gypsy curse that restored his human soul in the first place causes Angel, after consummating his relationship with Buffy in a moment of true happiness, to revert to the former soulless, vengeful Angelus. When his soul is later restored, he realizes that the kind of existence for which he had hoped will never be his, and instead takes up a kind of ministry as he "Helps the helpless." Spike, on the other hand, without soul, finds himself fighting alongside of Buffy, as she battles the forces of darkness. This is something that he can't explain, even to himself, since he doesn't have the excuse of a soul as his motive for joining up with the good guys. Clearly, the Powers of the Buffyverse work in different ways for different individuals. Redemption might come to Spike in spite of himself; for Angel, redemption is the goal he constantly seeks.

Spike and Xander: A Study in Redemptive Behavior

Spike and Xander Harris present an important contrast in character development through the course of the series that helps us to understand what the path to redemption is all about. Xander (human), is introduced in the series opener as a main character. Spike, and his mate Drusilla (both vampires), appear for the first time in Season Two ("School Hard"). From the first, Xander responds to Buffy in a typically adolescent hormonal way. As we move through the next four seasons, this kind of response to the opposite sex seems to be something that Xander never completely outgrows. Even after proposing marriage to Anya, a former demon-turned-human, whose principal task for over a thousand years had been to wreak vengeance on false lovers, he abandons her at the altar ("Hell's Bells"), apparently lacking the moral compass to follow through on his commitment.

Spike, on the other hand, although a soulless, ruthless killer, consistently demonstrates a kind of selfless love for his mate Drusilla, manifested in his steadfast willingness to put Drusilla's needs ahead of his own. Indeed, when she leaves him at the end of Season Two for not being "demon enough" for her, he is utterly heartbroken, if such a word can be used to describe the emotions of a creature whose heart doesn't beat, and who is ostensibly incapable of such a response.

In Season Three, we find Spike sitting in Joyce Summers's kitchen drinking hot chocolate, and pouring out his grief over the loss of Drusilla. He is appreciative of the opportunity to connect with a woman who is neither a "Happy meal on two legs," as he once referred to humans, nor a romantic interest. He passes on the opportunity to feed on Joyce, even though he could have done so. Xander, in a similar encounter with Joyce ("Restless"), evinces a sexual interest in her, made explicit in a dream sequence, that again demonstrates his inability to relate to the women around him without his hormones getting in the way.

To be sure, Spike's efforts to reprise his relationship with Drusilla are ruthless and single-minded. He has Xander and Willow as hostages, locked in an old factory while he cries into his hot chocolate with Joyce. However, his level of commitment to Drusilla is impressive, especially when contrasted with Angelus's utter lack of concern for anyone else, human or not. Yet they are both vampires without souls. Clearly, then, although by his nature Spike is "wired" for destructive, murderous behavior, he is capable of strong emotional commitment that goes beyond the simple fulfillment of his immediate needs for sex and affection. Further, when he allies with Buffy against Angelus to save the world, he appears capable of making moral choices for a greater good that go beyond any immediate benefit to himself. Of course, it could here be argued that his motivation is more to rekindle his romance with Drusilla, who has lately been seduced by Angelus's "pure" evil. However, there are many other ways in which Spike could have pulled this off, without aligning with Buffy. Taken in retrospect from where we are in Season Six, this could be seen as the beginning of Spike's regard of Buffy as something other than a complete enemy.

So, where does that leave Xander? Mr. Harris appears morally compromised in more ways than simply his inability to arrive at a mature expression of love. While Buffy is racing against the clock in her attempt to stop Angelus, Willow is having another go at performing the Gypsy ritual that will restore Angelus's soul. Xander knows this, but instead of telling Buffy (as he was asked to do by Willow) when he meets her on the road, he withholds this piece of information, perhaps as a last spiteful gesture towards Angel as his rival for Buffy's affection. Xander has never liked Angel, even when Angel was on Buffy's team, and he uses this opportunity as an attempt to get rid of Angel once and for all. In neglecting to relay this information to Buffy, Xander has not only broken his promise to Willow, but has taken the gamble that Buffy will destroy Angel without knowing that the recovery of his soul (and hence his humanity) is imminent. Xander's jealousy, tinged with revenge, informs his twisted moral justification for lying to Buffy, and the hubris of his presumption to know what is best for her.

Spike's Conversion

Spike's existence takes an unexpected turn when he is captured by the Initiative in Season Four. He is essentially "defanged" by the installation of a biochip in his brain that prevents him from harming any human by inflicting severe head pain whenever he attempts to do so. Demons, vampires, and other non-human creatures are apparently exempt from the chip's effects, allowing Spike to slake his thirst for violence as he works side by side with The Slayer. While this is helpful to the cause, one could assume that Spike's "good" behavior is simply a response to unpleasant stimuli.

This is only partially true. It would be more accurate to say that the chip has given Spike the *incentive* to behave differently. After several failed attempts to get this chip removed, he finds his un-dead life takes an even stranger twist when he awakes one day (literally) to the realization that he is passionately in love with Buffy, the vampire slayer ("Out of My Mind"). He finds himself making awkward attempts at moral choices in his intense desire to impress Buffy. This includes, in one episode, pointedly telling Buffy that he will not avail himself of the opportunity to feed off some recently dead humans (his chip prevents him from attacking the living), because he knows that she wouldn't approve. However, his behavior over time becomes more consistently social, and less driven by his demon-vampire need to kill. Drusilla, his former flame, when she makes a brief visit to Sunnydale, attempts to draw Spike back to his former killing ways ("Crush"). To bypass the effects of his chip, she offers him a human, fresh-killed, from which he feeds with obvious great reluctance. Spike has apparently discovered that despite his protests to the contrary, he cannot go back to being what he was, chip or no chip. The prescient Drusilla clearly senses this when she tells Spike that his love for Buffy has placed him beyond even her help.

It would be simple to explain Spike's transformation from killing machine to lovesick night-stalker by saying that his actions derive purely from his own self-interest. After all, he loves Buffy, and wants her in every way. His brain implant has removed the pleasure he once derived from killing people—a sort of behavior modification that has provided him with additional incentive to become more human, or, more accurately, to behave, in a more human, and less destructive manner. Unlike the animal that he once was, where his primary motivation was his own pleasure and satisfaction, his behavior now takes into account the feelings and needs of others, despite his ability (and willingness) to cause trouble when it suits his purpose.

Even when he begins to realize that he cannot have Buffy as he desires, Spike is unflagging in his commitment to her. He displays genuine sympathy and concern for Buffy and her sister Dawn after their mother's death ("The Body"). He endures a round of vicious torture at the hands of the nearly omnipotent, Glory, as she seeks to persuade Spike to reveal the location of "The Key," which has been concealed in the person of Buffy's sister, Dawn ("Intervention"). Xander is not convinced of the genuine nature of Spike's behavior, instead seeing every action on Spike's part as an effort to get Buffy into bed. However, it becomes increasingly clear that Xander resents *anyone* who evinces a personal interest in Buffy. He sees Buffy as kind of comforting mother figure—a safe haven to which he can always retreat. Anya would appear to agree when she sings, "When things get rough he just hides behind his Buffy / Now look he's getting huffy / 'Cause he knows that I know" ("Once More, With Feeling"). Xander apparently lacks the empathy that would help him to understand Buffy's complex relationships with others who are, in one way or another, not typically human, just as she herself is not.

When Buffy has given her own life in place of Dawn's to save the world from Glory's hell at the end of Season Five, Spike weeps passionately at the sight of her body ("The Gift"). After she is resurrected by Willow's dark magic, he feels an even closer bond with her. Like him, she has risen from the grave. Like him, she had to literally claw her way out of the ground, which Spike alone observes from her bloodied hands. For Spike, Buffy has become a kind of Beatrice to his Dante—a feminine ideal to be worshipped but, of whose affections he is not completely worthy. Like Dante, it is this love that moves him along the path to redemption. In contrast, Xander, in his little-boy way, expects that somehow life with Buffy will be exactly as it was before. Spike alone recognizes the trauma of what she has gone through, and indeed it is only in Spike whom she confides when she reveals that, rather than having been liberated from some hell dimension by her resurrection, as the Scooby gang has assumed from her behavior, Willow's spell has, in fact, wrenched her from heaven

Is Spike's "conversion" true, or valid? Or is it simply, as previously discussed, a Pavlovian response to desire? This might be a difficult question to answer were Spike's behavior radically different from our own. Arguably, at the core of most human behavior is the desire for survival and satisfaction without regard for the needs and wishes of others. It is out of a learned sense of enlightened self-interest that we develop the ability to deal with other people, to live comfortably with our neighbors, for example, even if we might not have chosen them as such were it ours to decide. Spike has much to overcome on his journey towards redemption—much more, say, than Xander, who is, after all, human. Xander has the opportunity to grow and learn, but he declines. Spike, on the other hand, is imbued with an evil nature, yet is motivated by his love for Buffy to overcome it. One should not assume from this that Spike is "good," and Xander is "bad." It would be more accurate to emphasize that Spike has far more to overcome on his way to redemption. It is perhaps this very fact that makes it possible for him to approach this goal; the greater challenge giving rise to a more heroic effort. Xander, on the other hand, possesses considerable virtue (he is often referred to as the "heart" of the Scooby gang), but is so insecure, that he backs away from any challenge that would help him to grow.

The sharp contrast between these two characters provides insight into the reality of salvation. There is not one universal measure against which all are judged. Rather, the standard is more like, "What have you done with what you've been given?" Spike strives to make the most of what he has; Xander behaves as though he is unable to face the challenge of growing up. Spike, although imbued with an intrinsically evil nature, is upfront and direct about who he is and what he wants, and far exceeds the innate ability of his kind in his service to others. Xander continues to hide his feelings and motivations behind an ongoing sophomoric banter.

In effect, Buffy and Xander express two opposing views on the nature of redemption—polar opposites that accurately reflect religious belief in contemporary life. To Xander, evil is evil, and can never change.[1] Hence, he views Spike as forever and completely malevolent, despite the many instances where

---

[1] To his credit, Xander later demonstrates, through his faith in evil Willow, that he also believes the obverse of this: that good is good, even if temporarily obscured by evil behavior. It is, of course, his faith in Willow that saves her from herself, and the world with her ("Grave").

he has shown himself to be otherwise. We might say that Xander's behavior implies a fundamentalist view that redemption is available only to a chosen group who subscribe to a particular set of beliefs. Within this mindset there isn't much of a mandate to grow and change; membership in the group is sufficient. If one (a vampire, for instance) is outside of that group or those beliefs, then that person is "unsaved," or unredeemable. Buffy, on the other hand, appears to take a universalist point of view that salvation is available freely to all, and all creatures have the potential for redemption. She demonstrates this belief in her willingness to accept Spike at face value, in spite of his being a creature that she would normally destroy. Without prejudice, she continues to evaluate and make decisions based on what she intuits and observes. To Buffy, it is not for her to decide who is redeemable and who is not. Her task is to protect and help—not to judge.

An almost disturbing question that is raised by this examination of Spike's redemptive behavior is, what does this say about the mission of The Slayer? If an inherently evil creature like Spike shows even a potential for redemption, is it right for the Slayer to go around killing every demon and vampire that she encounters? The answer to this is pretty straightforward: she doesn't. Once she perceives that Spike no longer poses a threat to the humans around him, she no longer feels it necessary to kill him. She often threatens to do so, out of her conflicted feelings for him, but she refrains from actually following through, even when she discovers that as a result of her resurrection experience, Spike's chip implant no longer prevents him from hurting her. Buffy intuits the mandate for careful judgment, even under the pressure of the fight, about when to slay and when to refrain.

The Purpose of Evil

The sense of balance between good and evil, between light and darkness, is a prominent feature in The Buffyverse. In *BtVS*, we meet a demon-like character called "Whistler" ("Becoming"), whose stated purpose is to maintain the balance between good and evil, between order and chaos. When one or the other starts to get out of hand, he intervenes to keep the balance intact. With the looming possibility that Angelus will succeed in his plan to destroy the world, Whistler provides Buffy with some essential information that she must use to prevent Angelus from achieving his goal.

Angel also takes up this theme repeatedly. The most pointed example comes in Season Three. Angel, seeking information that will help him recover his son, forces the Wolfram and Hart folks to give him access to the "White Room." Here, we meet a little girl, apparently a manifestation of The Powers That Be, seated in a chair, who knows everything about Angel, and why he is there. As she explains to him the history of a particularly violent species of demon, and why their physical form was taken from them, she says, "I *like* trouble—but I *hate* chaos" ("Forgiving"). Clearly, in the Buffyverse, good and evil must be held in tension with one another. The good guys must fight the good fight, and the bad guys continue to appear, like targets in a shooting gallery. Without this struggle, there would be no choices to make, no exercise of free will, no path to redemption.

After all, what distinguishes humanity from many of the other creatures we meet in Buffy's world, is the ability to choose. Vampires and (most) demons are inherently evil. Humans, on the other hand, are given the ability to choose which path to follow. Without the darkness, the light would go unrecognized. Without evil, there would be no struggle, no sacrifice, and hence no possibility of or need for redemption.

No Big Win

Each season Buffy and her gang are confronted with, and eventually vanquish, some terrible, world-threatening foe. To be sure, these year-end victories have not been without price. The final episode of each succeeding season has made the cost of her good works just a little higher. In Season Five, however, she is for the first time confronted with an apparently unbeatable enemy. When a possible means for destroying this enemy (Glory) is discovered, she finds herself in a moral dilemma that might involve killing her own sister. The "reward" for all her good works in prior years would appear to be increasingly difficult decisions without any obviously good choices. So why does she do it? Clearly, the reward is not an easier path; to the contrary, things become more difficult, culminating with Buffy accepting her own death as the price for saving the world. Nor does all her good work appear to result in a decline in the amount of evil that she must fight. To borrow a quote from the Christian tradition, "From everyone to whom much has been given, much will be required; and from the one to whom much has been entrusted, even more will be demanded."[2] When it appears that Buffy has given her all, yet more is demanded from her.

While *BtVS* poses the question, it is Angel, now in his own series, who provides the best answer. After several episodes during which Angel became totally consumed with the pursuit and destruction of the "Bad Guys," an endeavor that nearly cost him the friendships, not to mention the lives, of those closest to him, he has an experience that changes him completely. To this point, Angel has been "keeping score" as he knocks his foes down one at a time, in an attempt to fulfill an ancient prophecy that says that the "Vampire with a soul" (that is, Angel) will, through his work of fighting the powers of darkness, eventually redeem himself and become human.

Finally, he comes to the realization that his work isn't about winning this redemptive prize, but about helping everyone he can to suffer less. His path is not about what he will eventually win, but about how much he can do to lessen the suffering and pain of humanity, one encounter at a time. He says, "There's no grand plan, no big win . . . I wanna help because people shouldn't suffer as they do. Because, if there isn't any bigger meaning, then the smallest act of kindness is the greatest thing in the world" ("Epiphany").

Redemption is a process, not an event that happens in the course of doing the best we can with what we have. It is a much greater endeavor than anyone can realize individually, even though each individual is on a journey of their own. In the end, it is the collective struggle of all against the forces of darkness that moves the human race ahead on its path to redemption. Sacrifice along the way is the letting go, willingly or not, of all that is unnecessary for the completion of this task—a successive peeling away of the layers of an onion, as the Buddhist tradition

---

[2] Luke 12:48b. New Revised Standard Version Bible, ©1989, National Council of the Churches of Christ.

would say, to reveal more and more the essence of life's purpose. That purpose? In the Buffyverse, it is clearly not personal happiness, since none of the main characters manage to achieve any more than fleeting snatches of this. Rather, it is the process of growing, or "becoming" that *BtVS* really puts in our face. At the last, it isn't the destination, but the journey that really counts.

19

Old Familiar Vampires: The Politics of the Buffyverse

JEFFREY L. PASLEY

> Old familiar vampires are sucking our power.
> — The Mekons[1]

Of all the philosophical themes that run through the Buffyverse, the most elusive are the political ones. As the intelligentsia's favorite show and a pop-culture reference in heavy rotation, *Buffy the Vampire Slayer (BtVS)* has been analyzed many times, with amusingly bi-partisan results.[2]

It was initially greeted as an exemplar of "grrrl power," a highly cross-marketable trend that allowed TV shows and films featuring beautiful young girls in tight clothes to tout themselves as feminist as long as the young girls beat people up. Creator Joss Whedon presented the show as feminist in his many media appearances, and even earned a *Ms.* profile for his efforts.[3]

---

[1] "Take His Name in Vain," *OOOH! (Out of Our Heads)* Quarterstick Records CD, 2002.

[2] For much more thorough coverage of the feminist, liberal, and conservative interpretations of *BtVS* and *Angel*, see the extended online version of this chapter, "You Can't Pin a Good Slayer Down: The Politics, If Any, of *Buffy The Vampire Slayer* and *Angel*," http://jeff.pasleybrothers.com/writings/buffy.htm.

[3] Lewis Beale, "Attack of the Sexy-Tough Women: In Movies and TV, Sisters Are Kicking Butt for Themselves," *New York Daily News* final edition (19 October 2000), p. 52; Ken Tucker, "High Stakes Poker," *Entertainment Weekly* (5 October 1999), pp. 20 ff.; Heather Olsen, "He Gives Us the Creeps," *Ms.*, August-September 1999, pp. 79–80.

Whedon has repeatedly said that *BtVS* originated in his desire to re-imagine the horror genre on behalf of "that blonde girl who would always get herself killed," inverting its notoriously misogynistic sexual politics. He hoped that his literally empowered heroine would not only be better for girls to identify with, but also help reform the attitudes of boys who might resist feminism if it were presented directly or abstractly.[4] Academic feminists endorsed Whedon's view of his show's girl-empowering tendencies, anointing Buffy as a "transgressive woman warrior" offering "possibilities for re-imagining gendered relations and modernist American ideologies."[5]

Given this pedigree, it is not surprising that several avowedly liberal publications, including *The American Prospect*, *Salon*, and the British *Guardian*, along with their occasional fellow traveler, the *New York Times*, have featured appreciative analyses of *BtVS*.[6] It's also not surprising that the Buffyverse exudes Hollywood-style liberalism in other areas besides feminism, with social tolerance a particular emphasis. The pioneering Willow-Tara arc was apparently the first long-term lesbian sexual relationship ever featured on a broadcast network television series. Tolerance has been promoted on *BtVS* and *Angel* not only for lesbians and nerds and witches but also for certain categories of demon—a term used to denote a diverse array of supernatural beings, some "very, very evil," but some "considered to be useful members of society" ("Family"). Mercy and the chance for rehabilitation are offered even to the most depraved beings, such as lawyers and (defanged) vampires.

---

[4] Quotations from "Interview with Joss Whedon and David Boreanaz," *Buffy the Vampire Slayer: The Complete First Season on DVD*, Region 1 edition, Disc 1; Ginia Bellafante and Jeanne McDowell, "Bewitching Teen Heroines," *Time* (5 May 1997), pp. 82–84.

[5] Quotations from Frances H. Early, "Staking Her Claim: 'Buffy the Vampire Slayer' as Transgressive Woman Warrior," *Journal of Popular Culture* 35 (2001), pp. 11–27; and A. Susan Owen, "Vampires, Postmodernity, and Postfeminism: Buffy the Vampire Slayer," *Journal of Popular Film and Television* 27 (1999), p. 25.

[6] For examples, see Garrett Epps, "Can Buffy's Brilliance Last?," *The American Prospect* (28 January 2002); Zoe Williams, "The Lady and the Vamp: A Buff's Guide to Buffy," *Guardian* (London, 17 November 2001), www.guardian.co.uk/weekend/story/0,3605,593851,00.html; and the numerous articles on *BtVS* by Joyce Millman and Stephanie Zacharek at www.salon.com.

What's more surprising than the liberal endorsements is the fact that *BtVS* seems to resonate with many conservatives, too. The *National Review* has praised it as one of the "most morally serious" shows on television and, during the early seasons, conservatives delighted in the satire of psychobabbling liberal parents and ineffectual educators as well as the (very) occasional shots at political correctness. Buffy to Angel: "You're a vampire. Oh, I'm sorry, was that an offensive term? Should I say 'undead American'?" ("When She Was Bad")[7]

The conservative reading of *BtVS* is limited, and possibly ruled out, by the show's sharp divergences from the traditional, heterosexual, Judeo-Christian cultural norms that modern conservatives so strenuously advocate. The attitude toward Christianity is dismissive, encapsulated by the moment in "Triangle" when Buffy, looking to swear off men, visits a convent but quickly encounters a stumbling block: "Do you have to be, like, super-religious?" This stance and many other features of Buffyverse life, from the nonexistence of happy, intact nuclear families to the rampant premarital sex (in varieties that have included lesbian, oral, sadomasochistic, interracial, and interspecies), make it quite understandable that many or most conservative Christians regard *BtVS* as, in *Christianity Today*'s words, "Must Flee TV." The Parents' Television Council, a conservative media watchdog group, has consistently placed *BtVS* high on its annual list of "worst shows for families," and rated it the very worst show for 2001–2002.[8]

The distance between *BtVS* and conservative politics also can also be seen in the show's only explicit depiction of politics, the

---

[7] For conservative readings, see Jonah Goldberg, "Buffy, the U.N. Slayer," *Washington Times* (25 September 2002); Chandler Rosenberger, "Morality Tale . . . From the Crypt: Buffy the Vampire Slayer Is One of TV's Most Morally Serious Shows," *National Review Online* (26–28 May 2001), www.nationalreview. com/weekend/television-rosenberger052601.shtml; Alex Strachan, "An Old-fashioned Girl: In Her Own Sweet Way, Buffy the Vampire Slayer Drives a Stake through TV's PC Heart," *Vancouver Sun* (20 November 1999), final edition, p. E22; Brian Appleyard, "A Teenager to Sink Your Teeth Into," *Sunday Times* (London, 10 December 2000).

[8] Ted Olsen, "Buffy's Religion," *Christianity Today* (8 July 2002), p. 10; Parents' Television Council, "Top 10 Best and Worst Shows on Network TV," www. parentstv.org/PTC/publications/reports/top10bestandworst/main.asp.

Season Three arc centering on Sunnydale Mayor (and demon wannabe) Richard Wilkins, an obviously conservative Big Bad. As a smarmy gladhander, in office for a century and secretly mortgaged to the darkest forces imaginable, the Mayor character embodied a common stereotype of all modern American professional politicians. Yet his Fifties-sitcom-dad demeanor and vocal commitment to clean living and family values indicated that he was no permissive liberal. In a sly commentary on the political ruthlessness lurking behind the smiles and prayers of many a "compassionate conservative," the Mayor's nastiest threats were often linked with goofily prudish advice, as when he told his henchmen to "watch the swearing" after instructing them to kill Buffy's graduating class quickly and brutally ("Graduation Day, Part Two"). He also lectured Buffy and Angel on the Middle American virtues of civility, foresight, and personal responsibility while threatening Willow with evisceration: "You kids, you don't like to think about the future, don't like to plan; but unless you want Faith to gut your friend like a sea bass, you'll show a little respect for your elders" ("Choices").

Buffy the Revolutionist

> Oz: I'd call that a radical interpretation of the text. ("Doppelgängland")

More than one writer has detected radical or even Marxist tendencies in *BtVS* and *Angel* that go beyond Hollywood liberal pieties about tolerance and sexual freedom. Unsurprisingly, of the three major sets of commentators, self-consciously radical academics have been more likely to take this tack than entertainment journalists or fans. Yet it requires no great feats of exegesis to see what they mean.[9]

---

[9] The examples include Owen, "Vampires, Postmodernity, and Postfeminism"; Brian Wall and Michael Zyrd, "Vampire Dialectics: Knowledge, Institutions, and Labour," in Roz Kaveney, ed., *Reading the Vampire Slayer: An Unofficial Critical Companion to "Buffy" and "Angel"* (London: Tauris Parke, 2001), pp. 53–77; and James B. South, "'All Torment, Trouble, Wonder, and Amazement Inhabits Here': The Vicissitudes of Technology in *Buffy the Vampire Slayer*," *Journal of American and Comparative Cultures* 24 (2001), pp. 93–102.

In *BtVS* and *Angel* there is a persistent association of capitalist values—among them excessive self-interest, cut-throat competition, the accumulation of wealth, the rationalization of production, and the commodification of labor—with literal inhumanity. Following a long left-wing tradition of depicting economic exploiters as "bloodsuckers" and vampires as privileged figures exploiting a defenseless populace—like Bram Stoker's castle-dwelling nobleman, feeding off the peasants who should be under his feudal protection—the association of demonism and capitalist values is often made quite explicitly and directly.

The only really avid capitalist among the main cast members is the once and future vengeance demon Anya, whose greed and failure to master human behavior became running jokes. In "Doublemeat Palace," Anya even states her (shaky) motivation for fighting evil in narrowly capitalist terms: "Supervillains want reward without labor! To make things come easy. It's wrong! Without labor there can be no payment and vice versa! The country cannot progress!"

Globalization from Hell

When inhumans grow powerful on the show, so does capitalist excess. The hellgod Glory is depicted as an über-consumer, living in luxury and sending her scaly minions out to shop. The only things she seems to like about this dimension are the shoes ("Blood Ties"). In the alternate universe of "The Wish," the vampires' domination of Sunnydale leads directly to the industrialization of the human body. Bored with "the mindless routine of the predator," the Master introduces the vampire world to "a truly demonic concept: mass production," opening a blood factory where live humans will be transformed into a tasty, nutritious beverage. In *Angel*'s Los Angeles, capitalists of both the corporate and street-criminal variety are shown to be actual monsters whose interests are protected by the demonic law firm Wolfram and Hart.

The Buffyverse mythology identifies the essence of humanity with the capacity for non-capitalist, unselfish feelings and actions: compassion, altruism, love, and self-sacrifice. Indeed, the shows define the moral sense or conscience as the very function of the human soul and the most important thing separating humans and demons. When a human becomes a vampire, his or her soul departs, leaving behind most aspects of the original self—including memory, personality, appearance—except the conscience that restrained (or should have restrained) the former person from destroying others to serve his or her own needs. Separate a human being from his or her soul and he or she is liberated from the moral qualms and sentimental feelings that impede the ability to compete and dominate. As revealed in "Primeval," the evil plan of Professor Maggie Walsh and her demonic cyborg Adam is to create a new race of hybrids who would combine the intelligence and adaptability of humankind with the inhuman strength and killer instincts of demonkind. The first of their new warriors, Riley's former friend Forrest, sounds like a sales seminar graduate in describing his new hybridized state: "This is the best thing that ever happened to me. I'm free of all my weaknesses—my doubts."

BtVS frequently advances the idea that non-economic, altruistic values and structures are absolutely critical to the preservation of human freedom and must be protected from the selfish, aggressive forces that threaten them. The goal pursued by most of the seasonal Big Bads involved breaking down the barriers standing between the human world and the demonic ones: the forcefield keeping the Master in his underground prison, the magicks that banished pureblood demons from the Earth in prehistory ("The Harvest"), and most strikingly, the dimensional walls separating our reality from other far more horrifying ones where humanity faces some literally cutthroat competition. Angelus tried to get the Earth sucked into one of the many hells ("Becoming, Part One"), while Glory intended to use the Key (reshaped to be Buffy's sister, Dawn) "to open the gates that separate dimensions . . . all the gates" ("Spiral"). With the walls broken down, Giles explains in "The Weight of the World," "Dimensions will pour into one another . . . Reality as we know it will be destroyed, and chaos will reign on Earth." In "The Gift," we get to see a little bit of what this means. The world does not end so much as get opened up to free trade with many hellish, faraway places: A dragon suddenly cruises across the sky. An apartment building is suddenly exchanged for a nest of *Alien*-like monsters.

Allegorically, the Big Bads' schemes can be seen as nightmarish replications of the rise and globalization of capitalism. The history of capitalism has been a story of all structures blocking or impeding the free play of market forces gradually being neutralized, from physical obstacles to religious beliefs to local customs to cultural traditions to national boundaries.

In the Buffyverse, most humans can live relatively unaffected by, and ignorant of, the mighty magical forces lurking under and around their world. This is because a whole host of traditional structures and institutions (like religion and the nation-state in the real world) shelter them: the Slayers, the Watchers' Council, The Powers That Be, the magical limitations that constrain vampires and demons operating in this dimension, the dimensional boundaries themselves. The Big Bads want to knock these barriers down, and once they do, the *relatively* altruistic and communal human order would be replaced by a new *laissez-faire* regime of free competition between humans and supernatural creatures, where the only thing regulating their interactions would be raw power and the willingness to use it. In this new arena, as many *BtVS* villains have pointed out, the weaker, less aggressive, conscience-laden human race would be wiped out or become slaves or livestock. Compare this to Marx's description of the bourgeoisie's impact on traditional society and its institutions in the *Communist Manifesto*:

> The bourgeoisie, wherever it has got the upper hand, has put an end to all feudal, patriarchal, idyllic relations. It has pitilessly torn asunder the motley feudal ties that bound man to his "natural superiors," and has left no other nexus between man and man than naked self-interest, than callous "cash payment." It has drowned out the most heavenly ecstasies of religious fervor, of chivalrous enthusiasm, of philistine sentimentalism, in the icy water of egotistical calculation. It has resolved personal worth into exchange value, and in place of the numberless indefeasible chartered freedoms, has set up that single, unconscionable freedom—Free Trade. In one word, for exploitation, veiled by religious and political illusions, it has substituted naked, shameless, direct, brutal exploitation.[10]

---

[10] "Manifesto of the Communist Party," in Robert C. Tucker, ed., *The Marx-Engels Reader* (New York: Norton, 1978), p. 475.

Demonic Dependency

For orthodox Marxists, of course, the dissolution of traditional society represents progress on the road to communism. The dimensional portal-opening metaphor in *BtVS* comes much closer to the ideas of neo-Marxist "dependency" and "world-system" theorists who describe the destructive impact of intercourse between developed capitalist nations and the poorer, less developed, formerly isolated places they colonized. Such theorists, and the scholars influenced by them, cast a sympathetic eye on the less individualistic, less economically competitive traditions of tribal and peasant societies.[11]

Historians of Native American culture have been particularly eloquent on this theme. Brought into contact with the world market and European culture, Richard White writes, Indians who "had once been able to feed, clothe, and house themselves with security and comfort" and maintain political self-determination, soon found their accustomed means of subsistence impossible, their political and economic choices dictated by outsiders, their cultures rapidly and involuntarily changing, and their societies divided, impoverished, and collapsing. The evocative title of Elizabeth A.H. John's book on southwestern American Indian history captures this idea in a way that closely tracks the fiery tableaux of dimensional conversion seen in "The Gift": *Storms Brewed in Other Men's Worlds*.[12]

The heroes of *BtVS* (and *Angel*, to a slightly lesser extent) are specifically set up as champions and users of traditional, non-technological, uncommodified forms of knowledge and power. Buffy and her friends operate as an informal collective altruistically serving the common good. Beginning undercover in the high school library with funding from the Watchers' Council of

---

[11] For overviews of development theory, see Alvin Y. So, *Social Change and Development: Modernization, Dependency, and World-System Theories* (Newbury Park: Sage, 1990); Colin Leys, *The Rise and Fall of Development Theory* (London: James Currey, 1996).

[12] Richard White, *The Roots of Dependency: Subsistence, Environment, and Social Change Among the Choctaws, Pawnees, and Navajos* (Lincoln: University of Nebraska Press, 1983); Elizabeth A.H. John, *Storms Brewed in Other Men's Worlds: The Confrontation of Indians, Spanish, and French in the Southwest, 1540–1795*, second edition (Norman: University of Oklahoma Press, 1996).

England, the Scooby Gang's demon-slaying operation has moved systematically away from sanction or association with any hierarchical, bureaucratic organization, be it the police, the Watchers' Council, or the military.

Buffy herself is too absorbed with her personal life and Slayer duties to pay attention to money matters or procedural niceties. Yet even when left destitute after the death of their mother, she and Dawn angrily reject Anya's suggestion that they "start charging" for killing monsters ("You provide a valuable service to the whole community. I say, cash in" ["Flooded"]). Buffy thinks of Slaying as anything but a service to be exchanged for money: it is her calling, her destiny, and she will not have it "stripped of its halo" and converted to a form of wage labor, as Marx observed that capitalism had done to "every occupation hitherto honored and looked up to with reverent awe."[13] Angel Investigations is a more complicated case—something must be paying all those salaries and maintaining that hotel. Yet money is rarely shown changing hands, and Angel's biggest battles are clearly handled on a *pro bono* basis.

Social Banditry in Sunnydale

Armed with pointed sticks, crossbows, axes, dusty old tomes, and magic (supplemented only by Willow's plot-convenient computer hacking and the occasional rocket launcher or bomb for magically unkillable foes), Buffy and her friends are the "primitive rebels" of leftist lore and scholarship. As developed by postwar social historians such as E.J. Hobsbawm, E.P. Thompson, and George Rudé, this interpretation transforms the criminal classes of world history—the bandits, poachers, gangsters, and rioters—into proto-revolutionaries, resisting by the traditional means the forces threatening the common folk and their traditional way of life. Robin Hood, Jesse James, and the pirates thus become "social bandits" in the eyes of some historians.[14]

---

[13] "Communist Manifesto," p. 476.

[14] For examples, see E.J. Hobsbawm, *Primitive Rebels: Studies in Archaic Forms of Social Movement in the Nineteenth and Twentieth Centuries* (New York: Norton, 1965); Richard White, "Outlaw Gangs of the Middle Border: American Social Bandits," *Western Historical Quarterly* 12 (1981), pp. 387–408; E.P. Thompson, "The Moral Economy of the English Crowd in the Eighteenth

Buffy's experience with the Initiative in the second half of Season Four established her most clearly as a "primitive rebel." Buffy briefly joined this secret, demon-fighting branch of the military, even carrying a gun for one episode ("The 'I' in Team"), but it all backfired: the gun was sabotaged, and it was revealed that Professor Walsh, the Initiative leader, wanted the Slayer dead. Later discovering that Adam, the Initiative's own Frankenstein, cannot be hurt by their technology, the "young radical" Buffy ("The Yoko Factor") realizes that she can only defeat the menace with the traditional, supernatural means that are her birthright. Marching into the Initiative's lair with only her friends, a spellbook, and a magic gourd ("Primeval"), Buffy warns the facility's clueless replacement commander to butt out:

> BUFFY: This isn't your business. It's mine. You, the Initiative, the boys at the Pentagon . . . You're in way over your heads. Messing with primeval forces you've got no comprehension of.
> COLONEL McNAMARA: And you do.
> BUFFY: I'm the Slayer. You're playing on my turf.

Colonel McNamara does not listen and gets killed along with most of his men. Buffy and her friends combine their essences into a glowy-eyed super-Slayer and tear Adam's nuclear heart out.

A Revolution Will Not Be Televised: Superheroism and the Limits of Buffy's and Angel's Radicalism

> Willow: Congratulations, you're now an official capitalist running dog. ("No Place Like Home")

Unfortunately for the radical interpretation of the Buffyverse, the Slayer and her friends are "primitive rebels" in one other way. Theirs is only a piecemeal resistance rather than any sort of revolution. Viewers and heroes alike are constantly reminded that

---

Century," in *Customs in Common: Studies in Traditional Popular Culture* (New York: The New Press, 1993), pp. 185–258.

the fight can never be conclusively won, that evil will abide no matter how often it is defeated. "For us, there is no fight," explains the ghost of Holland Manners, top official of Wolfram and Hart, after Angel has killed one of their "senior partners." "We go on, no matter what. Our firm has always been here in one form or another. The Inquisition, the Khmer Rouge . . ." ("Reprise"). Though their efforts are frequently hindered by corrupt or incompetent human institutions, which they have seen to be permeated by demonic evil and its minions, the heroes have never developed any strong sense that the larger social order is unjust enough, or changeable enough, to overturn. Based on their conversations and the posters on their walls, the embattled youth of Sunnydale seem to be enthusiastic consumers of popular culture and generally seem to regard their prosperous California suburb as a place worth saving rather than one in need of revolutionizing.

Moreover, the anticapitalist themes have been balanced by other storylines that depict money-making in a far more positive light. In the *Angel* series and the post-high school *BtVS* episodes, running a small business like Angel Investigations or the Magic Box is presented as a perfectly decent and darkness-free activity if one doesn't get carried away.

At the beginning of Season Five, Whedon and company seemed to be following the uncritically procapitalist *Zeitgeist* of the late 1990s when they shifted *BtVS*'s primary setting from the university to a retail store. While investigating the latest murder of a local magic shop owner, the unemployed Giles made a startling discovery in the deceased's account books: "I had no idea the profit margin for a shop like this could be so high" ("The Real Me"). Giles eagerly went into business, and he and the other characters were rather genial about the fact that the magic supply business involves a good deal of mystification, turning miscellaneous junk into valuable commodities and deriving inflated profits from the ignorance of the clientele—the truly useful stuff was kept mostly away from the customers in a loft or behind the counter. Willow made the parodic crack quoted above as Giles burbled over his first sales. Even "Doublemeat Palace," a satire on the horrors of life on the bottom rung of the economy (and the only episode so far to get *BtVS* in hot water with the advertisers), ended with our heroine concluding that her fears of corporate conspiracy were unjustified and resigning herself to a career in burger-flipping.

The Superhero As Liberal Reformer

Finally, the standards of heroic behavior expressed and modeled on the shows hew much more closely to liberal notions of incremental reform and the rule of law, though sometimes a higher-than-institutional law, than to the radical drive for "justice now" "by any means necessary." These standards are rooted in a comic-book tradition that Joss Whedon has acknowledged as a major influence on his development as a writer and the conception of *BtVS*. Buffy and Angel are essentially superheroes, and the superhero concept has always been liberal, rather than radical, at heart.[15]

Superman originated during the New Deal years as the Liberal Reformer of Steel, punishing corrupt businessmen, exposing stock market swindles, and freeing death-row prisoners before moving on to supervillains later. Superman also pioneered the code that most costumed heroes came to live by in later years: he avoided the use of firearms, protected helpless creatures at all costs, and never killed human beings, or even allowed them to die if he could help it, no matter how great the justification. In the 1960s, Marvel's signature hero Spider-Man debuted, committing himself to the same superhero code and adopting a motto that incorporated the principles of selfless community service and the duties of the powerful to the powerless: "With great power there must also come—great responsibility."

This new liberal hero was a significant revision of the heroic model presented in older genres like the western and the hard-boiled detective story, where everyone had guns and the heroes took vengeance and killed all the time. Though much bloodied

---

[15] On the influence of comics on *BtVS*, see Christopher Golden and Nancy Holder, *The Watcher's Guide* (New York: Pocket Books, 1998), p. 242, and Whedon's introduction to Jim Krueger's graphic novel *Earth X* (New York: Marvel Comics, 2000). Whedon has actually written a number of Buffy-related comics himself, including the Dark Horse Comics series *Fray*, about a Slayer of the future, and several sections of the anthology *Tales of the Slayers* (Milwaukie, Ore.: Dark Horse Comics, 2001).

and battered, the superhero code survived in comics and comic-book films, and preserved a liberal bent, even through the vogue for cynical, violent, adult-oriented comics, often featuring murderous former villains like Wolverine, the Punisher, and Venom, that swept the industry in the 1980s and 1990s.[16]

Though both Buffy and Angel have temporarily gone dark and abandoned the superhero code, usually incurring serious repercussions, they have always come back and occasionally even vocalized the code's precepts on the shows. In "She," Angel aids Princess Jhiera's campaign to save the enslaved women of Oden Tal, but warns her not to kill any more humans who happen to get in her way. Their last exchange is a fairly classic rendition of liberal reformist vs. radical revolutionary tactics, as well as Angel's adherence to Supermanian canons of heroism:

> ANGEL: If you've vowed to protect the innocent, Jhiera—it shouldn't matter which dimension they're from.
> JHIERA: An easy sentiment, when your people are free.
> ANGEL: I'm not saying you shouldn't fight—just know I'll be here to stop you if you cross the line.

Angel fights for the oppressed, but he could never condone revolutionary bombings, shootings, or hijackings no matter how good the cause.

The most stirring endorsement of the superhero code in Buffyverse history came near the end of Whedon's "The Gift." Buffy has finally defeated Glory but cannot bring herself to execute the now defenseless human, Ben, whose body the hellgod shared. With Buffy engaged elsewhere, Giles takes it upon himself to kneel down and suffocate Ben, destroying Glory forever while preserving Buffy's liberal values: "Sooner or later, Glory will re-emerge and make Buffy pay for that mercy, and the world with her. Buffy even knows that, and still she wouldn't take a human life," Giles explains, with great admiration in his voice, to the man he is about to kill. "Because she's a hero, you see. She's not like us."

---

[16] Bradford W. Wright, *Comic Book Nation: The Transformation of Youth Culture* (Baltimore: Johns Hopkins University Press, 2001), pp. 10–13, 210–11, 262–278.

Murder, terror, and other radical or final solutions are for ordinary humans; liberalism is for heroes, who must at least model the superhuman values of mercy and altruism for the rest of us. The 2002 season premiere of *Angel* featured an actual lecture on this theme, delivered to the hero's vengeful, wayward son Connor ("Deep Down"): "Nothing in the world is the way it ought to be. It's harsh, and cruel. But that's why there's us. Champions. It doesn't matter where we come from, what we've done or suffered, or even if we make a difference. We live as though the world was what it *should* be, to show it what it *can* be." That is as clear a statement of Joss Whedon's liberal, incrementalist vision as we are likely to get.

Codex 5

You're all slaves to the television

Watching Buffy

20
Morality on Television: The Case of *Buffy the Vampire Slayer*

RICHARD GREENE and WAYNE YUEN

Buffy the Vampire Slayer (BtVS) can be viewed as a morality play: every week, Buffy and her friends fight evil in some form and in so doing make complex moral decisions. The moral principles that underwrite Buffy's relationships with her non-human counterparts can be explained with an eye toward developing a clear picture of her overall moral system.

Buffy's Seven Principles of Morality

To understand Buffy's moral system, one needs only to look at her relationships with other characters in the show. Start with Buffy's relationship with Angel (a vampire who has had his soul restored by a gypsy curse): it speaks immediately to the fact that not all vampires are evil. What makes Angel stand apart from other vampires is that he has a soul, or more specifically, that because he has a soul he has no desire to harm people (More precisely, since plenty of persons with souls do desire to harm others, perhaps the correct thing to say is that because Angel has a "good" soul he has no desire to harm people). It follows then, that Buffy slays vampires not because they are soulless or because they are vampires, but because they harm human beings.

So we can summarize Buffy's first moral principle as *Do not harm those who typically do not pose a threat to human beings.*

271

(By "typically" we mean under normal everyday circumstances. Lions, for example, under certain circumstances pose a threat to human beings, but we don't want to say that they typically pose a threat to human beings. Vampires, on the other hand, do typically pose a threat to the human citizens of Sunnydale). We can also, as a first approximation, adopt the related moral principle, namely, *One ought to stop (either by killing or by incapacitating) those who typically can or will harm other human beings.* This principle, however, stands in need of revision. In the episode "Ted," Buffy kills Ted, believing him to be a human being, because he poses a direct threat to her mother and herself. Even though Ted poses a threat that is equal in severity to the threat posed by vampires (albeit the threat is different in kind), Buffy is despondent when she thinks that she has actually killed a human being, and she is subsequently relieved when she discovers that Ted is an android and not a human. Thus our second principle becomes *One ought to stop (by killing or incapacitating) all non-humans that typically can or will harm other human beings.*

Further evidence that Buffy is operating in accordance with something akin to this principle is seen in the episode "Bad Girls," in which Faith (another slayer) kills one of the human henchmen of the evil town Mayor. Despite the fact that the human poses a significant danger to humans (he is assisting the Mayor, who is attempting to become an omnipotent demon), Buffy admonishes Faith for killing a human. Moreover, Faith is unable to reconcile the fact that she, up to that point, a protector of humans, has actually killed a human. This event drives Faith to become a rogue slayer in the employ of the forces of evil. Humans, therefore, have a special status in Buffy's moral system. This special status makes them exempt from being seriously harmed by her, even if they do harm others. (A noteworthy exception to the exemption—Giles's killing of Ben—will be discussed below.) This status is partially explained in the episode "Villains." When Dawn and Xander express the view that Willow's killing Warren (out of revenge for Tara's death) would not be a bad thing, Buffy responds that Willow does not have the right to take a human life, and that their actions involving relations with the human world are bound by human laws. Buffy later explains that human-to-human evils are beyond the duties of the Slayer.

A third moral principle comes into play when the evil vampire Spike becomes a permanent character: *Do not harm those who pose no immediate threat.* When The Initiative (a top secret branch of the U.S. Military which does research and experiments on demons and vampires) embeds a chip in Spike's head to prevent him from hurting humans, a new dynamic in the relationship between Buffy and Spike is created. There are several reasons why Buffy should eliminate Spike while he is incapacitated. First, at least on those occasions when he is not in love with her, Spike desires to kill Buffy, and should he get the chip removed he would be in a good position to do so; second, he can still harm her in a variety of ways, as illustrated when he aids Adam (an Initiative-created cybernetic human-demon soldier which could not be controlled) in causing dissension among Buffy and her friends. Buffy has no reason to believe that Spike will not take advantage of any situation in which he can harm her.

So why doesn't Buffy spike Spike? There appear to be three moral factors working in Spike's favor. First, in his incapacitated state, there can be no "fair" fight between him and Buffy. This factor also exemplifies another reason why Buffy does not harm humans; in general, they are not a fair match against her superior strength (although the members of the Initiative are, because of their mechanically and drug-enhanced bodies). On numerous occasions, members of Buffy's team reassure Spike that it would be wrong to harm him while he is in this state. Our heroes are operating on the general moral principle that defenseless people and animals should not be harmed. Giles summarizes this in the episode "Something Blue," when he says, "Look, look, Spike . . . we have no intention of killing a harmless . . . uh, creature." Thus the second factor that serves to protect Spike is the principle that potentially harmful agents should not be harmed provided that they can be controlled. This principle is best illustrated by the case of Oz (a werewolf who is a contributing member of Team Buffy when not in wolf form). Being a werewolf, Oz has an instinct to hurt people while he is a wolf. However, since locking him up during a full moon can largely control him, more permanent forms of control are not required. Similarly, the chip in Spike's head functions as his "prison."

While both factors serve to keep Spike alive, there remains a compelling reason for killing him, namely, that he still poses a threat. So one wonders why Buffy doesn't, in fact, spike Spike. An important reason is that Spike has utility. Spike has access to information about demon and vampire activity in the area, which at times proves to be invaluable to Buffy. In return for this information, Buffy and company provide money, occasional protection from The Initiative, a place to stay, or sometimes even butcher's blood. Spike has also proven helpful in a number of episodes fighting demons and vampires alongside Buffy, since his chip allows him the freedom to harm non-humans, and humans that have been raised from the dead. Spike has also proven to be helpful at times as a protector and caretaker of Joyce and Dawn. Without this utility, given the long-term threat he poses, killing Spike would be just as permissible as killing a rabid dog that has been temporarily restrained.

Buffy's relationship with Spike, however, is not always one of *quid pro quo*. In a number of episodes Buffy and the gang have blackmailed Spike for information, while appearing to derive a great deal of pleasure from doing so. Whereas blackmailing Spike appears to raise no moral concerns for our heroes, blackmailing humans is considered to be both intuitively morally impermissible and inconsistent with Immanuel Kant's formula of humanity: *Act in such a way that you treat humanity, whether in your own person or in the person of another, always at the same time as an end and never as a means.*[1] This further illustrates the difference in status between humans and non-humans in Buffy's moral reasoning. Thus, in addition to the principles stated above, the following moral principles emerge: 4) *No harm should be done to those who don't harm humans*; 5) *Unless there is some urgent pressing matter, fairness should be taken into account*; 6) *Those that do harm humans but can be controlled should be controlled*; 7) *When the benefits of a good opportunity outweigh the risks of a dangerous situation, the good should be attempted.*

---

[1] Immanuel Kant, *Groundwork of the Metaphysics of Morals*, §429, translated by Mary J. Gregor (Cambridge: Cambridge University Press, 1988).

Testing Buffy's Moral Principles

The above principles seem intuitively sound, but how applicable are they to the real world? After all, they are derived from a fictional television show about demons and vampires. Although the majority of people in the real world (perhaps all) never slay demons and vampires, *BtVS* nevertheless has pedagogical value. Through allegorical depictions of ethical situations, it reflects the complexity of the moral world in which we live.

Buffy's sophisticated moral universe does not assume that difficult decisions can be made without consequences. Unlike many other television shows, decisions made in the show affect subsequent episodes, and sometimes permanently change the characters in the show; the moral universe is not simplified in order to allow appropriate decisions whose repercussions fully unfurl within an hour. Moreover, the show does not ignore competing value systems. Most notably, the Initiative's "institutional" ethics is presented, at least nominally, as a viable ethical alternative. The Initiative's ethics seem to follow the standard military guidelines: avoid harm to civilians, while anything identified as an enemy may be eliminated or captured. In this case, it is especially easy to identify enemies: they are demons and vampires. But historically this "institutional" ethic has led to questionable activities, such as the U.S. internment of Japanese during World War II. And although Buffy's moral decisions tend to be the most favorably portrayed in the show, the Initiative also presents compelling arguments for some of their actions.

In the episode "The Gift," the natural tension that exists between consequentialist and deontological moral theories is highlighted. Buffy has an opportunity to kill Glory (a god who inhabits the body of a human—Ben) by killing Ben. Buffy refrains as doing so would violate her duty not to harm humans. Giles, on the other hand, kills Ben by strangling him while explaining that he does not have the luxury of adopting a nonconsequentialist position. Buffy's decision not to kill Ben was made as a result of following certain principles of fairness and respect of Ben's own autonomy, while Giles decides that the threat that Glory presents outweighs the respect due to Ben's autonomy.

Willow also deviates from Buffy's values when she delivers vigilante justice to Warren and attempts to do the same to

Jonathan and Andrew ("Villains"). Buffy's value system is not without flaws. No character in the show is portrayed as perfect, as each of the characters has been morally faulted at one time or another. For example when Buffy kills Ted, since at the time she believes that he is human, her causing him to fall down the stairs is considered to be morally objectionable.

Further evidence that *BtVS* is reflective of real-life ethical situations can be adduced from various quotidian circumstances in which the characters find themselves. A dominant conceit of the show is that Buffy is an extraordinarily (even supernaturally) gifted teenage girl who nevertheless maintains her "normal" teenage personality and concerns. Teenagers often find themselves having to weigh their moral obligations (as well as other obligations) against their desire to fit in, be cool, be accepted, and feel normal. Buffy, on more than one occasion, opts to put her moral responsibilities aside in order to pursue a "normal" teenage lifestyle, often with negative consequences. Similarly, the largely ineffectual Spike, whose instincts incline toward mischief and violence, finds that he must co-exist with and occasionally even assist people he dislikes (for example, Buffy and the "Scooby Gang," as they mockingly refer to themselves) in order to survive. Again, the problem of working with people whose sensibilities are different from, even antithetical to, our own is part of our everyday lives. Xander must deal on a regular basis with feelings of inadequacy caused by two factors. First, he has no remarkable personal skills (for much of the series he lived in his parents' basement). On occasion he has had to drive an ice cream truck to make money, and he is physically uncoordinated as we see in his slap-fight with the vampire Harmony in the episode "The Harsh Light of Day." Second, those around him are not only skilled, but have supernatural abilities: Buffy and Faith are slayers, Willow is a practicing witch, his girlfriend Anya is a recovering demon, Giles at times is able to use borrowed magic, and Oz is a guitarist in a popular alternative rock band. It goes without saying that young people routinely experience insecurities like Xander's, albeit generally in less fanciful contexts.

BtVS also explores the moral dimension of being a social animal. What does one do when one's social obligations conflict with one's occupation, or birthright as the case may be? Early in the show, the tensions between the father-figure Giles and Buffy exemplified such conflicts; later Buffy struggles with them internally. How should a person act when he discovers that his girlfriend has been in love with a person he finds morally reprehensible? Riley Finn struggles with this question when he discovers that Buffy had been romantically involved with the vampire Angel. Similarly, Xander (who has had a crush on Buffy) is troubled by Buffy's involvement with Spike and had earlier been troubled by her relationship with Angel.

In addition to the above considerations *BtVS* addresses a number of other moral issues that bear on issues that confront the real world. For example, parallels can be drawn between the moral status of demons and the moral status of animals in our society, thus raising important questions regarding animal rights (the unexplored evils of kitten poker notwithstanding). Demons are routinely treated as means to an end—roughed up for information, or used to run interference. Thus, it is clear that in Buffy's moral universe in many cases non-humans enter the moral sphere only to the extent that they have utility, and more importantly their moral status does not grant them rights and privileges (unless via some agreement to that effect). Interestingly, on this matter, Buffy and the gang are not acting in accordance with Kant's Formula of Humanity as many demons (such as Doyle, Angel's demon sidekick, and Angel himself) are rational creatures (whatever their other shortcomings may be), and not merely animals. *BtVS* also touches on the related questions of precisely what makes a person bad, and how we ought to treat those who differ from us. Drug use and the issues it raises are paralleled in Season Six with Willow's "addiction" to magicks.

Shades of Moral Complexity in TV Shows

If we look at various types of television programs that in one way or another present moral situations or depict persons as moral agents, we can imagine these programs as existing along a spectrum of complexity, with varying degrees of reflexivity and allowance for shades of moral ambiguity.

On one end of the spectrum we might expect to find shows like *Full House*, *Touched by an Angel*, *Seventh Heaven*, and *Highway to Heaven*—shows that exemplify what we call "after-school special" morality. On programs like these, moral situations are presented as relatively clear-cut instances of right and wrong where it only remains for characters to find their way to a patently correct answer. Typically, good characters are the protagonists, and will choose to do the "right" thing (recognizing it as such); bad characters are the antagonists, and will invariably choose to do the "wrong" thing (except when a central theme of the show is their conversion from an erroneous moral position to an ethically correct position). Good characters are generally rewarded for their virtuous actions, and bad characters are punished for their selfishness and malice.

A typical scenario might be one in which a teenager is tempted to smoke marijuana in order to fit in with his peers, but comes to realize the folly of such a course of action. He is "rewarded" by landing a date with the head cheerleader, who as it turns out thinks that "drugs are bogus," while the pot-smokers end up in an automobile accident. The pedagogical efficacy of these shows lies chiefly in their potential for instilling productive values in the very young or in persons with limited cognitive ability. A key element in Aristotelian moral philosophy[2] is the claim that in order to achieve *eudaimonia* (roughly, "happiness"), one must develop proper moral habits well before one can engage in proper moral reasoning; the shows mentioned above aim to satisfy this requirement by leading viewers through rote motions of ethical indoctrination, with little or no room for interpretation.

A second category of moral programming, slightly further along the spectrum of complexity, exemplifies what we call "culpable clown morality." Shows in this category—*All in the Family, The Jeffersons, Married with Children*, and *Just Shoot Me*—operate along the lines of classical satire, lampooning recognizable "types" who appear as ridiculous by virtue of their selfish, crude, or prejudiced social attitudes. Such shows exhibit an increased level of sophistication over shows in the first category in that their protagonists are often weak moral agents, and in that it is often this very weakness that makes the characters endearing or at least sympathetic on some level. For example, the character of Archie Bunker on *All in the Family* is

---

[2] See Aristotle, *Nicomachean Ethics*, Book II, translated by Terence Irwin (Indianapolis: Hackett, 1985).

on one level a reprehensible bigot who makes slurs against various ethnic, religious, and social groups (as well as against women); on another level, he is a loveable father figure whose shortcomings serve to enhance his all-too-human fallibility. Moreover, characters like Bunker (or even the more absurdly degraded Al Bundy on *Married with Children*) are not fully responsible for their shortcomings, as they are presented as subjects within an ideological system that promotes such attitudes, and in which they are ultimately victims to the same or a greater extent as the persons or groups they denigrate. The pedagogical thrust of shows like these presumes a viewer with a more advanced moral awareness than those at whom the "after-school special" programs are directed: this viewer has developed the ability to make moral judgments, and (it is hoped) may recognize his or her own shortcomings in the satirical mirror held up by the buffoon-figure, and accordingly amend his or her behavior.

Related in a morally relevant way to "culpable clown" shows are voyeuristic "realistic" shows such as *The Real World*, *Survivor*, *Road Rules*, and *Big Brother*. These shows are not written with morality *per se* in mind (for that matter they are not written at all); rather they are constructed in such a way as to place persons with conflicting personality types into stressful and somewhat claustrophobic circumstances. The result is always the same: at least some of the persons on the program behave in bad ways (for example, resorting to name calling, back-stabbing, scheming to have the person or persons with whom they are at odds removed from the situation, rallying support against that person with the others on the show). Again, the limited pedagogical value of "reality" shows is that they can teach the reflective and somewhat morally sophisticated agent something about him or herself. On the one hand, the fact that these shows actually depict real life (to some extent) may increase their pedagogical force over that of "culpable clown" programs. On the other hand, this type of show suffers from the shortcoming that they offer no guidance for moral decision-making. One might identify with an unethical agent to some degree or recognize bad properties in oneself, but one is not offered an alternative way of behaving, or worse, that the unethical agent is rewarded with a million dollars; whereas with "culpable clown" programming there is typically another equally sympathetic character presenting an alternative "correct" course of action.

A third category of moral programming, again moving further along the spectrum of complexity, exemplifies what we call "*faux* realistic morality." Shows in this category— *ER*, *Chicago Hope*, *NYPD Blue*, and *Law and Order*—operate by appearing to present complex moral dilemmas from a detached objective viewpoint, thus claiming a sense of moral authority while retaining a non-committal stance with respect to resolving tough moral dilemmas. The veneer of realism absorbs the audience but fails to deliver any actual moral guidance; morality is merely used to generate dramatic tension. Once the dramatic tension has been relieved the focus on the moral issue tends to vanish. One virtue of these shows is that the moral dilemmas they depict are not simple cases composed of clear-cut instances of right and wrong; rather, they are often "no-win" situations in which every alternative has both an upside and a downside, as is the case with many real-life moral dilemmas. A typical scenario might involve a physician who must choose to violate hospital policy or perhaps the physician's code of ethics in order to save someone's life (perhaps by using a treatment procedure that has not been approved for use). The moral and dramatic tensions are intertwined as both sides of the issue are presented and argued for by sympathetic characters on the show. The pedagogical value of these shows is that they provide us with a good sense of the varieties of tough ethical choices with which one might be confronted.

The Moral Sophistication of
Buffy the Vampire Slayer

BtVS, by contrast, exemplifies the chief pedagogical virtues of the above categories of moral programming while avoiding the shortcomings of each. While "*faux* reality" shows raise moral concerns in order to create dramatic tension, *BtVS* appears to consciously "take on" moral issues for their own sake, occasionally laughing at itself in the process, as we see in the episode "Who Are You?" when Faith inhabits Buffy's body (and vice versa). Here Faith practices impersonating Buffy in front of the mirror by saying, "You can't do that—it's *wrong*. You can't do that because it's naughty. Because it's wrong. Because it's wrong. You can't do that. It's wrong."

BtVS provides us with a vast array of moral dilemmas ranging in complexity and sophistication from the clear-cut cases of the "after-school special" program to the no-win situation of the "*faux* realistic" program, and is, thus, reflective of the type of moral situations that confront us in real life. *BtVS*, however, goes further than these shows by taking a sophisticated moral stand on complex moral issues. In most cases the stand that Buffy and company take is the intuitively correct stand, but *BtVS* doesn't rest on intuition alone; rather, and this is the show's greatest virtue with respect to issues of morality, it supports the stand it takes by clever use of allegory and by appeal to general moral principles—a necessary feature of sound moral reasoning.[3]

---

[3] We would like to thank Kasey Silem Mohammad for helpful comments on an earlier version of this chapter. An earlier version of this chapter appeared in *Slayage* 2, www.slayage.tv (March 2001).

21

High School Is Hell: Metaphor Made Literal in *Buffy the Vampire Slayer*

TRACY LITTLE

"High School is Hell!" "My boyfriend is a monster!" "I feel invisible!" "My mother is just clueless!" "I would kill to get on the cheerleading squad!" "After we slept together he became a totally different person"—All common metaphors spoken among today's youth. Such lines speak to the complexities faced by teenagers in today's culture. We recognize them for what they are, just metaphors, but sometimes the metaphor is more the reality than the fiction.

Today's teens live in a world where their classmates plot their murders, where the threat of gun violence is always present, where there is a high rate of sexually transmitted diseases, date-rape, and stalking. Now step into the world of *Buffy the Vampire Slayer* (*BtVS*)—here you will find that the monsters under your bed at night are real, that there actually are demons lurking outside your bedroom window. Also, more often than not it's the teens and young adults of the Buffyverse who see this reality for what it is, and it's the adults who are often the ones existing in a collective state of denial. Here we find the metaphors of our contemporary fears played out and made literal through the deliberate efforts of the show's writers and creator Joss Whedon. In Sunnydale, high school is not just hell; it sits on top of a "Hellmouth." In Sunnydale one does not fear having a monster for a boyfriend; werewolves and vampires are date material. In Sunnydale the lunch lady really is trying to poison the cafeteria food, and people really do kill to get on the cheerleading squad.

From a philosophical and sociological perspective the literal use of such metaphors serve to represent the fears present among today's teens and young adults growing up in a post-industrial world. Such metaphors taken to their literal extreme were the driving force behind many of the early episodes of *BtVS*. Here the "monster of the week" could stand in for themes like fear of relationship violence, feelings of low self-esteem, teenage lust and heartbreak, and giving in to strong social pressure. This chapter explores how the metaphors of high school life help to build and construct the dialogue, plot, and themes of *BtVS*. While metaphor is richly present in each season of the series, we shall focus on how metaphor is used during the first three seasons, that is, the high-school years.

Researchers argue that as the fears and threats in a society change, so does the way that we represent such fears and threats as a culture. A new set of norms is often required to address and respond to these fears and threats, as well as to allow for the development of a common frame of reference and understanding. Metaphors are often utilized in this way because they allow us to communicate about events, fears, and emotions that may not yet be understood fully by members of a society. Thus, metaphor serves as a way to discuss topics for which we do not yet have a language, or for which our vocabulary cannot reach in a one-dimensional way. Through making a comparison to something else, metaphor creates layered dimensions of understanding by which the speaker and the listener can better communicate and through which a level of emotional or philosophical understanding can be reached that would not be possible with a straight description of the situation or feeling. Speaking of language, metaphor, and the postmodern reality, Rosenthal holds:

> What can be said operates within the limits of the already said. Instead of the struggle for coherent reference points of modernist identity, postmodernism's "nowness" suggests that identity is just a set of stories that we tell ourselves about who we are and that these stories are thoroughly permeated by all the stories that we've absorbed about who we can be.[1]

---

[1] Michael Rosenthal, "What was Postmodernism?" *Socialist Review* 22 (1992), p 91.

Metaphor has the capacity to get at this reality or identity by calling upon common references, and placing these references in a new context. The writers and producers of *BtVS* have utilized this approach not just as an effective story-line motivator, but also as a valid way to appeal to viewers on several levels. In this context, such metaphors have the capacity to help viewers put their own fears and emotions into perspective, deal with such fears and emotions in a more effective way, to provide a point of comparison with the reality of the viewer and that of the show, to recognize that the fears and the emotions played out by the show's characters may be similar to their own, and, finally, to legitimize the feelings of the viewer. The complex nature of such metaphors also allows for multiple interpretations on the part of the viewer, providing the viewer with a means of agency for interacting with the show on a deeply personal level.

Of Monsters and Metaphor

The use of metaphor in the horror genre is by no means a new one. In fact, writers of classic horror fiction have commonly utilized metaphor as a means to address larger social issues— issues that, for political or emotional reasons, could not be written about in a straightforward manner, or would not have had the same philosophical impact on the audience without the underlying metaphor. Metaphors in horror have often been used as an "Aha!" kind of experience. For example, when one figures out that Mary Shelley's *Frankenstein* is a treatise about the impending changes involved with nineteenth-century fears of the industrial revolution and science, the story takes on a different character, becoming infused with greater philosophical meaning. Indeed, stories of vampires have long stood as metaphors for the social drain of work and age, while the werewolf has represented the metaphor of the beast within, and the zombie can signify the fear of losing one's mental faculties.

Folklorists have noted that local beliefs around the world of demons, monsters, and vampires are representations of the collective fears of a culture, often speaking to the reality of an incomplete understanding of the epidemiology of a disease or the decomposition process. When placed in a cultural framework of ancestor observances and spirits, we see the emergence of our monsters: the vampire, the zombie, the ghoul. Folklorists make the observation that certain stories about vampires in particular may have some basis in reality, as the process of decomposition would often appear to show bodies with blood on their lips and the appearance of long fingernails or other signs of growth.[2] Other folktales, such as *Cinderella* and *Snow White*, speak equally to the horrors of social stratification. Anthropologists have noted that the myths of zombies in Haiti may relate to the actual use of powdered blowfish in zombie powder that may in some cases cause the slowing of the processes of the central nervous system, so that the person appear dead, only to "come back to life" later.[3]

Does this mean that at some level, the metaphors are more real than we first expected and that there is some truth behind the myth? Might it be that truth is scarier than all the collective monsters put together? From the perspective of the horror genre that often seems to be the point, and that also seems to be part of the point in the "Buffyverse" as well. Xander clearly alludes to this idea in "Gingerbread" during the following exchange with Oz:

XANDER: Whoa! Whoa! I'm still spinning on this whole fairy tales are real thing.
Oz: So what do we do?
XANDER: I don't know about you, but I'm gonna go trade my cow in for some beans. No one else is seeing the funny here.

The way that metaphor is utilized in *BtVS* takes on a new and more postmodern twist, however, than that employed in classic horror or folklore. In the classic horror genre the metaphors are often moving in only one direction. That is, they are written as

---

[2] This theory is discussed in several texts on Vampire Folklore. See Paul Barber, *Vampires, Burials and Death: Folklore and Reality* (New Haven: Yale University Press, 1990), for a thorough discussion.

[3] The connection between Haiti's zombies and the ingredients of the "zombie powder" was first explored by anthropologist Wade Davis. For an overview of Davis's discoveries see Gino Del Guercio's, "The Secrets of Haiti's Living Dead", originally published in *Harvard Magazine* (January–February 1986), and republished in *Annual Editions: Anthropology 2000–2001* (Guilford: Dushkin, 2001), edited by Elvio Angeloni.

fiction that represents something else. In Mary Shelley's *Frankenstein* the story unfolds with Dr. Frankenstein's creation of a monster made from the parts of deceased humans and through scientific intervention—given life. The fictional story points to the potential of science to overstep its boundaries and create something that cannot be controlled. By contrast, in the Buffyverse the writers begin with the idea that teens struggle with social pressures, violence, and other social horrors. They then take those metaphors, used to speak about the realities of life, and make them real. Finally the viewers are left with a show where the characters' worst horrors are not just the monsters they are fighting but the grim reality of such ultimate high-school horrors as parent-teacher night, not having a date for the prom, being made fun of in class, and not getting a spot on the cheerleading team.

Thus the metaphor is made literal—high school really is hell—but that is not the worst thing about high school for Buffy and her friends. What this procedure serves to do is to take the metaphor further than simple correspondence. While fighting demons and the forces of evil is by no means easy for Buffy and her friends, it is by no means the toughest problem that they have to deal with. In this sense the metaphor has the ability to say the unsayable, thus haunting us with the idea that the metaphor and the reality may not really be that far apart. Metaphor thus embodies Baudrillard's concept of the simulacra: the idea that the copy—in this case the metaphor—is more real than the original. As Powell explains:

> For Baudrillard one of the characteristics of postmodern society is that we are all similarly entranced by surfing the simulacra. In the universe of Hollywood, Pop Art, TV, cyberblitz and the dazzling spectacle of the mediascape—signs and images no longer bear any correspondence to the "real" world, but create their own hyperreality—an order of representation that is not the unreal, but has replaced reality and is more than real, more real than real . . . These hyperreal worlds are presented as imaginary only to lead us to believe that the rest of Los Angeles and America are real. But they are not. They too are hyperreal—pure simulacrum.[4]

---

[4] Jim Powell, *Postmodernism for Beginners*, (New York: Writers and Readers, 1998), p. 58.

The writers and creator of *BtVS* have done just that: taken what seems unreal and made it more real than the real. In Buffy's world, High School really is Hell, but isn't it that way for everybody?

On the Irony of Metaphor

The idea that fairytales and other supposedly mythical monsters actually exist continues as a point of irony throughout the series. Characters often call upon such irony to make that observation: "Yeah, he's some kind of demon looking for an all-powerful thingimibob and I've got to stop him before unholy havoc's unleashed and it's another Tuesday night in Sunnydale" ("Revelations"). Or, consider Oz and Willow discussing a spell:

> WILLOW: Arr! This is so frustrating!
> Oz: Nothing useful?
> WILLOW: No, it's great. If we want to make ferns invisible or communicate with shrimp, I've got the goods right here.
> Oz: Our lives are different than other peoples. ("Graduation Day, Part One")

The irony in such remarks lies in their reflexive nature: the ability to look at the situation from the point of view of others outside the Buffyverse, that is, a world in which demons and the Hellmouth do not exist.

The idea that the monsters that Buffy and her friends are fighting are not necessarily the worst of their worries shows the new dimension of metaphor present in the show. The lines between metaphor, reality, and irony are so blurred that it is difficult to sort out which is which. Giles make this clear as he and Buffy discuss test scores:

> BUFFY: She saw these scores and her head spun around and exploded.
> GILES: I've been on the Hellmouth too long. That was metaphorical, yes? ("Lovers Walk")

Rarely do the writers of the show include metaphor that in some way do not have such an ironic twist. One example is the episode "Earshot" in which Buffy, accidentally infused with the power to hear the thoughts of others, overhears someone say, "This time tomorrow, I will kill them all." Upon discovering that there is a student with a rifle in the school clock tower, the conclusion seems obvious, and her efforts become focused on stopping the impending school shooting. As it turns out, the student, Jonathan, is only trying to kill himself, and says, "I wouldn't hurt anybody." The story displays a new plot twist as Buffy, having experienced the thoughts and the collective pain and angst of the entire study body, is able to speak to those feelings of isolation and not fitting in. By doing so she prevents the suicide from taking place. The metaphorical irony is that the true killer is the lunch lady who is putting rat poison in the cafeteria food. Thus, the school lunch really is poison. In an additional twist of irony, the episode was actually pushed back from its original airdate, as that was too close in time to an actual school shooting.

This delicate balance of irony, the literal, and metaphor infuses the show with multiple layers of meaning for the audience to dissect and identify with. Even the show's title, *Buffy the Vampire Slayer*, is an ironic tribute to the show's premise of a blond, fashion-obsessed high-school girl having the supernatural power to defeat the forces of evil that lie in the world. Many critics dismiss the show off-hand because of this intentionally campy title, but they fail to grasp this irony as setting the premise of the story and providing a context for the very real social issues that lie just beneath the surface of the show's metaphors.

In Sunnydale, one must always be careful what one wishes for as it might come true. One example occurs in "The Wish" where Cordelia Chase wishes that Buffy had never come to Sunnydale. What ensues is the harsh reality of a "bizarro world" where Xander and Willow are vampires, Giles is a nearly mentally ill librarian who did not fulfill his watcher duties, and The Master is alive and making new and better machinery to extract blood from his victims. The irony of course consists in the fact that in the wished-for world Cordelia winds up dead. Another examples occurs in "Something Blue" where Willow, after being left by her boyfriend Oz, casts a spell to make her will come true. It is her spoken metaphors, however, that come true. Here, Xander, to whom she metaphorically refers as a "demon magnet," finds himself being chased by demons. When Willow, in anger, tells Giles metaphorically that he "can't see anything,"

Giles finds himself going blind. Both of these scenarios speak to the metaphor of the evil twin in a bizarro world where things are not the way they are supposed to be.

The Evolution of the Metaphor

The idea that metaphor is a driving factor in many of the early shows is only part of the story. In fact, the show progresses from the reliance on the metaphor of the "monster of the week," representing a version of teenage angst, to using metaphor as a way to treat the weighty questions of life, death, love, friendship, and ultimate reality. Let's trace this development out over the course of the first three seasons.

Season One: Identity and Perception

In Season One we see overarching metaphors that refer to moving to a new school, finding a peer group, making friends, and coming to grips with teenage self-esteem and self-identity issues. Such themes are apparent in the first episode, as Buffy struggles to deny her Slayer heritage in the face of obvious vampire activity, and as Buffy's new friends struggle with the reality that vampires and the Hellmouth are real.

"The Pack" is pervaded by the metaphor of peer pressure and the negative influence that such unchecked peer pressure can have. In this episode Xander and several other students, who are already known for their misbehavior, are magically infused with the spirit of the hyena and in turn wreak havoc at the school. It is in fact the bullying that the "pack" engages in that makes the metaphor come close to the reality of high-school cliques. The irony is not lost on the viewer at this point, however, as Giles says to Buffy following her description of Xander's cruel behavior, "It's devastating—he's turned into a sixteen-year-old boy. Of course, you'll have to kill him."

"Witch" is another episode that deals directly with the problems of fitting in, high school cliques and the importance of certain roles. Here we find a mother taking over the body of her high-school daughter, Amy, so she can once again live her glory days of being on the high-school cheerleading squad. The plot takes a serious turn when we find that Catherine (Amy's mother in Amy's body) has also taken to using magic to knock off the other contenders for the spot on the cheerleading squad. Again, we see a case where the reality is often not so far away from the metaphor since we often receive media reports involving Olympic skaters hiring "hit-men" to rough up the competition, parents at little-league games killing each other over their children's performances, and young girls plotting each other's murders out of jealousy.

Self-esteem and self-identity are addressed most prominently in "Out of Mind, Out of Sight." In this episode, students at Sunnydale High find themselves plagued by an invisible force. Through investigation, Buffy uncovers evidence that someone is living in the school. The person is Marcie Ross whom no one seems to remember at all. Marcie, having felt invisible for so long, literally becomes invisible and in turn seeks to take her revenge on those who previously ignored her. The story points to the feelings of isolation, invisibility and getting lost in the crowd that so many teens experience on a daily basis, hitting on themes of self-esteem, self-identity, and Charles Horton Cooley's idea of the "looking-glass self." The "looking-glass self" refers to the idea that a person's sense of self is derived from their idea of how they are perceived (or in Marcie's case not perceived) by others. In Cooley's theory the self only develops through contact with others and "self and society go together as phases of a common whole. I am aware of the social groups in which I live as immediately and authentically as I am aware of myself."[5]

Season Two: Love Gone Wrong

In Season Two the metaphors of high-school love, dysfunctional relationships, and finding out that the person you love isn't who you thought they were, become the show's principle theme: love gone wrong. The strongest example occurs in the developing relationship between Buffy and Angel. Buffy and Angel meet in Season One and very soon their relationship turns to one of romance. As Giles states, "A vampire in love with the

---

[5] Charles Horton Cooley, *Human Nature and the Social Self* (New York: Schocken, 1902), reprinted in *On Self and Social Organization: Charles Horton Cooley*, edited by Hans Joachim Schubert (Chicago: University of Chicago Press, 1998), pp. 155–175.

Slayer; now that's poetic." Now, though, we start to see signs that their love is in for a rocky ride as the following exchange between Buffy and Angel hints:

ANGEL: This isn't some fairytale: When I kiss you, you don't wake up from a deep sleep and live happily ever after.
BUFFY: When you kiss me, I want to die. ("Reptile Boy")

The Season Two story arc changes its direction in the episodes "Surprise" and "Innocence." After escaping from the Judge, Buffy and Angel take refuge in each other and finally make love. The plot twist arrives in the form of the gypsy curse that had returned Angel's soul many years before. The catch is that if Angel experiences one true moment of happiness, he will once again lose his soul. He finds this one moment of happiness in Buffy's arms. When he wakes up, he has literally become a different person, the evil Angelus, providing us with an old metaphor made literal: "After we slept together, he was a different person." In the second half of Season Two, Buffy finds a new villain to fight, her past lover, Angel/Angelus. The relationship also becomes a site for the struggle between relationship and duty. Buffy is eventually forced to kill Angel in order to save the world, even after learning that his soul has once again been restored. Here the metaphor can be seen as the bittersweet end to a relationship where the person is once again viewed from the original perspective of love, but the relationship is ended nonetheless. It also contains the theme of sacrificing something you love for some higher good or purpose.

In addition to the set of metaphors surrounding Buffy and Angel, "You are not the person I though you were" is a constant metaphorical theme of the season. The new exchange student from South America turns out to be a mummy ("Inca Mummy Girl"). The cool frat boys turn out to be part of a demon-snake worshipping secret society that has to sacrifice teenage girls ("Reptile Boy"). Buffy's old friend Billy Fordham turns out to be part of a vampire-wannabe cult ("Lie to Me"). Buffy's mother's new boyfriend, Ted, turns out to be a robot with a tendency to kill his wives ("Ted"). Willow learns that Oz is a werewolf ("Phases"). Giles learns that Jenny is really a gypsy sent to keep track of Angel ("Innocence"). The Scooby Gang learns that Giles has a dark past as a rebel and a demon-summoning magician

("The Dark Age"). All of these hidden identities speak to the struggles over the self, identity and the moral ambiguity that are woven throughout the series.

Season Three: The End of the World

Season Three brings us to the senior year of Buffy and the Scooby Gang, and to those classic high-school metaphors: "Graduation is like the end of the world;" "The prom is the most important night of my life;" and "I'll just die if I don't win Homecoming Queen." Additionally, several metaphors that began in the first two seasons, such as those for love, betrayal and questions of self-esteem and identity, continue into Season Three.

The first episode of the season, "Anne," begins with Buffy, having left for Los Angeles after killing Angel and taken on a new identity, being thrown back into the world of slaying as she tries to help Lily find her missing boyfriend. It turns out that Lily's missing boyfriend has fallen victim to Ken, a demon who is disguising himself as the co-ordinator of a teen shelter. To continue his demon mining operation, Ken enslaves the kids from the shelter, has them work until they are old and used up, and then returns them to their own world to die. In Ken's hell dimension time moves differently, so what would seem to be only a few days for Ken's victims turns out to be decades in the real world. Ken and his minions subdue their teen captives by repeatedly announcing that the captives are "no one." After a time the captives lose their former identities. Ironically, once in this dimension Buffy is able to reclaim her identity that she abandoned after leaving Sunnydale. The metaphor of the loss of self-esteem and identity that so many teens go through is dealt with head on, and the underlying message is "Be yourself."

The season also takes up the challenge of dealing with two of the largest traumas involved in high school: the Prom and Graduation. Buffy and her friends are preoccupied with the prospect of having the one perfect high-school moment—the moment that all high-school students dream about, plan for, and anticipate—the Prom. Overshadowing the Prom, however, is the impending ascension of the Mayor into a demon and the student who has been training "hellhounds" to attack the night of the prom. Ironically, the episode "The Prom" points to the false hopes that are often placed upon single high-school rituals, with the subtext that even given all the anticipation and planning, everyone is being set up for an even greater let-down. Buffy overcomes even this dilemma however, by battling the hell-hounds, changing into her Prom dress and being met, to her great surprise, by Angel (who had previously been returned from his death at the end of Season Two) for a dance.

For many high-school seniors the prospect of leaving the familiar high school setting, of leaving their friends, of moving away to college or into the workforce seems like the end of the world. At Sunnydale High it is, or at least would have been, if the Mayor had had his way. Sunnydale High's graduation coincides exactly with the scheduled time of the Mayor's ascension. The only way to defeat the mayor is to go outside the Scooby Gang and recruit the entire Sunnydale High student body for the fight. The metaphor of graduation as the one last coming together of the group before they go their separate ways, along with the looming struggle they will all face to stay together as friends, is not lost here. Buffy and the students triumph in the end, resulting in the Mayor, in his form as a big snake-demon, being blown up—along with the school. The act of blowing up the high school sets the stage for the metaphor of the finality of graduation; of having no other choice but to move on to new and different paths of life. The final ironic shot of the episode is that of a Sunnydale High yearbook, tattered and lying on the ground with the inscription: "Sunnydale High '99—The Future is Ours."

In Sunnydale the monsters are sometimes more human than the humans, the metaphors are sometimes more real than the reality, and being the Slayer does not excuse one from the stresses of the teenage years or from deciding what to wear to the high-school prom. The show's writers and creator have provided the metaphors, the actors have played them out, and the task is now placed on the viewer to interpret, to legitimize, and to incorporate these into their own socially-constructed realities.

22
Feeling for Buffy:
The Girl Next Door

MICHAEL P. LEVINE and
STEVEN JAY SCHNEIDER

Where they love they do not desire and where they desire they
cannot love.

— Sigmund Freud[1]

Deflating *Buffy*

There have been numerous and diverse accounts among academics, particularly those in Film, Cultural Studies, and English, as to what it is that has made *Buffy the Vampire Slayer* (*BtVS*) such a successful television series. By "successful," most have in mind not just commercial success or high entertainment value—these can hardly be challenged—but artistic success as well. In other words, *BtVS* is often seen as—and frequently assumed to be—a show that has considerable merit beyond "mere" entertainment. The scholars in question think it is a fine and intriguing program, one that reinforces important moral messages and deals creatively with significant issues involving teenagers and their families, all the while challenging the audience on various levels.

---

[1] "On the Universal Tendency to Debasement in the Sphere of Love (Contributions to the Psychology of Love II)," *The Standard Edition of The Complete Psychological Works of Sigmund Freud*, edited and translated by J. Strachey (London: Hogarth, 1953–74 [1912]), p. 183.

According to Richard Greene and Wayne Yuen, for example, *BtVS* "is reflective of the complexity of the various moral dilemmas one encounters in the real world and the intuitions that tend to guide our moral decision making, and through clever use of allegory it takes well-supported stands on a number of pressing moral issues."[2] And as Janet K. Halfyard argues, "[Buffy's] behavior, her narrative function, and her music all indicate a subversion of behaviors, narratives, and music that are more usually a male preserve. This is, perhaps, the essence of her 'girl-power' . . . the appropriation for herself of territory (and music) that has previously been largely unavailable to women."[3]

Unfortunately, the arguments offered in support of these and similar hypotheses often consist of little more than the presentation of plot précis. Needless to say—or rather, it seems it is necessary to say—one cannot establish, for example, the show's subversion or reversal of traditional gender roles by pointing out that Buffy is the most powerful person in the diegesis (the narrative world of the film or TV show). Nor does the fact that Buffy has problems with her mother suffice to show that *BtVS* engages seriously with real-world familial issues. And so on.

For many, *BtVS* has attained—or has been reduced to—cult status. On the one hand, the "cult" label is employed to emphasize the level of passion and commitment felt towards the show by its teenage fan base. On the other hand, it is used to explain why *BtVS*, despite its commercial success and pop cultural *cachet*, has consistently failed to garner critical respect from the mainstream television establishment. As the show's creator and producer Joss Whedon notes, the negative side of being a so-called cult series is that "it does sort of put you in a niche that

---

[2] Richard Greene and Wayne Yuen, "Why Can't We Spike Spike?: Moral Themes in *Buffy the Vampire Slayer*," *Slayage* 2, www.slayage.tv (March 2001). See also Chapter 20 in this volume and Rhonda Wilcox, "'Who Died and Made Her The Boss?' Patterns of Morality in *Buffy*," in *Fighting the Forces: What's at Stake in Buffy the Vampire Slayer*, edited by Rhonda V. Wilcox and David Lavery (Lanham: Rowman and Littlefield, 2002), pp. 3–17.

[3] Janet K. Halfyard, "Love, Death, Curses and Reverses (in F minor): Music, Gender, and Identity in *Buffy the Vampire Slayer* and *Angel*." *Slayage* 4, www.slayage.tv (December 2001).

some people are just [put off by]."[4] "Cult" is less a descriptive term than a rhetorical expression loaded with a variety of personal and ideological meanings. However, we think it makes sense to ask what the term really means here, other than that *BtVS* is, for the time being at least, located in the "cult" section of the local video store.

Erroneous Theories of *Buffy's* Success

If we are going to understand the real reasons for *BtVS*'s success and why it has proven such a draw, we must first dispel some odd suppositions that appear to have gripped the show's scholars. Dismissing these strange notions will serve as an introduction to our thesis, which is that the popularity and effectiveness of *BtVS* does not rest on innovation in genre or in any other area, nor does it rest on anything remarkable (much less unique) about the series, its scripts, acting, language, or message.[5] Instead, *BtVS*'s potency, its success and influence, rest precisely, and for the most part unabashedly, on its conventional or archaic dimensions. Forget the vampire stuff: it's just window-dressing. Buffy Summers is the classic "girl next door": a paradoxically unstable object of both love and desire. She, and to a lesser extent Willow, are a voyeur's delight, perfectly-suited objects for teenagers—both boys and girls—to project and direct their narcissistic (and other) fantasies towards.

Firstly, in many respects and to a large extent *BtVS* repeatedly plays off familiar themes of jealousy, envy, and insecurity; teenage angst, desire, and sexuality; relationships between boyfriends and girlfriends, mothers and daughters, and the like. There is little, if any, substantive connection with the great gothic themes present in *Dracula, Frankenstein,* or other masterpieces of gothic literature, nor for that matter is there any serious engagement with the traditional folklore surrounding vampires. Indeed, many episodes focus on a *pot-pourri* of cartoon demons and newly-concocted denizens from other

---

[4] Allan Johnson, "Why Can't *Buffy* Creator Get Any Respect?" *Chicago Tribune* (30 September 2001).

[5] By way of contrast, see, for example, the introduction by Rhonda V. Wilcox and David Lavery to *Fighting the Forces.*

worlds rather than vampires proper. Stacey Abbott takes a different view, arguing that, while *BtVS* "has used the past four years to painstakingly dismantle and rebuild the conventions of the vampire genre and work toward gradually disembedding the vampire/slayer dichotomy from religious ritual and superstition," the show effectively subverts and modernizes the symbols present in early vampire literature, along with their significance.[6] But the symbols in question are employed in *BtVS* superficially and willy-nilly. To subvert a symbol in the ways Abbott suggests, the show's writers would have to be intent on engaging with the symbols as they occurred in their original historical and literary context. In *BtVS*, however, crucifixes, wooden stakes, and holy water are merely props and jokes that serve functional purposes in the forwarding of the serial narratives.

Secondly, despite its gothic trappings and its knowing (if not quite reflexive) use of generic conventions, there is really no horror in *BtVS* at all. This must be intentional. How many times can you watch a hand come up from a grave and be afraid? (We more or less know when a hand or something else is going to appear from a grave, and so we sit back and wait for it.) Contrasted with shows like *The Twilight Zone* and, more recently, *The X Files*, *BtVS* has a noticeable *lack* of any genuine fear-provoking devices. Episode after episode seems to rely almost wholly on such well-worn tension-generating devices as having someone walk into a room when the viewer knows in advance that something is going to happen (it always does), or having a malevolent figure suddenly dart across the frame from off-screen space. Indeed, these particular devices—intended as they are to generate the so-called "startle effect,"[7] rather than true chills, uncanniness, or horror-proper—are used in the show *ad nauseum*.

None of this is meant to deny that *BtVS* is often entertaining, amusing, gripping—even exciting and titillating. But it is little more. Primarily, *BtVS* scholars are the ones who attempt to

---

[6] Stacey Abbott, "A Little Less Ritual and a Little More Fun: The Modern Vampire in *Buffy the Vampire Slayer*," *Slayage* 2, www.slayage.tv (March 2001).

[7] See Robert Baird, "The Startle Effect: Implications for Spectator Cognition and Media Theory," *Film Quarterly* (Spring 2000), pp. 12–24

make the show out to be something else or something more than this. In our view, the basic interest in and appeal of *BtVS* lies not in its innovation or wit, let alone its moral messages about self-reliance and family. Rather, its success lies in its ability to entertain and engage viewers *psychologically*. For teenagers in particular the show evokes emotion and fantasies about love and desire—including repressed love and desire—along with other aspects of sexuality, envy, narcissistic revenge, good girl/bad girl dichotomies, and the like.

Serious Treatment of Everyday Problems?

Some scholars argue that what distinguishes *BtVS* from certain other television series is that it deals with the real everyday problems of adolescents—albeit somewhat transformed. Rhonda V. Wilcox and David Lavery, for example, claim that: "In the world of *Buffy*, by contrast [to *The Wonder Years*, *Party of Five*, and *Seventh Heaven*], the problems that teenagers face become literal monsters."[8] While it is true that *BtVS* contains storylines involving issues of authority, friendship, love, and other aspects of life that take on a special form and focus during teenage years, the idea that *BtVS* somehow takes these problems seriously, where these other programs do not, is just false. The show does not treat distinctly teenage problems seriously and only addresses these problems in superficial and stereotypical ways. *BtVS* is, for many, an enjoyable show, a fun show. But those who seek to make it something more than that—to suppose that there are important moral issues and messages to take from it; that pedagogically-speaking its principal usefulness lies in its ethical teachings; and that it delivers its teachings better than shows like *NYPD Blue*, *ER*, and so on—are simply off-base. *BtVS* is not a serious show. It can be used for serious academic purposes, but the mistake that many *BtVS* scholars make is in taking the show *itself* seriously. It can, after all, be clever, witty, and moving, be interesting, entertaining, and exciting, *without* being particularly serious—even when it purports to be, or when it touches on serious topics. Teenagers understand this. For the most part, the critical literature on *BtVS* offers a clear example of teens once again being misunderstood by well-

---

[8] Wilcox and Lavery, "Introduction," in *Fighting the Forces*, p. xix.

meaning adults who—seeking to be "hip" and trying too hard to relate—miss the boat. Wilcox, Lavery, and other *BtVS* scholars are thinking family issues and adolescent problems, when they should be thinking sex and fantastic escapism.

What is so peculiarly wrong with much of the scholarship on *BtVS* is that it misplaces the show's value and appeal. The appeal does not lie in its innovation or its intellectual or moral content or in the fact that it somehow brilliantly represents real-life teenage problems in a way that other shows simply fail to do. If Joss Whedon is in fact a "genius,"[9] this is not because he manages to do any of those things that *BtVS* scholars bizarrely claim he does by erecting their own fictions and fantasies about what is going on in the various episodes, and by being unduly impressed with some clever and entertaining dialogue. *BtVS* scholars are, in psychoanalytic parlance, repressing, projecting, and "acting out" their own fantasies in relation to the program. They love *BtVS*.

Questionable Values and Stereotypes

There is also something ironic in the claims of those who unduly praise *BtVS* as something other and more than mere entertainment, and who—like Camille Bacon-Smith—berate others who write on the show for not taking it seriously (or seriously enough).[10] The irony here is that, in attempting to bring scholarship or serious discussion to bear on *BtVS*, the scholars in question evince their own lack of understanding of, and insight into, the show, and perhaps more importantly, into the kinds of tasks, purposes, and methods that cultural theorists and others who engage with popular culture set for themselves and employ. To claim that *BtVS* is frequently entertaining, though without embodying the virtues theorists often attribute to it, does not necessarily signal one's adherence to any sharp distinction, or any distinction at all, between high and low culture. It need not reflect snobbery or even an especially good critical eye. It requires only ordinary evaluative standards.

---

[9] David Lavery, "Afterword: The Genius of Joss Whedon," in *Fighting the Forces*, pp. 251–56.

[10] Camille Bacon-Smith, "Foreword: The Color of the Dark in *Buffy the Vampire Slayer*," in *Fighting the Forces*, pp. xi–xvi.

Bacon-Smith blasts those, layman and scholars alike, who adhere to "old-think presuppositions" and see the show as pandering to a teenage market by feeding their fantasies, desires, likes and dislikes, and so forth. Though she is correct about the nature of the presuppositions, Bacon-Smith makes no attempt to challenge them seriously. Simply pointing to such presuppositions does not suffice to prove that, as applied to *BtVS* (and few would wish to apply them universally to all television programming), they are false or misleading. Many of the academics who engage with *BtVS* confuse the limited extrinsic value the show may have from a scholarly point of view—for example as the paradigm for a kind of genre—with some intrinsic merit that they allege the show (along with its writers, music, set and costume designers, and so on) must possess in order to be so successful and appealing.

Far from being subversive in any positive sense, *BtVS* in fact embodies questionable values and stereotypes on a number of levels. Thus, for example, the show does not challenge sexual and gender stereotypes (except superficially), or those about romance and true love, but instead reinforces them. Nor does it do justice to the complexity of the everyday life of adolescents, or of child-parent relations. Rather, it plays down such complexity and difficulty with its characteristically one-dimensional treatments. *BtVS* does not address serious moral problems or even accidentally, in the context of a particular plot, succeed in illustrating them. There is no indication that there is any real insight into what the moral issues are that teenagers must peculiarly face—just a bit of the emotional turmoil. The morality and morality tales in *BtVS* are on the level of cartoon morality—played out in narcissistic fantasy—just like the show's violence. How can so many of those who "study" *BtVS* be so taken in by the choreography, clever dialogue, and pretty faces—so flummoxed—as to argue for the show's worth as something other than entertainment?

One *BtVS* scholar who does *not* appear to have been seduced by the show in this way is Elyce Rae Helford. In a recent essay,[11] Helford clearly illustrates—with respect to the

---

[11] Elyce Rae Helford, "'My Emotions Give Me Power': The Containment of Girls' Anger on *Buffy the Vampire Slayer*," in *Fighting the Forces*, pp. 18–34.

expression of women's anger—just how *BtVS* reinforces, even exemplifies, rather than challenges or weakens existing cultural (here, gender) stereotypes. According to Helford, while the show succeeds in countering "the message that anger is entirely inappropriate for nice, middle-class girls," it is crucial to recognize that "not just any display of anger will do. Over the course of the first four seasons, we learn that 'proper' display means, above all, to enact anger in a contained manner through the employment of wit and humor" (p. 19). Buffy's potentially subversive (because traditionally "masculine") demonstrations of toughness are effectively undermined through cutesy jokes and one-liners, "a witty pun delivered just before she drives the stake through the vampire's heart, etc."[12]

There has been much less of the kind of self-reflective work about the nature of *BtVS* scholarship—what it is about and what it is trying to accomplish versus what it should or could be about—than there should be, or than there in fact is within various disciplines in the humanities generally as regards their objects and methods of study. It is *BtVS* scholarship that warrants study at this point, not *BtVS* itself. Those in English, Film and Television, and Cultural Studies departments would be better off investigating the nature of the unreflective and narrow critical responses to *BtVS* instead of responding to the show unreflectively, narrowly, and mistakenly themselves. As a paradigmatic instance of a superficial but immensely popular TV series, *BtVS* merits a degree of scholarly attention. This does not require that the show be regarded as anything but a well-made and fairly unremarkable instance of pop culture.

Debasing *Buffy*

It is against this background of odd and insupportable claims about the success and value of *BtVS* that we argue for the show's potency, its success and effectiveness, as resting precisely on its conventional and archaic dimensions. Stacey Abbott argues that:

---

[12] Deborah Netburn, "Media Studies Does Buffy: And Buffy, as Always, Prevails," book review, *New York Observer* (25 March 2002), p. 26.

What makes *Buffy the Vampire Slayer* such an effective television program is that the evil that she battles is not a product of an ancient world but the product of the real world itself. *Buffy* has used the past four years to painstakingly dismantle and rebuild the conventions of the vampire genre and work toward gradually disembedding the vampire/slayer dichotomy from religious ritual and superstition. The removal of religious dogma and superstition from the genre and the transformation of the vampire into a physical rather than ethereal being, acknowledges that what we describe as "evil" is a natural product of the modern world.

Contrary to this and similar views, we wish to argue that Buffy Summers, as the archetypal "girl next door" (albeit one with a helluva secret identity), embodies certain central themes of love and desire, themes that psychoanalytically understood help to explain at least one central aspect of the show's appeal. In what follows we forgo discussing other central aspects of the show's appeal, aspects that are by no means specific to *BtVS* but are part of the nature of cinematic and televisual spectatorship generally, such as the show's tendency to elicit voyeuristic, sadistic, masochistic, and narcissistic responses from its viewers.

In his 1912 essay, "On the Universal Tendency To Debasement in the Sphere of Love," Freud posits that love, in the sense of deep and abiding affection, and sexual desire were usually, although not universally, incompatible (179). He claims that the reason most men seek psychoanalytic help is because of some degree of impotency, and that this impotency is usually psychical rather than physical. He seeks to explain the rather strange fact that more often than not, even if a man is able to have sex with the person he claims to love, the sex is generally unsatisfactory in varying degrees, and often is highly unsatisfactory. Thus, he took men at their words when they claimed to be impotent with the very person they loved.

According to Freud, the reason for this is as follows: due to the incest barrier that psychically comes into play as the boy succeeds in surmounting the Oedipal complex—the desire to sleep with his mother and be like his father—the affectionate current and the sexual current that were previously united in the boy's love/desire for the mother each take a different path and must now be kept separate. As a result of the incest barrier, sex and affection must be kept apart; therefore, impotency results when, psychically speaking, the object of desire also becomes the object of love. In other words, if and when the object of desire also becomes an object of love, it will, psychically speaking, represent the mother with whom it is forbidden to have sex. Freud is thus able to conclude: "*Where they love they do not desire and where they desire they cannot love*" (183).

What are some of the other implications of Freud's essay? It purports to explain why all marital relationships or their equivalent, even when they are desirable overall, are doomed to be, to greater or lesser degrees, unsatisfactory; why "love" and "sex" (good sex that is) is more or less like trying to mix water and oil. It also explains, or presupposes, the nature of the love object: why we are attracted to the particular people we are attracted to, over and over again. (It is apparently quite common for people who have been divorced to remarry the very same person; alternatively, perhaps you know of people who have been divorced or simply get out of one relationship only to get into another one with a person who is remarkably similar to the previous partner.) Freud's essay helps to explain why—despite sometimes heroic efforts—people are so often not sexually attracted to those whom they would like to love or be sexually attracted to.

As the "girl next door"—sweet, charming, and virginal on the one hand; attractive, alluring, and always potentially (if not actually) accessible on the other—Buffy is depicted as a young woman whom one loves and holds on a pedestal but also whom one sexually desires and fantasizes about. People (notably men) should therefore be more or less impotent around her. Psychically speaking, she is, as the girl next door, not only the woman men lust after, but also, after all, our mother. Not only the male characters in the show (notably Xander, Giles, Angel, and Spike), but also male viewers will behold, or psychically represent, Buffy in this inherently unstable and conflicted way. Love, according to Freud, is anaclitic;[13]

---

[13] As Charles Rycroft explains, "Freud . . . distinguished two types of object choice: narcissistic and anaclitic. . . . *anaclitic object-choice* occurs when the choice is based on the pattern of childhood dependence on someone unlike himself . . . the implication is that the man rediscovers a mother and the woman rediscovers a father. . . . Alternatively, . . . in narcissistic object-choice the sexual choice follows a path laid down by the self-preservative instinct"

that is, it is based on the young child's original love object: the mother. The way to overcome impotency and achieve a level of sexual satisfaction with someone whom one loves, that is, feels affection for, is to psychically distance that person from the original love object (the mother) that she represents. Sexual satisfaction or potency relies on this strategy. To psychically distance oneself from the primary love object is effectively to "debase" it, to get the object off its pedestal and thereby stop "overvaluating" (Freud's term) it, in order that the sexual current not be undone or defeated by the affectionate current. This accounts for the presence of the term "debasement" in the title of Freud's 1912 essay.

Freud does not explicitly describe how one goes about achieving such debasement, and there is nothing in his account that requires the methods be even more or less univocal. As long as the methods in question do the job of psychically distancing the object of desire from the original object of affection, it doesn't really matter. The implication in Freud is that the most common method of debasement is the performing of certain sexual acts (oral and anal sex, perhaps) that one would not, at the time of those acts, perform with a woman that one regarded highly. Accordingly, women as love objects are psychically encountered or represented as either whores or Madonnas. And if a man wants to have good sex it had better be with an object psychically represented as a "whore." As Freud says, "It is possible . . . [that] the tendency so often observed in men of the highest classes of society to choose a woman of a lower class as a permanent mistress or even as a wife is nothing but a consequence of their need for a debased sexual object, to whom, psychologically, the possibility of complete satisfaction is linked" (185).

Freud does not wish to claim that sex is impossible with an object of love, and he even admits that sometimes the two may occur together. He holds that "there are only a very few educated people in whom the two currents of affection and sensuality have become properly fused; the man almost always feels

---

(*A Critical Dictionary of Psychoanalysis* [London: Penguin, 1970], p. 6). See Michael P. Levine, "Lucky in Love: Love and Emotion," in *The Analytic Freud: Philosophy and Psychoanalysis*, edited by Michael P. Levine (London: Routledge, 2000), pp. 231–258.

respect for the woman acting as a restriction on his sexual activity" (185). Nevertheless, even if sex is more or less satisfying, the satisfaction will nearly always be diminished to some extent if the sexual object is also "respected" or is an object of affection.

Freud's theory offers an explanation as to why impotency in various degrees is such a problem for men, and why men should be believed when they say that, despite the love, sex with the one they love is often unsatisfactory. The theory explains a variety of other things as well, such as why erotica, insofar as it does not debase women, can never do the job of stimulating men in the way that pornography does, insofar as the latter *does* debase women. Pornography involves an element of subjugation or debasement, if for no other reason (though there are other reasons) than that it depicts sexual acts that many men at least would like to do but their female partners do not or will not. The theory goes a long way towards illuminating the attraction of "trashy" lingerie for men and various other dynamics, intra-personal and interpersonal, of relationships. For example, Freud writes, "Psycho-analysis has shown us that when the original object of a wishful impulse has been lost as a result of repression, it is frequently represented by an endless series of substitutive objects, none of which, however, brings full satisfaction. This may explain the inconstancy in object-choice, the 'craving for stimulation' . . . which is so often a feature of the love of adults" (p. 189).

Thus far we have been discussing Freud's theory as applied to men. However, in the same essay he briefly discusses sexual satisfaction of women as well. As the "girl next door," Buffy not only embodies for others the unstable and paradoxical combination of affectionate lover and sensual object choice, she also embodies youth, sexual desire, and the virginal. According to Freud,

> In the case of women there is little sign of a need to debase their sexual object. This is no doubt connected with the absence in them as a rule of anything similar to the sexual overvaluation found in men. But their long holding back from sexuality and the lingering of their sensuality in phantasy has another important consequence for them. They are subsequently often unable to undo the connection between sensual activity and the prohibition, and prove to be psychically impotent, that is, frigid, when such activity is at last

allowed them. This is the origin of the endeavour made by many women to keep even legitimate relations secret for a while; and of the capacity of other women for normal sensation as soon as the condition of prohibition is re-established by a secret love affair: unfaithful to their husband, they are able to keep a second order of faith with their lover. The condition of forbiddenness in the erotic life of women is, I think, comparable to the need on the part of men to debase their sexual object. Both . . . aim at abolishing the psychical impotence that results from the failure of the affectionate and sensual impulses to coalesce. (p. 186)

People sometimes fool themselves into thinking that the conditions of the forbiddenness of sex for young women have been overcome, rather than loosened somewhat, in contemporary society. *BtVS* is an excellent example of a pop cultural text that belies such a view. The show reinforces, through various means (for example, parental prohibition, the ethics of slaying, severe negative consequences), the forbiddenness of sex for young women. As in so many other respects, this is a case in which *BtVS* reinforces rather than subverts or undermines traditional gender stereotypes.

Psychical Dynamics of Love and Lust

We have been building to the conclusion that there is plenty about Buffy's sex life—which is, after all, the show's predominant focal point—that illustrates central aspects of Freud's thesis and gives both young (and not so young) male and female viewers something to fixate on, fantasize about, and projectively identify with. Buffy's first sexual encounter, an encounter that is delayed week after week in Season Two, is certainly with a forbidden object: Angel. The sex between them is very special, and presumably very good, because if ever there was a "condition of forbiddenness," it is present here between a slayer and a vampire. It is network television's psychical equivalent of having sex in the backseat of a car or "dangerously" when one's parents are sleeping upstairs. Buffy's subsequent sexual encounters are simply nowhere near as good— not for Buffy and not for the show's viewers/voyeurs.

However, it should be remembered that even for Freud, "bad" sex—sex with less than full potency and desire—is often better than no sex at all, and may in fact be quite satisfying even without being completely satisfying. Buffy's sexual encounters and her perennially incipient sexuality imbue the show with an element that goes a long way towards explaining the audience's interest and the cinematic pleasure viewers get from watching week after week, season after season. It is simply the draw of schoolgirl sex—a well-known fetish that can be elucidated in no small part with reference to Freud's 1912 essay (as we have attempted to demonstrate). To reiterate our earlier point, it is not the case that *BtVS* has modernized Gothic themes, let alone subverted archaic gender stereotypes and put them in a "short skirt." *BtVS* has no serious gothic themes; it only has the skirt.

The principal theme in Freud's essay, the universal tendency towards debasement in love, can be most clearly illustrated with respect to various relationships in the show. Not counting some funky and fairly implausible late-season plot twists, Xander respects and feels ample affection for the chaste, faithful (not exactly sexy) Willow—he does not desire her. The nature of his respect for Buffy is far less straightforward. We know from the very beginning that he has the hots for her, and we also know that he holds her on a kind of pedestal. As long as such a dynamic holds, it is unlikely that there could be any satisfying sexual encounter either for them or for the audience; this is registered through the appropriately awkward handling of Xander's attempted rape of Buffy while under demonic possession in an early episode ("The Pack").

Angel, on the other hand, is no nervous high-school boy, but rather very much a man about town—a man/vampire of the world. At 240, there is necessarily going to be some aspect of debasement, even perversion, in his sexual encounters with Buffy, a sixteen-year-old virgin. Angel is at one and the same time a Prince Charming catering to a young girl's fantasies, a forbidden object, and also a "dirty old man," a horny (and vampire-ugly) wolf in romantic sheep's clothing. Meanwhile, some of the show's female characters—Drusilla especially, but also Cordelia to an extent—insofar as they are depicted as promiscuous, uninhibited, or literally demonized, are already debased. These are the girls that one has sex with according to the rules of the diegesis, not the ones who are love objects.

Consider too the brief but passionate relationship between Giles and Jenny Calendar. She is the forward one—effectively (and then quite literally, at least for a while) the bad girl—while any sexual relationship between Giles, the Watcher/father, and Buffy remains unthinkable due to the incest barrier. As we have attempted to show in the preceding paragraphs, it is precisely the existence of this barrier, one that is erected in the face of the young male child's profound sexual desire towards his own mother (as primary love object), that eventually leads to unsatisfying sex or else full-blown impotence in the lives of so many men, and that goes a long way towards accounting for the success and popularity of *BtVS*, a show in which the psychical dynamics of love and lust are hyperbolically enacted and rigorously complied with, week in and week out. It is only the *BtVS* "scholars" who fail to see the writing on the wall, and it is their loss, since it is herein that the show's most delectable pleasures lie.[14]

---

[14] Sincere thanks to Janet Fletcher, Stephanie Green, and James South for their helpful comments and suggestions on an earlier draft of this chapter.

I have a hard enough time remembering what happened last week

BtVS SEASON ONE

Episode	Airdate	Title	Writer(s)
1/1	3/10/97	"Welcome to the Hellmouth"	Joss Whedon
1/2	3/10/97	"The Harvest"	Joss Whedon
1/3	3/17/97	"Witch"	Dana Reston
1/4	3/25/97	"Teacher's Pet"	David Greenwalt
1/5	3/31/97	"Never Kill a Boy on the First Date"	Rob Des Hotel, Dean Batali
1/6	4/7/97	"The Pack"	Joe Reinkemeyer, Matt Kiene
1/7	4/14/97	"Angel"	David Greenwalt
1/8	4/28/97	"I Robot . . . You Jane"	Ashley Gable, Thomas A. Swyden
1/9	5/5/97	"The Puppet Show"	Rob Des Hotel, Dean Batali
1/10	5/12/97	"Nightmares"	David Greenwalt, Joss Whedon
1/11	5/19/97	"Out of Mind, Out of Sight"	Thomas A. Swyden, Ashley Gable, Joss Whedon
1/12	6/2/97	"Prophecy Girl"	Joss Whedon

BtVS SEASON TWO

Episode	Airdate	Title	Writer(s)
2/1	9/15/97	"When She Was Bad"	Joss Whedon
2/2	9/22/97	"Some Assembly Required"	Ty King
2/3	9/29/97	"School Hard"	David Greenwalt, Joss Whedon
2/4	10/6/97	"Inca Mummy Girl"	Matt Kiene, Joe Reinkemeyer
2/5	10/13/97	"Reptile Boy"	David Greenwalt
2/6	10/27/97	"Halloween"	Carl Ellsworth
2/7	11/3/97	"Lie to Me"	Joss Whedon
2/8	11/10/97	"The Dark Age"	Dean Batali, Rob Des Hotel
2/9	11/17/97	"What's My Line? Part One"	Howard Gordon, Marti Noxon
2/10	11/24/97	"What's My Line? Part Two"	Marti Noxon
2/11	12/8/97	"Ted"	David Greenwalt, Joss Whedon
2/12	1/12/98	"Bad Eggs"	Marti Noxon
2/13	1/19/98	"Surprise"	Marti Noxon
2/14	1/20/98	"Innocence"	Joss Whedon
2/15	1/27/98	"Phases"	Rob Des Hotel, Dean Batali
2/16	2/10/98	"Bewitched, Bothered, and Bewildered"	Marti Noxon
2/17	2/24/98	"Passion"	Ty King
2/18	3/3/98	"Killed by Death"	Rob Des Hotel, Dean Batali
2/19	4/28/98	"I Only Have Eyes for You"	Marti Noxon
2/20	5/5/98	"Go Fish"	David Fury, Elin Hampton
2/21	5/12/98	"Becoming, Part One"	Joss Whedon
2/22	5/19/98	"Becoming, Part Two"	Joss Whedon

BtVS SEASON THREE

Episode	Airdate	Title	Writer(s)
3/1	9/29/98	"Anne"	Joss Whedon
3/2	10/6/98	"Dead Man's Party"	Marti Noxon

BtVS SEASON THREE (continued)

Episode	Airdate	Title	Writer(s)
3/3	10/13/98	"Faith, Hope, and Trick"	David Greenwalt
3/4	10/20/98	"Beauty and the Beasts"	Marti Noxon
3/5	11/3/98	"Homecoming"	David Greenwalt
3/6	11/10/98	"Band Candy"	Jane Espenson
3/7	11/17/98	"Revelations"	Douglas Petrie
3/8	11/24/98	"Lovers Walk"	Dan Vebber
3/9	12/8/98	"The Wish"	Marti Noxon
3/10	12/15/98	"Amends"	Joss Whedon
3/11	1/12/99	"Gingerbread"	Thania St. John, Jane Espenson
3/12	1/19/99	"Helpless"	David Fury
3/13	1/26/99	"The Zeppo"	Dan Vebber
3/14	2/9/99	"Bad Girls"	Douglas Petrie
3/15	2/16/99	"Consequences"	Marti Noxon
3/16	2/23/99	"Doppelgängland"	Joss Whedon
3/17	3/16/99	"Enemies"	Douglas Petrie
3/18	9/21/99	"Earshot"	Jane Espenson
3/19	5/4/99	"Choices"	David Fury
3/20	5/11/99	"The Prom"	Marti Noxon
3/21	5/18/99	"Graduation Day, Part One"	Joss Whedon
3/22	7/13/99	"Graduation Day, Part Two"	Joss Whedon

BtVS SEASON FOUR

Episode	Airdate	Title	Writer(s)
4/1	10/5/99	"The Freshman"	Joss Whedon
4/2	10/12/99	"Living Conditions"	Marti Noxon
4/3	10/19/99	"The Harsh Light of Day"	Jane Espenson
4/4	10/26/99	"Fear, Itself"	David Fury
4/5	11/2/99	"Beer Bad"	Tracey Forbes
4/6	11/9/99	"Wild at Heart"	Marti Noxon
4/7	11/16/99	"The Initiative"	Douglas Petrie
4/8	11/23/99	"Pangs"	Jane Espenson
4/9	11/30/99	"Something Blue"	Tracey Forbes
4/10	12/14/99	"Hush"	Joss Whedon
4/11	1/18/00	"Doomed"	Marti Noxon, David Fury, Jane Espenson

BtVS SEASON FOUR (continued)

Episode	Airdate	Title	Writer(s)
4/12	1/25/00	"A New Man"	Jane Espenson
4/13	2/8/00	"The I in Team"	David Fury
4/14	2/15/00	"Goodbye Iowa"	Marti Noxon
4/15	2/22/00	"This Year's Girl"	Douglas Petrie
4/16	2/29/00	"Who Are You?"	Joss Whedon
4/17	4/4/00	"Superstar"	Jane Espenson
4/18	4/25/00	"Where the Wild Things Are"	Tracey Forbes
4/19	5/2/00	"New Moon Rising"	Marti Noxon
4/20	5/9/00	"The Yoko Factor"	Douglas Petrie
4/21	5/16/00	"Primeval"	David Fury
4/22	5/23/00	"Restless"	Joss Whedon

BtVS SEASON FIVE

Episode	Airdate	Title	Writer(s)
5/1	9/26/00	"Buffy vs. Dracula"	Marti Noxon
5/2	10/3/00	"Real Me"	David Fury
5/3	10/10/00	"The Replacement"	Jane Espenson
5/4	10/17/00	"Out of My Mind"	Rebecca Rand Kirshner
5/5	10/24/00	"No Place Like Home"	Douglas Petrie
5/6	11/7/00	"Family"	Joss Whedon
5/7	11/14/00	"Fool for Love"	Douglas Petrie
5/8	11/21/00	"Shadow"	David Fury
5/9	11/28/00	"Listening to Fear"	Rebecca Rand Kirshner
5/10	12/19/00	"Into The Woods"	Marti Noxon
5/11	1/9/01	"Triangle"	Jane Espenson
5/12	1/23/01	"Checkpoint"	Douglas Petrie, Jane Espenson
5/13	2/6/01	"Blood Ties"	Steven S. DeKnight
5/14	2/13/01	"Crush"	David Fury
5/15	2/20/01	"I Was Made to Love You"	Jane Espenson
5/16	2/27/01	"The Body"	Joss Whedon
5/17	4/17/01	"Forever"	Marti Noxon
5/18	4/24/01	"Intervention"	Jane Espenson
5/19	5/1/01	"Tough Love"	Rebecca Rand Kirshner
5/20	5/8/01	"Spiral"	Steven S. DeKnight
5/21	5/15/01	"The Weight of the World"	Douglas Petrie
5/22	5/22/01	"The Gift"	Joss Whedon

BtVS SEASON SIX

Episode	Airdate	Title	Writer(s)
6/1	10/2/01	"Bargaining, Part One"	Marti Noxon
6/2	10/2/01	"Bargaining, Part Two"	David Fury
6/3	10/9/01	"After Life"	Jane Espenson
6/4	10/16/01	"Flooded"	Jane Espenson, Douglas Petrie
6/5	10/23/01	"Life Serial"	David Fury, Jane Espenson
6/6	10/30/01	"All the Way"	Steven S. DeKnight
6/7	11/6/01	"Once More, with Feeling"	Joss Whedon
6/8	11/13/01	"Tabula Rasa"	Rebecca Rand Kirshner
6/9	11/20/01	"Smashed"	Drew Z. Greenberg
6/10	11/27/01	"Wrecked"	Marti Noxon
6/11	1/8/02	"Gone"	David Fury
6/12	1/29/02	"Doublemeat Palace"	Jane Espenson
6/13	2/5/02	"Dead Things"	Steven S. DeKnight
6/14	2/12/02	"Older and Far Away"	Drew Z. Greenberg
6/15	2/26/02	"As You Were"	Douglas Petrie
6/16	3/5/02	"Hell's Bells"	Rebecca Rand Kirshner
6/17	3/12/02	"Normal Again"	Diego Gutierrez
6/18	4/30/02	"Entropy"	Drew Z. Greenberg
6/19	5/7/02	"Seeing Red"	Steven S. DeKnight
6/20	5/14/02	"Villains"	Marti Noxon
6/21	5/21/02	"Two to Go"	Douglas Petrie
6/22	5/21/02	"Grave"	David Fury

Angel SEASON ONE

Episode	Airdate	Title	Writer(s)
1/1	10/5/99	"City of . . ."	Joss Whedon, David Greenwalt
1/2	10/12/99	"Lonely Hearts"	David Fury
1/3	10/19/99	"In the Dark"	Douglas Petrie
1/4	10/26/99	"I Fall to Pieces"	David Greenwalt, Joss Whedon
1/5	11/2/99	"Rm w/a Vu"	David Greenwalt, Jane Espenson
1/6	11/9/99	"Sense and Sensitivity"	Tim Minear
1/7	11/16/99	"The Bachelor Party"	Tracey Stern

Angel SEASON ONE (continued)

Episode	Airdate	Title	Writer(s)
1/8	11/23/99	"I Will Remember You"	Jeannine Renshaw, David Greenwalt
1/9	11/30/99	"Hero"	Tim Minear, Howard Gordon
1/10	12/14/99	"Parting Gifts"	Jeannine Renshaw, David Fury
1/11	1/18/00	"Somnambulist"	Tim Minear
1/12	1/25/00	"Expecting"	Howard Gordon
1/13	2/8/00	"She"	Marti Noxon
1/14	2/15/00	"I've Got You Under My Skin"	Jeannine Renshaw, David Greenwalt
1/15	2/22/00	"The Prodigal"	Tim Minear
1/16	2/29/00	"The Ring"	Howard Gordon
1/17	4/4/00	"Eternity"	Tracey Stern
1/18	4/25/00	"Five by Five"	Jim Kouf
1/19	5/2/00	"Sanctuary"	Tim Minear, Joss Whedon
1/20	5/9/00	"War Zone"	Gary Campbell
1/21	5/16/00	"Blind Date"	Jeannine Renshaw
1/22	5/23/00	"To Shanshu in L.A."	David Greenwalt

Angel SEASON TWO

Episode	Airdate	Title	Writer(s)
2/1	9/26/00	"Judgment"	David Greenwalt, Joss Whedon
2/2	10/3/00	"Are You Now or Have You Ever Been?"	Tim Minear
2/3	10/10/00	"First Impressions"	Shawn Ryan
2/4	10/17/00	"Untouched"	Mere Smith
2/5	10/24/00	"Dear Boy"	David Greenwalt
2/6	11/7/00	"Guise Will Be Guise"	Jane Espenson
2/7	11/14/00	"Darla"	Tim Monier
2/8	11/21/00	"The Shroud of Rahmon"	Jim Kouf
2/9	11/28/00	"The Trial"	Douglas Petrie, Tim Minear, David Greenwalt

Angel SEASON TWO (continued)

Episode	Airdate	Title	Writer(s)
2/10	12/19/00	"Reunion"	Tim Minear, Shawn Ryan
2/11	1/16/01	"Redefinition"	Mere Smith
2/12	1/23/01	"Blood Money"	Shawn Ryan, Mere Smith
2/13	2/6/01	"Happy Anniversary"	David Greenwalt, Joss Whedon
2/14	2/13/01	"The Thin Dead Line"	Jim Kouf, Shawn Ryan
2/15	2/20/01	"Reprise"	Tim Minear
2/16	2/27/01	"Epiphany"	Tim Minear
2/17	4/17/01	"Disharmony"	David Fury
2/18	4/24/01	"Dead End"	David Greenwalt
2/19	5/1/01	"Belonging"	Shawn Ryan
2/20	5/8/01	"Over the Rainbow"	Mere Smith
2/21	5/15/01	"Through the Looking Glass"	Tim Minear
2/22	5/22/01	"There's No Place Like Plrtz Glrb"	David Greenwalt

Angel SEASON THREE

Episode	Airdate	Title	Writer(s)
3/1	9/24/01	"Heartthrob"	David Greenwalt
3/2	10/1/01	"That Vision Thing"	Jeffrey Bell
3/3	10/8/01	"That Old Gang of Mine"	Tim Minear
3/4	10/15/01	"Carpe Noctem"	Scott Murphey
3/5	10/22/01	"Fredless"	Mere Smith
3/6	10/29/01	"Billy"	Tim Minear, Jeffrey Bell
3/7	11/5/01	"Offspring"	David Greenwalt
3/8	11/12/01	"Quickening"	Jeffrey Bell
3/9	11/19/01	"Lullaby"	Tim Minear
3/10	12/10/01	"Dad"	David H Goodman
3/11	1/14/02	"Birthday"	Mere Smith
3/12	1/21/02	"Provider"	Scott Murphey
3/13	2/4/02	"Waiting in the Wings"	Joss Whedon
3/14	2/18/02	"Couplet"	Tim Minear
3/15	2/25/02	"Loyalty"	Mere Smith
3/16	3/4/02	"Sleep Tight"	David Greenwalt

Angel **SEASON THREE** (continued)

Episode	Airdate	Title	Writer(s)
3/17	4/15/02	"Forgiving"	Jeffrey Bell
3/18	4/22/02	"Double or Nothing"	David Goodman
3/19	4/29/02	"The Price"	David Fury
3/20	5/6/02	"A New World"	Jeffrey Bell
3/21	5/13/02	"Benediction"	Tim Minear
3/22	5/20/02	"Tomorrow"	David Greenwalt

Oh yeah? Let's look at
your bio

ANDREW ABERDEIN is Lecturer in Philosophy at the University of Edinburgh. His research is primarily concerned with the interplay between logic and the philosophy of science, and his most recent publications have explored topics in informal and non-classical logic. He is not miserable about it, just really British.

WENDY LOVE ANDERSON is Assistant Professor of Theological Studies at Saint Louis University. She specializes in medieval church history, concentrating on such freaky topics as mysticism, apocalypticism, and heresy. The book she is currently writing deals with the late medieval evolution of guidelines for distinguishing between true and false revelations, so she can take most of the third season of *Angel* as a shout-out to her work. She also agrees with Wesley Wyndham-Pryce that apocalyptic prophecies aren't exactly a science.

TOBY DASPIT is Assistant Professor in the Department of Teaching, Learning and Leadership at Western Michigan University in Kalamazoo, Michigan. He is co-editor of *Popular Culture and Critical Pedagogy* (Garland, 2000) and the forthcoming *Science Fiction Curricula, Cyborg Teachers, and Youth Culture(s)* (Peter Lang). Toby was the focus of the Initiative's earlier Project 313, a failed attempt to clone Bruce Springsteen.

GREG FORSTER is a senior research associate at the Manhattan Institute for Policy Research. His dissertation was on religion and politics in the thought of John Locke, but he now studies education reform. He draws inspiration from Buffy's groundbreaking work in this field in the finale of Season Three, when she demonstrated that even the most appalling schools can be dramatically improved.

RICHARD GREENE received his Ph.D. in Philosophy from the University of California, Santa Barbara. He is currently an Assistant Professor of Philosophy at Weber State University. He has published papers in epistemology, metaphysics, and ethics. Richard suspects that Anya may be right about bunnies.

JACOB M. HELD is a graduate student in Philosophy at Marquette University in Milwaukee, Wisconsin. His research interests include nineteenth-century German philosophy, political and social philosophy, and Marx. He has published on natural law theory and is currently writing his dissertation on Marxian ethics. He is relieved that to date his wife has yet to procure the services of a vengeance demon.

THOMAS S. HIBBS is Professor and Department Chair of Philosophy at Boston College. He has written two scholarly books on Aquinas and is the author of *Shows About Nothing: Nihilism in Popular Culture from The Exorcist to Seinfeld* (Spence, 1999). He is presently working on another book, *Paint It Black: Philosophy and Film Noir*. Still suffering from the YV viewing habits of his youth, he enjoys the vampires of *BtVS* but insists that Barnabas Collins is the hippest vampire ever.

JASON KAWAL is Assistant Professor of Philosophy at the University of Tennessee at Chattanooga. He works primarily in ethics and environmental ethics, and has published in such journals as *Philosophical Studies*, the *Journal of Applied Philosophy*, and the *Journal of Value Inquiry*. He's still looking for his business-class ticket to cool with complimentary mojo after take-off.

SHARON M. KAYE is Assistant Professor of Philosophy at John Carroll University. She has published several articles in medieval philosophy and is co-author of *On Ockham* and *On Augustine*. When reading primary sources she is careful not to mutter under her breath.

NEAL KING is Associate Professor of Humanities and Women's Studies at Virginia Tech. He is author of *Heroes in Hard Times: Cop Action Movies in the U.S.*, and co-editor of *Reel Knockouts: Violent Women in the Movies*. He studies media violence and regrets its effects on his four cats, who will need chips installed in their heads before humans may sleep in safety.

CAROLYN KORSMEYER is Professor of Philosophy at the University at Buffalo, State University of New York. She writes in aesthetics and related fields and is the author or editor of several books, including *Making Sense of Taste: Food and Philosophy* (1999) and *On Disgust* (2003). She herself lives over a hellmouth and visits there on occasion to use the oven.

JAMES LAWLER teaches philosophy at the State University of New York at Buffalo. He has written a book on Jean-Paul Sartre and one criticizing the biological explanation of IQ tests, and is currently working on the relation between metaphysics and ethics in the philosophy of Kant. In his spare time he likes to shop and hang out and save the world from unspeakable demons.

MICHAEL LEVINE is Professor of philosophy at the University of Western Australia and Baruch College City University of New York. His recent work includes *Integrity and the Fragile Self* (co-authored with Damian Cox and Marguerite La Caze), and *Racism in Mind* (co-edited with Tamas Pataki). He has not written a book on eating disorders and he is not Michael Levin. He has a thing for Buffy, and is jealous of Spike.

TRACY LITTLE is an Instructor of Sociology and Anthropology at Columbus State. Her research interests include popular culture, religion and folklore. Her dissertation involved a study of the Neo-Pagan religious movement, its festivals and folklore. From this work, she is accustomed to being surrounded by witches and is still holding out for some proof that demons exist so she can add the occupation of "Watcher" to her curriculum vitae.

MIMI MARINUCCI is Assistant Professor of Philosophy and Women's Studies at Eastern Washington University, near Spokane. Her research interests currently include epistemology, feminist theory, and anything related to gender. Convinced that she will be the next Slayer, Mimi is patiently awaiting a call from the Watchers' Council.

MELISSA M. MILAVEC is a student at John Carroll University, and she is studying to become a high school English teacher. She loves to dance, especially ballet, Pointe, tap, and jazz. By night, she can be found practicing her hip hop Kool-Aid funky Satan groove.

JESSICA PRATA MILLER has published articles on ethics and feminist theory and is the author of *Trust: A Philosophical Approach* (forthcoming on Broadview Press). She is Assistant Professor of Philosophy at the University of Maine, where she enjoys teaching courses such as introduction to pies and advanced walking.

MADELINE MUNTERSBJORN is an Associate Professor of Philosophy at the University of Toledo where she teaches an on-line course, The Self in Science-Fact and Science-Fiction. She has published in *Philosophia Mathematica* and *Synthese*. Dr. M., her husband and daughter are the only Muntersbjorns; as Buffy says, "Love makes you do the wacky."

JEFFREY L. PASLEY is Associate Professor of History at the University of Missouri's main campus in Columbia. He is author of *"The Tyranny of Printers": Newspaper Politics in the Early American Republic* and numerous scholarly articles on early American history. He also writes a "historical punditry" column for the online history magazine *Common-Place* and keeps a weblog at *History News Network* (http://hnn.us). He is much less snooty than the history professors at UC-Sunnydale.

GREGORY SAKAL is an academic librarian in Boston, Massachusetts. He holds a Bachelor's degree in music, and a Master's degree in Library Science, both from Rutgers University and a Master of Divinity degree from Episcopal Divinity School in Cambridge. As a fellow librarian, Greg has always found Giles to be an inspiration. However, despite the many rare books he has dealt with in the graduate libraries where he has worked, Greg has yet to find anything as obscure, dangerous, or fascinating as Rupert Giles once kept in the library at Sunnydale High.

STEVEN JAY SCHNEIDER is a Ph.D. candidate in Philosophy at Harvard University, and in Cinema Studies at New York University's Tisch School of the Arts. He is the author of *Designing Fear: An Aesthetics of Cinematic Horror* (Routledge), editor of *Freud's Worst Nightmares: Psychoanalysis and the Horror Film* (Cambridge University Press) and *New Hollywood Violence* (Manchester University Press), and co-editor of *Horror International* (Wayne State University Press) and *Understanding Film Genres* (McGraw-Hill). He majored in slaying at U.C. Berkeley, with a minor in Hellmouth history.

KARL SCHUDT teaches philosophy at Lewis University in Romeoville, Illinois. In addition to watching too much television, he has written articles on business ethics, bioethics, and Christian philosophy. He is continually amazed that *BtVS* wasn't canceled after the first season like his other favorite show, *The Adventures of Brisco County, Jr.*

JAMES B. SOUTH is Associate Professor of Philosophy at Marquette University in Milwaukee, Wisconsin. His numerous articles on Late Medieval and Renaissance Philosophy have appeared in such journals as *The Review of Metaphysics*, *Rivista di storia della filosofia*, *Vivarium*, and *Medieval Philosophy and Theology*. Since he never wanted to be a florist, James still has hopes that one day he's gonna be on the cover of *Sanity Fair*.

SCOTT R. STROUD is a doctoral student in the Department of Philosophy at Temple University. His research and publication efforts focus on Kantian ethics, ancient Indian philosophy, and aesthetics. In his spare time, Scott loves to play kitten-poker with the boys.

WAYNE YUEN received his MA from San Jose State University. He currently teaches at several community colleges in the Bay Area. His next project will be researching the moral permissability of house-smashing necrophilia.

We've got a lot of important work here, a lot of filing, giving things names